MW01017274

NO MIRACLE

Global Finance Series

Edited by
John Kirton, University of Toronto, Canada,
Michele Fratianni, Indiana University, USA and
Paolo Savona, University of Rome Guglielmo Marconi, Italy

The intensifying globalization of the twenty-first century has brought a myriad of new managerial and political challenges for governing international finance. The return of synchronous global slowdown, mounting developed country debt, and new economy volatility have overturned established economic certainties. Proliferating financial crises, transnational terrorism, currency consolidation, and increasing demands that international finance should better serve public goods such as social and environmental security, have all arisen to compound the problem.

The new public and private international institutions that are emerging to govern global finance have only just begun to comprehend and respond to this new world. Embracing international financial flows and foreign direct investment, in both the private and public sector dimensions, this series focuses on the challenges and opportunities faced by firms, national governments, and international institutions, and their roles in creating a new system of global finance.

Also in the series

The European Union in the G8
Promoting Consensus and Concerted Actions for Global Public Goods
Edited by Marina Larionova
ISBN: 978-1-4094-3323-1

European Union Economic Diplomacy
The Role of the EU in External Economic Relations
Stephen Woolcock
ISBN: 978-0-7546-7930-1

The New Economic Diplomacy
Decision-Making and Negotiation in International Economic Relations
Edited by Nicholas Bayne and Stephen Woolcock
ISBN: 978-1-4094-2541-0

Full series listing at the back of the book

No Miracle
What Asia Can Teach All Countries About Growth

MITCHELL WIGDOR

ASHGATE

Published by
Ashgate Publishing Limited
Wey Court East
Union Road
Farnham
Surrey, GU9 7PT
England

Ashgate Publishing Company
110 Cherry Street
Suite 3-1
Burlington, VT 05401-3818
USA

www.ashgate.com

British Library Cataloguing in Publication Data
Wigdor, Mitchell.
  No miracle : what Asia can teach all countries about growth. -- (Global finance series)
  1. Information technology--Economic aspects.
  2. Institution building--Economic aspects. 3. Digital divide. 4. Investments, Foreign--Developing countries.
  5. Economic development--Singapore. 6. Economic development--Malaysia.
  I. Title II. Series
  338.9'27'09595-dc23

Library of Congress Cataloging-in-Publication Data
Wigdor, Mitchell.
  No miracle : what Asia can teach all countries about growth / by Mitchell Wigdor.
      p. cm. -- (Global finance)
  Includes bibliographical references and index.
  ISBN 978-1-4094-3811-3 (hardback) -- ISBN 978-1-4094-3812-0 (ebook)
  1. Information technology--Asia. 2. Economic development--Asia. 3. Digital divide--Asia. I. Title.

  HC415.I55W54 2012
  338.9--dc23

                                                                    2012020464
ISBN 9781409438113 (hbk)
ISBN 9781409438120 (ebk – pdf)
ISBN 9781409474630 (ePUB – pdf)

Printed and bound in Great Britain by the
MPG Books Group, UK.

Contents

Acknowledgements

I am indebted to so many people who have contributed in so many ways that it is impossible to thank them adequately and I regret not being able to mention all of their names or to thank them all personally. Most of all, I would like to thank my family, to whom this book is dedicated, and without whose love, patience and perseverance it would not have been possible to complete. I am extremely grateful, in particular, to Michael Trebilcock of the University of Toronto for all of his help and support. Words fail to express fully my appreciation of his guidance, insights and encouragement. I am also very grateful to Katharina Pistor of Columbia University and Edward Iacobucci and Mariana Mota Prado of the University of Toronto for their invaluable suggestions and comments upon reading drafts of my doctoral dissertation, as well as Kevin Davis of New York University who reviewed early drafts of several chapters.

The University of Toronto, School of Graduate Studies was generous in awarding travel grants to me to conduct research in Malaysia and Singapore. I am thankful to all those who have taken the time to meet with me and for their generosity in sharing their insights with me. I would especially like to thank Francis Loh of University Sains Malaysia, Boonler Somchit of the Penang Skills Development Centre, K. Gopalan, formerly of the Penang Development Corporation, Y. T. Tan, Honorary Consul for Canada in Penang, Rajah Rasiah of the University of Malaya, S. Gopinathan of the National Institute of Education, Singapore, Wong Poh Kam of the National University of Singapore, Matti Pohjola of the Helsinki School of Economics and Peter Nunnenkamp of the Kiel Institute for the World Economy. This is but a short list of all those who have helped me.

I would also like to thank the entire team at Ashgate for making this book a reality, John Kirton, series editor and his colleague Madeline Koch, and Suzanne Leblanc for all of her efforts to impose a modicum of consistency upon my manuscript. All shortcomings, of course, remain my own.

List of Abbreviations

CMA	Communications and Multimedia Act (Malaysia)
CMC	Communications and Multimedia Commission (Malaysia)
CNC	Committee on National Computerization (Singapore)
CPTE	Council on Professional and Technical Education (Singapore)
DBS	Development Bank of Singapore
EAP	East Asia and the Pacific
ECA	Eastern Europe and Central Asia
EDB	Economic Development Board (Singapore)
EIC	East India Company
FELCRA	Federal Land Consolidation and Rehabilitation Authority (Malaysia)
FELDA	Federal Land Development Authority (Malaysia)
FDI	Foreign Direct Investment
FIDA	Federal Industrial Development Authority (Malaysia)
GATT	General Agreement on Tariffs and Trade
GDP	Gross Domestic Product
GPT	General Purpose Technology
HBA	Home Base Augmenting
HBE	Home Base Exploiting
HDB	Housing & Development Board (Singapore)
HP	Hewlett-Packard Company
IBRD	International Bank for Reconstruction and Development (World Bank)
ICT	Information and Communications Technology
IDA	Infocomm Development Authority (Singapore)
IMF	International Monetary Fund
iN2015	Intelligent Nation 2015 (Singapore)
Infocomm21	Information and Communications Technology of the 21st Century (Singapore)
IRA	Independent Regulatory Authority
ISIS	Institute of Strategic and International Studies (Malaysia)
iTA	Infocomm Training and Attachment Program (Singapore)
ITU	International Telecommunications Union
ITU Toolkit	ICT Regulation Toolkit published by the ITU
JTC	Jurong Town Corporation (Singapore)
JTM	Jabatan Telekomunikasi Malaysia
LAC	Latin America and the Caribbean

LSE   London School of Economics and Political Science
MARA   Majlis Amanah Ra'ayat (Council for the Trust of the People)
                (Malaysia)
MCA   Malayan Chinese Association (Malaysia)
MDC   Multimedia Development Corporation (Malaysia)
MENA   Middle East and North Africa
MFP   Multifactor Productivity
MIC   Malaysian Indian Congress (Malaysia)
MIDA   Malaysian Industrial Development Authority (Malaysia)
MIDF   Malaysian Industrial Development Finance Ltd. (Malaysia)
MNC   Multinational Corporation
MNE   Multinational Enterprise
MSC   Multimedia Super Corridor (Malaysia)
NCB   National Computer Board (Singapore)
NCP   National Computerization Plan (Singapore)
NDP   New Development Plan
NECTEC   National Electronics and Computer Technology Center
                (Thailand)
NEP   New Economic Policy
NES   New Education System (Singapore)
NGBE   National Board of General Education (Finland)
NGO   Non-governmental Organization
NTP   National Telecommunications Policy (Malaysia)
NUS   National University of Singapore
OECD   Organization for Economic Cooperation and Development
OPP2   Second Outline Perspective Plan (Malaysia)
PAP   People's Action Party (Singapore)
PDC   Penang Development Corporation (Malaysia)
PISA   Programme for International Student Assessment
POLCON   Data base of political constraints
PSDC   Penang Skills Development Centre (Malaysia)
R & D   Research and Development
RCM   Resources, Capabilities and Markets
SAR   South Asia Region
SEDC   Selangor Economic Development Corporation
SingTel   Singapore Telecom
SSA   Sub-Saharan Africa
STM   Syarikat Telekom Malaysia
TAS   Telecommunications Authority of Singapore
TEKES   National Technology Institute (Finland)
TFP   Total Factor Productivity
TIMMS   Trends in International Math and Science Study
TMB   Telecom Malaysia Berhad
TNC   Transnational Corporation

TSLN	Teaching Schools, Learning Nation (Singapore)
UMNO	United Malay National Organization (Malaysia)
UNCTAD	United Nations Conference on Trade and Development
VITB	Vocational and Industrial Training Board
VTT	Technical Research Centre (Finland)
WEF	World Economic Forum
WTO	World Trade Organization

To Blossom, Clare, Lara and Emilie with all my love and thanks.

Introduction
ICT and the Digital Divide

The Bumper Sticker

This book is about institutions and economic development. Specifically, it is about the role of institutions in bridging the Digital Divide. Its thesis, shared by others, is that the governments of less economically developed countries must foster consistently increased use of information and communications technology (ICT) throughout their societies if they hope to foster sustained economic growth. At one level, the Digital Divide is concerned with differences between wealthy and poor countries in the access to, and usage of, ICT. More profoundly, the Digital Divide is about the extent to which less economically developed countries have integrated into an increasingly global economy. Without ICT permeating throughout their societies there is little hope that those nations will come to enjoy prosperity.

What is the Purpose of this Book?

Institutions have been identified as playing a central role in both the theoretical literature of economic development and the economic literature specifically concerned with the relationship between ICT usage and growth. This book addresses three perceived shortcomings in those bodies of literature. First, proponents of the importance of institutions use the term vaguely, often obscuring basic distinctions between policies, laws, institutions and organizations. Institutions must be clearly understood and defined. If institutions cannot be clearly defined, then the role they play in economic development cannot be precisely analysed. Second, highly influential writers in the field of the New Institutional Economics (NIE) have argued that a country's economic status is a result of its institutions and that institutions change only exceedingly slowly. The reform needed for growth is portrayed as a highly protracted process due to the interaction of social and economic institutional structures that are beyond the reach of governments' grasp. This view, however, does not explain how many countries, most prominently in East Asia, were able to transform their economies in the relatively short time since 1960. Third, despite emphasizing the importance of institutions, the literature does not adequately address which institutions are salient to growth or how to create them, providing little guidance to the governments of less economically developed countries.

The book's primary goals are, first, to provide some insight into why the literature is incapable of producing a clear, commonly accepted, workable definition of institutions that can provide guidance to the governments of less economically developed countries and other concerned with development and, second, to shift the focus of the development debate from whether institutions are important, which now seems to be broadly accepted in the literature, to which institutions are important for growth and how to build them, which does not generate much academic attention. Sufficient consideration of the role of institutions has been devoted to the question of whether they are important to economic development to conclude that they are, regardless of whether they are *the* most important factor, as some writers contend, or 'merely' very important, in the view of others. Several suggestions are offered in an attempt to identify some key institutions. If, as will be argued, the evidence supports the conclusions that ICT usage has become essential to sustained economic growth and that institutions play a critical role in that relationship, then it would seem to be beneficial to attempt to identify the specific institutions that help mediate that relationship and to offer suggestions about how those institutions might be built. These recommendations should be viewed as amongst the first words in that line of inquiry, not as the last.

A secondary goal of the book is to broaden participation in the study of international development and to encourage new perspectives on why some countries are rich and others poor. Understandably, economists dominate the field, but economic development is not simply about economics and economic policy. Countries are complex as are the factors that lead to growth or result in enduring poverty. No two counties are identical in their demographic composition, history, geography, natural resource endowments, or social or governance structures, to name but a few. The entire range of social science disciplines is devoted to trying to understand how and why individuals and the societies they form behave as they do. Yet, the voices of far too few of the sociologists, historians and psychologists, for example, who are concerned with how individuals, societies and countries function within the context of their respective areas of expertise have joined with economists in trying to understand the development process. The role of institutions, in particular, offers a unique challenge to economists, highlighting why additional voices are needed. From one perspective, institutions determine economic behaviour and structures, but the social and cultural forces that create those structures often fall within the field of expertise of other social scientists. From another perspective, government-created institutions are used to implement public policy, including economic policy. This field of study falls normally within the domain of other social scientists, such as political scientists and lawyers.

For decades, economists have placed institutions at the heart of international development. In *Economic Backwardness in Historical Perspective*, one of the first major studies of the economic development process, Alexander Gerschenkron (1962) attributed 'differences in the speed and character of industrial development' to the application of 'institutional instruments' (7). Published at a time of heightened American insecurity about its technological prowess – after Sputnik and the Bay of Pigs and before John Glenn's space flight and the Cuban Missile Crisis – Gerschenkron's main interest was the industrial transformation of the Soviet Union from an agrarian society to a military superpower. Industrialization could not be achieved in pre-Soviet Russia, he maintained, 'as long as certain formidable institutional obstacles (such as the serfdom of the peasantry or the far-reaching absence of political unification) remained' (Gerschenkron: 8). Many of those impediments were swept away by the Russian Revolution, but others remained. England had accumulated the capital needed for investment in new enterprises over a slow, lengthy period of industrialization. This 'obviated the pressure for developing any special institutional devices for provision of long-term capital to industry' (Gerschenkron: 14). 'Backwards' countries, lacking the capital, needed to create 'institutional devices', such as investment banks, to finance industrialization projects.

Economic Backwardness influenced development thinking profoundly. It stands as an eloquent exposition of the then prevailing 'stages of development' theory that viewed economic development as a series of clearly identifiable phases which countries traverse in an effort to become prosperous. Gerschenkron's description of the activist role played by government in developing and implementing industrial policy found echo and was expanded upon in the work of Chalmers Johnson (1982), Alice Amsden (1989) and Robert Wade (2004), whose studies of rapid post-World War II economic growth in Japan, South Korea and Taiwan, respectively, contributed to what has become known as the 'developmental state' school of analysis. The concept of the developmental state as one where government guides a country's growth in a far more interventionist manner than contemplated in neoclassical or, more recently, neoliberal economic theory, provides important insights into how countries are able to industrialize relatively quickly, and will be discussed in greater detail in connection with the introduction to the case studies of Singapore and Malaysia.

Gerschenkron's work also serves to illuminate an ongoing challenge of the institutions literature that partially explains its inability to give practical guidance. Like many economists, Gerschenkron stresses the role of institutions, but does not define them. He uses institutions in two senses in the quoted passages. 'Institutional obstacles' refers to historical structures that govern human interaction such as serfdom. 'Institutional devices' or 'instruments', in contrast, are more concrete. They are deliberately created bodies that carry out specific functions. A police force is a law enforcement institution. The concepts are distinct from each other. Gerschenkron rarely uses the noun 'institutions'. He predominantly uses 'institutional' as an adjective and it is relatively simple to determine in his work which concept is being described. Modern writers fail to make that distinction. They tend simply to use the word 'institutions' to cover both concepts.

Douglass North is a winner of the Nobel Prize for his work in the NIE field and is possibly the most influential contemporary writer concerned with the impact of institutions on development. North states: 'Institutions are the rules of the game in a society or, more formally, are the humanly devised constraints that shape human interaction' (North 1990: 3). The vast scope of the meaning bestowed upon 'institutions' is readily apparent. Given this definition, in contrast to Gerschenkron, North would likely have written that industrialization could not have occurred in Russia as long as certain 'formidable institutions' blocked the path. North would refer to an institutional device, such as a legislature, as an organization. In common parlance and in most writing, a legislature is an institution. Although North's definition allows for great insights into why some countries are poor while others are rich, which is the focus of much of his writing, it is too broad to be workable as a tool in understanding what actions nations can undertake in order to achieve prosperity.

The analytical approach this book follows most closely is the one advocated by Mary Shirley (2008) in *Institutions and Development* and Dani Rodrik (2007) in *One Economics Many Recipes*. They call for the use of both large scale, cross-country regressions and case studies to determine which variable factors contribute to economic growth. Shirley and Rodrik echo Nicholas Crafts (1997) who ten years earlier engaged in an examination of the evolution of endogenous growth models. He called on economists and economic historians to work together to understand better the political economy of growth which would be more likely to be achieved 'through a portfolio of detailed case studies of individual countries than through regressing growth rates against standard variables' (Crafts 1997: 69).

Regressions are a commonly used tool in economic research. Case studies are more frequently used in other social sciences. No one case study purports to provide a definitive understanding of an issue or a prescription for future conduct. Their greatest value comes once a sufficient body of studies has been compiled so that common themes and patterns can be discerned. The better those concerned with development can understand what works, or has failed to work, in a number of national settings, the better the advice they can provide to the governments of nations still struggling to achieve prosperity. Rodrik succinctly expresses the rationale for relying upon both regressions and case studies:

> Econometricians are still hard at work looking for the growth-promoting effects of policies that countries in Latin America and elsewhere embraced enthusiastically a quarter century ago. I am not a purist when it comes to the kind of evidence that matters. In particular, I believe in the need for both cross-country regressions and detailed country studies. Any cross-country regression giving results are that [sic] not validated by case studies needs to be regarded with suspicion. But any policy conclusion that derives from a case study and flies in the face of cross-national evidence needs to be similarly scrutinized. Ultimately, we need both kinds of evidence to guide our views of how the world works. (Rodrik 2007: 4)

The Nature of the Challenge

Understanding ICT

Like the Digital Divide, a distinction can be drawn between the meaning of ICT and what it represents. The term 'ICT' refers to a wide variety of electronic goods such as computers and cell phones as well as software and intangibles such as know-how, proprietary processes and other forms of intellectual property. Based on definitions of ICT developed by the OECD and the World Bank, Qiang and Pitt (2004) summarize neatly the technical meaning of ICT as follows:

> ICT, as defined in the Information & Communication Technology Sector Strategy Paper of the World Bank Group consists of hardware, software, networks, and media for collection, storage, processing, transmission, and presentation of information (voice, data, text, images). ICT-producing sectors are defined by the OECD as a combination of manufacturing and services industries that capture, transmit and display data and information electronically. Manufacturing includes office, accounting and computing machinery; insulated wire and cable; electronic valves and tubes and other electronic components; television and radio transmitters and apparatus for line telephony and line telegraphy; television and radio receivers, sound or video recording or reproducing apparatus and associated goods; instruments and appliances for measuring, checking, testing, navigating and other purposes, except industrial process equipment; and industrial process equipment...Services include wholesaling of computers, computer peripheral equipment and software; wholesale of electronic and telecommunication parts and equipment; renting of office machinery and equipment (including computers); telecommunications; computer and related activities. (1, footnotes omitted)

The lengthy definition serves to emphasize the vast scope of the products and services encompassed by the term 'ICT', but it fails to capture certain of its intangible aspects. Powerful computers, innovative software and fast internet connections are merely tools that do nothing on their own. Their economic impact depends upon the abilities of the people using them and the context in which they are used. An employee may be taught relatively easily to use a forklift, but there will always be a limit upon what can be done with that forklift. A person trained to use a computer will be unlikely to exhaust its functions. Daron Acemoglu (1998) forcefully argues, 'new technologies are not complementary to skills by nature, but by design' (1055). Computers and other ICTs were first created in the 1940s specifically to enhance the productivity and capabilities of highly educated people by allowing them to analyse and manipulate large amounts of data far more quickly than they could manually. Unlike earlier technology that is mechanical and geared towards reducing the physical labour required to complete a task, ICT is a tool designed to enhance the productivity of the human brain.

Previously, poor countries could substitute for machinery with excess labour. The same is not true with ICT.

The critical importance of technology and knowledge to economic development has long been recognized. As Joseph Stiglitz (2003) noted: 'But today we recognize that what separates developed from less developed countries is also a gap both in knowledge and in technology' (2). This traditional view, suggesting that closing the gaps in knowledge and technology represent parallel challenges to governments, has been reflected in numerous econometric studies which have examined the relationship between economic growth and technology, on the one hand, and human capital, usually measured as a function of education, on the other. The importance of ICT, however, lies not merely in what it enables people to do, but for what it potentially represents – the intersection of technology and knowledge. Governments may be better served by adopting a unified approach to ICT, viewing it as being equally comprised of the hardware and software that embody it and human capital. Simply buying computers without educating people or, as is less often the case, providing a good system of education without modern tools, such as in Cuba, will not result in positive outcomes. Fostering the usage of ICT will be more successful where governments, particularly those in less economically developed countries, are able to raise incrementally, but methodically, their levels of technology usage and human capital in tandem.

What is the Digital Divide?

The Digital Divide, as stated, is a concept that is concerned not simply with differences between countries in the usage of ICT, but more profoundly with their ability to participate in a global economy. Several international organizations devote strenuous efforts to determining whether the Digital Divide is growing or shrinking. Focusing extensively on definitional and quantification issues, however, serves to obscure the larger issue that the twin forces of ICT and international economic integration have compelled, and will continue to compel, countries to adapt their economic development thinking by striving to incorporate ICT usage into every aspect of their societies in order to improve the well-being of their citizens. The Digital Divide is about the gaps between the predominantly wealthy societies that create and use ICT extensively, allowing them to become more productive and enjoy greater economic growth, and those that must devise the means to acquire it and learn how to use it effectively. It can be seen as a proxy for economic development and not merely as another measure of economic disparities.

The OECD first addressed the Digital Divide in a 2001 study of differences in ICT usage in member countries. It defined the Digital Divide as follows:

> ... the term 'digital divide' refers to the gap between individuals, households, businesses and geographic areas at different socio-economic levels with regard to both their opportunities to access information and communication technologies

(ICTs) and to their use of the Internet for a wide variety of activities ... The
digital divide reflects various differences among and within countries. (5)

The definition still finds broad acceptance and the OECD continues to refer to it.[1]
As the definition makes clear, divides exist between and within countries, both
regionally and between groups. Only the differences between countries will be
addressed in this book.

The 2001 OECD study also noted that quantifying the Digital Divide poses
inherent difficulties as it does 'with all efforts to measure new phenomena'
(5). In particular, it underlined the fact that its initial efforts at collecting data
were hindered by the lack of standardized techniques in place across the OECD
members subject to the study. Consequently, 'the figures are often not comparable
in terms of time and coverage' (OECD 2001: 5). The study looked primarily at
telephone lines per 100 inhabitants and internet hosts as key indicia of the Digital
Divide as they can be the first determinants of access to ICT. It found that in 1998
in OECD countries there was an average of 72.1 fixed plus mobile phone lines per
100 people compared to 7.8 in non-OECD states. The gap in internet hosts was
even more striking in 2000. OECD countries enjoyed an average of 82 internet
hosts per 1,000 people whereas in non-OECD countries the average was only 0.85
(OECD 2001: 7–8).

Not everyone agreed with the OECD and others concerned with the negative
economic development consequences of a potentially growing gap between
nations in ICT usage. Some noted economists suggested that the Digital Divide
was merely a temporary phenomenon. Carsten Fink and Charles Kenny (2003),
World Bank economists, maintained that one should be more concerned with
relative gaps than absolute gaps. As less economically developed countries
showed faster rates of growth in adopting ICT than the more economically
developed, they argue that 'the developing world would eventually catch up to
the developed world' (1). They propose that 'ICT use per unit of GDP may be a
better measure of the potential scale of the problem than ICT use per capita' (14).
By using such a measure they claim the less prosperous were not only rapidly
catching up to the wealthy with respect to a variety of ICTs but in many respects
'developing countries already 'digitally leapfrog' the developed world' (1). Their
method of calculation allowed them to conclude that by 2000 middle income
countries had surpassed high income countries in mobile phone usage and that low
income countries were on track to do so (10). Consequently, they were of the view
that, with time, the Digital Divide would disappear. In retrospect, their analysis
failed to understand the evolutionary nature of ICT. Technological advancement
did not reach its zenith with early mobile telephones and projecting shrinking

---

1 See, for example the OECD's on Line Glossary of Statistical terms; http://stats.
oecd.org/glossary/. The International Telecommunications Union states that the 'difference
between the "have" and the "have-nots" is something known and defined' referring to the
definition formulated by the OECD in its 2001 study (ITU 2009: 45).

differences in computer ownership rates based on per capita spending patterns did not appreciate that computer ownership, regardless of its quality, would be only the threshold price of entry into the ICT age.

Robert Wade (2002) was considerably more sceptical in his estimation of those promoting ICT usage and the alleged dangers of the Digital Divide. Casting himself as a devil's advocate guarding against a misguided campaign to encourage the expanded use of ICT, he sought to 'challenge what John Stuart Mill once called "the deep slumber of decided opinion"' (443). He argues that 'a kind of groupthink grips the burgeoning ICT-in-development field.' (460) Those who warned of a growing Digital Divide are essentially portrayed as a homogeneous mob that simplistically proclaims that supplying ICT products to less economically developed countries is a panacea that will allow them to leapfrog over other, more complex, development issues on their way to prosperity. (443; 445; 460) Such naïve thinking had to be expected from the proponents of ICT usage:

> The missionary [World] Bank literature cited earlier comes from a set of people who are marginal to the organization as a whole. The operational managers tend to know very little about ICT potentials and are inclined to think that ICT applications are too complex and fast-changing for them to get involved. (462)

As an example, he cites a World Bank paper that describes a World Bank ICT promotion program in Andhra Pradesh, India that it was hoped would provide a number of benefits by simplifying the dealings by individuals with their state government. According to Wade, the report merely emphasizes potential, but unrealized, benefits. More reliably, an 'informal survey of friends who live in Andhra (where I used to live)' (446) confirmed to him that the program's successes were minimal and achieved at a high cost.

Of greater benefit to poor nations, Wade suggests, would be an overhaul of the international system's standards and rules that permit Western technology suppliers to benefit most greatly from the integration of ICT into poorer countries' economies. (462) It is thus not surprising, according to Wade, that Microsoft, Hewlett Packard, Siemens and Alcatel are amongst the greatest supporters of ICT-for-development in the same way that 'tractor companies facing stagnant tractor sales and seeing LDC markets as their vent for surplus' (463) pushed the tractors for Africa fad of the 1960s and 1970s. ICT-for-development could similarly be dismissed as a fad. (461)

Assessing the Digital Divide

UNCTAD published its first comprehensive examination of the Digital Divide in 2005. It identified the Digital Divide as a policy matter of 'increasing concern' (UNCTAD 2005:1). While noting that technological gaps have been a persistent problem in economic development, 'the size and scale of the potential benefits foregone through failure to participate in the new "digital society" are likely to be much greater' (UNCTAD 2005: 1). It compared data collected from 1995 to 2002 for 165 countries focusing slightly more widely than the OECD (2001) by trying to compare figures for fixed telephone lines, mobile subscribers, computers, internet hosts, and internet users. UNCTAD found that little had changed between 1995–2002 ICT diffusion rankings. OECD countries continued to dominate at the top of the rankings while South Asian and African countries remained at the bottom. While some countries, particularly those in transition to capitalist economies in Eastern Europe and the former Soviet Union, made notable progress overall, '[l]evels of inequality in access to ICTs remain high still, *around twice average levels of income inequality*' (UNCTAD 2005: 2, emphasis original).

Whether the Digital Divide is shrinking or growing depends upon what one measures and what one determines is important. According to UNCTAD, the gap in telephone ownership and internet access is closing as prices for what are now considered basic services decline and infrastructure is built. The dramatic rise in mobile telephony usage, the sector where usage gaps may have closed the most, is producing a significant economic impact in rural Africa. Mobile telephony, however, also illustrates the challenges in measuring these gaps. As 'smart' phones, with broadband internet access and such a multitude of applications that they resemble pocket computers, grow in popularity in wealthier countries they make cell phones that 'only' allow users to make calls and send text messages obsolete. The importance and economic significance of such new devices compared to older ones is difficult to determine. Unlike electricity, to which ICT is often compared in terms of its impact on economic growth, ICT is not static. Electricity is electricity. Computer ownership and internet access alone are no longer sufficient to determine the Digital Divide. In the late 1990s dial-up internet connections in wealthy countries were the norm. By the late 2000s such connections had become antiquated and inefficient. Internet speed has become an important economic determinant and despite more people in poorer countries enjoying internet access 'there is a widening gap between high-income and low-income countries in the area of broadband connectivity' (UNCTAD 2009: xi).

UNCTAD (2009) also recognized that the relationship between ICT usage and 'economic growth and development is greatly affected by the way such technologies are used in the productive sector' (37). It emphasized that measurement issues remain a problem in precisely determining differences in ICT usage in wealthy and poor countries and that the size of those gaps can vary widely depending on which economic sector, for example, is being examined. The UNCTAD (2009) 'analysis confirms the existence of huge gaps both between and within countries in the use of different ICTs' (37).

More recently, the ITU and the World Economic Forum (WEF) have also attempted to measure the Digital Divide and ICT usage. The ITU has created an ICT Development Index based on a number of sub-indices it prepares which, it believes, allows for the grouping of several key factors to present a more comprehensive picture of where countries stand in their evolution towards an information society. While it emphasizes that its results have to be read with caution as the creation of such an index can result in broad generalizations that mask important individual changes, its 2009 report concludes that their results 'suggest that globally the digital divide is as prevalent as before, but is slightly closing between countries with very high and low ICT levels' (ITU 2009: 2). Although there was some movement, 29 of the top 30 countries remained unchanged in the two indices (ITU 2009: 22). The bottom 30 also showed little change. The 2010 report showed limited further progress. Although all countries improved their aggregate scores between 2000 and 2008, the most recent year for which information was available, there was little movement out of the top or bottom groups. The report found:

> The analysis shows that the digital divide is still significant, although it is slightly shrinking, especially between those countries with very high ICT levels and those with lower levels. This is partly explained by the flattening of ICT growth in the group of countries that are most advanced. At the same time, countries with reasonably high levels of ICT have made strong improvements thus increasing the gap with those towards the lower end of the scale. (ITU 2010: x)

The WEF, in conjunction first with the Harvard Center for International Development and subsequently with the French-based business school, INSEAD, has published a Networked Readiness Index annually since 2001 that covered 133 countries in its 2010 report. The significance of the Index, according to the WEF website is that it 'underlines that good education fundamentals and high levels of technological readiness and innovation are essential engines of growth' (www.weforum.org). While the WEF index thus does not purport to measure the Digital Divide, the purpose of the index is similar to those of UNCTAD and the ITU. The WEF ranks countries on over 60 factors highlighting the challenges in quantifying the Digital Divide as ICT evolves. Again, the wealthiest countries are generally found at the top of the aggregate index and the very poor at the bottom, although the WEF (2009) does note that certain countries, such as China, and regions, such as the Middle East, have made notable progress over the time that the index has been developed. The concern that continues to be expressed by the ITU, UNCTAD and the WEF is that differences in ICT usage will bring about ever greater differences in wealth between rich and poor. The economic prospects for countries that fail to keep pace are bleak.

The G-8 – Raising Awareness of the Digital Divide

The need to address the Digital Divide and the underlying gaps in ICT usage and access became evident in the early 2000s and has since become a priority issue for those concerned with economic development. Much of the credit for recognizing and publicizing the importance of the issue can be attributed to the leaders of the world's largest economies, as expressed through their annual G-8 meetings. By the end of the 1990s it was clear that computer usage had spread throughout the economically developed world as a business and personal tool as well as a means of almost instantaneous, cheap, global communications. ICT's potential for economic change became the central focus of the July 2000 G-7 meeting of Finance Ministers and the G-8 Heads of State meeting later that month.

The G-7 Finance Ministers (2000) report, *Impact of the IT Revolution on the Economy and Finance*, predicted that ICT could become 'a major force in the global economy, in improving productivity, raising potential output, and promoting higher living standards' (paragraph 1). The document is quite remarkable in its prescience as the view that ICT could lead to significant productivity gains was not, at that time, commonly accepted wisdom. Much of the empirical analysis supporting this point of view was only just beginning to emerge. Although they acknowledged that it was too early to determine accurately the timing, nature and strength of the ICT revolution, the Finance Ministers underscored ICT's potentially profound implications for economic productivity and growth. Employing language that demonstrated their understanding of the implications of ICT usage, the suggested:

> The increase in production potential due to IT will not be limited to IT-related industries, but will extend to the overall economy. First of all, the IT revolution can increase the rate of growth of the capital stock by stimulating active IT-related investment. This kind of investment leads to increasingly sophisticated IT technology being built into capital and, accordingly, raises the quality of capital as well. More importantly, by increasing the speed with which information is disseminated and shared inside and outside corporations, the IT revolution can drastically alter the combination of capital and labor, bring about greater efficiency in conducting business, facilitate corporate restructuring, induce a synergistic effect, and thus lead to productivity increases that cannot be attributed to either capital or labor (total factor productivity). (G-7 2000: paragraph 3)

If ICT could lead to productivity gains and economic growth amongst the wealthy nations that led in its usage, then the failure to adapt could result in even greater differences in wealth between nations. Capturing ICT's benefits was not guaranteed, they underlined, as doing so would also require sound policies. The onus was on governments to create 'an environment that is conducive to private-sector creativity and entrepreneurship' (G-7 2000: paragraph 7).

The Finance Ministers report was followed quickly by the *Okinawa Charter on Global Information Society* (2000) issued by the G-8 leaders. The Okinawa Charter similarly recognized ICT as 'fast becoming a vital engine of growth for the world economy' (2000: paragraph 1). Less focused on productivity than the Finance Minister's Report, it stressed the social and cultural benefits of ICT use, in addition to the economic benefits, and called upon all countries to create national and international strategies to bridge international information divides. It placed the responsibility on governments to create the policy and regulatory environment necessary for the information society.

The leaders' meeting resulted in the creation of a Digital Opportunities Task Force, known as the DOT Force. The DOT Force was given the exceptionally broad and somewhat nebulous task to:

> ...facilitate discussion with developing countries, international organizations and other stakeholders to promote international co-operation with a view to fostering policy, regulatory and network readiness; improving connectivity, increasing access and lowering cost; building human capacity; and encouraging participation in global e-commerce networks... (G-8 2000: paragraph 18)

In addition, the DOT Force's mandate included encouraging the G-8's own efforts with respect to ICT pilot programs and projects; examining contributions from the private sector and other interested stakeholders; promoting policy dialogue and global public awareness of ICT's challenges and opportunities. It was to report to the leaders at the following year's summit.

The DOT Force did as it was instructed and presented its report at the G-8 meeting the following year at Genoa, Italy. The substance of the report is sparse from an operational point of view, offering broad policy initiatives but very little concrete guidance to governments, international organizations or other policymakers concerned with the Digital Divide about how to narrow existing gaps or promote ICT usage. Developing countries are urged to seek new digital opportunities proactively and to use 'ICT on a wider scale by creating their own ICT productive sector or through more intensive use within their own economies' (DOT Force 2001: 6). Governments are that told they need to create the right policy environment, particularly pro-competitive policies in the communications sector in order to develop the needed infrastructure and to develop human capacity. A proposed Genoa Plan of Action was incorporated into the DOT Force Report as a framework for future action. Adopted by the heads of state, it encouraged all countries to pursue national e-strategies enjoying 'the highest level of national political commitment' generated through 'a consultative process involving all relevant interested parties' (DOT Force 2001: 9).

Given the breadth of its mandate and the relatively short time it had to perform its work, it is questionable whether one could have expected a detailed report to emerge. While it is admirable that the Finance Ministers and leaders recognized early the importance of ICT to productivity and economic growth and the potential dangers of the emerging Digital Divide, the magnitude of the issue did not, and does not, lend itself to simple solutions. The DOT Force report is largely a recitation of little more than vague policy goals. If it represents the final word of the G-8 then its seriousness in addressing the challenges of the Digital Divide remains an open question, given that the Digital Divide has effectively disappeared from the agenda at subsequent meetings. As the University of Toronto G8 Working Group pointed out a year later, the submission to the G-8 leaders of a business plan by the DOT Force 'will offer little benefit to developing countries if not accompanied by concrete tangible resources' (University of Toronto G8 Working Group 2002: 4).

The G-8 and its companion organization, the G-20, are somewhat unique given their prominent stature. These groups do not have a permanent secretariat, staff or funding and they do not collectively carry out programs to implement their proposals. It may be that the annual meetings and their ancillary preparatory work lead to shifts in the domestic policy of member states and to changes in the instructions of their representatives to international organizations such as those under the United Nations umbrella or at the World Bank. Those organizations, of course, do have permanent secretariats, staff, budgets and programs, but they are structured to be insulated from political pressure that might be applied by their members' governments of the day. Consequently, even where the G-8 leaders genuinely desire to implement their proposals, their ability to take concerted collective action with respect to economic development is limited. The individual members can coordinate their efforts on specific matters such as debt relief, but they face structural issues that impede their ability to implement their development recommendations.

The World Summit on the Information Society

G-8 interest in the Digital Divide may have ceded its place to other matters, but the international community has remained engaged in the issue through a number of international organizations, most prominently the ITU which has spearheaded the World Summit on the Information Society (WSIS). WSIS was mandated by a UN General Assembly resolution in December 2001. Held in two phases, Geneva in 2003 and Tunis in 2005, the summit meetings each attracted heads of state, ministers and other high ranking officials from over 170 countries among their 11,000 and 19,000 participants, respectively. The main results, aside from a continuing consultative process primarily through the holding of an annual international forum, were the Geneva Declaration of Principles and the Geneva Plan of Action emanating from the first meeting and the Tunis Agenda for the Information Society. The annual forum provides an important venue for interested parties to meet, exchange ideas, learn of new developments and become aware of how others have confronted common problems. WSIS thus performs an extremely useful function in coordinating activity and the flow of information.

Both the Plan of Action and the Agenda provide a comprehensive paradigm of activities for governments, the private sector, international organizations and everyone else concerned with bridging the Digital Divide. Like the Okinawa Plan and the DOT Force report, they describe a vast array of activities that should be undertaken. By way of example, the Geneva Plan of Action prescribes, in part, the following actions for governments and all stakeholders in promoting ICT for development:

> a) Development of national e-strategies, including the necessary human capacity
> building...taking into account different national circumstances.

b) Initiate at the national level a structured dialogue involving all relevant stakeholders, including through public/private partnerships, in devising e-strategies for the Information Society and for the exchange of best practices.

c) In developing and implementing national e-strategies, stakeholders should take into consideration local, regional and national needs and concerns. (World Summit on the Information Society 2003: 2)

Undoubtedly, this is good advice, but its generalities and broad policy imperatives provide little concrete, operational guidance to those seeking to bridge the Digital Divide.

Structure of the Book

Part I – ICT and Institutions

The last quarter of the twentieth century witnessed a profound change in economic structures occasioned by the confluence of several contemporaneous events. Each of those events – the spread of ICT within and between countries; the shift from import substitution to export orientation growth strategies; the lowering of tariffs and trade barriers; falling transportation costs; and the collapse of the Soviet bloc – would have generated economic consequences on their own, but collectively they became mutually catalytic; each accelerated the pace of the others. Their combined effect produced an increasingly integrated global economy where the ability to innovate has superseded the capacity to produce goods as a generator of wealth. Just as electrification a century ago changed the nature of economies so that prosperity without electricity became inconceivable, the same is true about the effect of ICT on today's economies. The task for less economically developed countries has become even more challenging. They must find methods to allow ICT usage to permeate throughout their societies. Failure to do so will result in enduring poverty. Chapter 1 will examine the changing nature of ICT and the Digital Divide.

Chapter 2 examines the relationship between ICT and economic growth. As with the gradual adoption of electricity and other forms of new technology, the growing use of computers at first was more apparent to the casual observer than it was to those examining national economic indicators as many wealthy countries experienced recession in the late 1980s. ICT's impact on economies only began to be observed in the late 1990s when sizable gains in productivity attributable to ICT were first felt in the United States, then in Western Europe and other wealthy countries and, subsequently, in the Asian 'tiger' economies of South Korea, Hong Kong, Taiwan and Singapore. Four factors were found to be critical to the process by which ICT usage leads to economic growth. The first is telecommunications infrastructure. Second, government, firms and individuals must consistently invest in ICT goods. Third, the level of human capital must be sufficiently high to provide the skilled labour needed to make effective use of ICT. The fourth factor, institutions, has been identified, but poorly described. The literature provides very little elucidation of which institutions are important to the relationship or how they help to create an enabling environment in which growth can occur.

If one accepts that fostering the use of ICT is essential for sustained economic growth, then the governments of less economically developed countries may be forced to obtain the ICT they need to expand their economies through foreign direct investment (FDI), particularly as most commercial applications are privately developed and owned. Chapter 3 examines the relationship between FDI and economic growth. Governments cannot simply open their doors and hope that any FDI they are able to attract will bring the technology or other desired benefits. They need to understand the motivations that underlie the actions of multinational corporations (MNCs) and the factors that attract FDI to one country instead of another. Even when a sought-after investment is obtained, its benefits do not simply flow throughout the host economy. Countries need to build their 'absorptive capacity' in order to take advantage of the 'spillovers' that can potentially take place, thereby building linkages with local industries and spurring virtuous cycles of growth and investment. Economists have identified three critical, and familiar, factors that mediate the relationship between FDI and economic growth: ICT; human capital; and institutions. The literature in this field of study, however, also does little to provide a better understanding of institutions.

Chapter 4 looks primarily at the NIE literature which is focused upon the relationship between institutions and economic growth, but is not specifically concerned with the impact of either ICT or FDI on growth. The chapter seeks to determine whether governments can influence the institutions that affect economic growth or whether a country's institutional legacy precludes them from doing so as North suggests. North argues that an country's institutions constitute the rules of the game and as they interact with organizations, which he calls society's players, in a mutually self-reinforcing manner they lead to path dependent behaviour that brings enduring prosperity in some cases and poverty in others. Contrary to North, others have argued that the institutions that determine economic growth lie within the control of governments. This view finds particular support in the work of Dani Rodrik and Daron Acemoglu who empirically test the role of institutions against other 'deep determinants' of economic growth. Rodrik's (2004) conclusion is stated in the title of his article: 'Institutions Rule'. Rodrik confesses in the same article, however, that the finding that institutions rule does not provide much direction to governments. The chapter examines the reasons for the inability of the literature to give actionable advice.

Chapter 5 shifts the discussion from the theoretical to the practical. Having concluded that the institutions that matter for economic growth tend to be the ones that governments bear the primary responsibility for creating, the chapter provides suggestions of which institutions help mediate the relationship between ICT usage and economic growth and how to build them. It argues that building institutions is about the implementation of policy objectives. The chapter then attempts to provide some guidance to governments of less economically developed countries by suggesting that if they wish to increase ICT usage the institutions that they might focus upon first are those specifically related to telecommunications infrastructure, investment in ICT and human capital. It seeks to identify some of the policies, laws and institutions that have been demonstrated to be critical to each.

Part II – Case Studies

The Developmental State   Despite East Asia now often being considered the most economically dynamic region in the world, such was far from the case for much of Southeast Asia from 1960 – 2000. The war in Vietnam continued until the mid-1970s, spilling over to its neighbours in Laos and Cambodia, where the Khmer Rouge were not overthrown until 1979. Indonesia lived through internal violence in the early 1960s, followed by decades of dictatorship under Suharto. Burma succumbed to a repressive military regime in the early 1960s which may only be lifting fifty years later. Singapore and Malaysia were not buoyed by a rising tide of prosperity around them for much of the period examined. Nevertheless, their development did not take place in isolation. It is unlikely that their economic trajectories would have been comparable had they been magically transported to sub-Saharan Africa in 1960. In contrast to Southeast Asia, some Northeast Asian economies expanded significantly in the 1960s and 1970s providing investment and examples for Malaysia and Singapore to follow.

The literature examining industrialization in Japan, South Korea and Taiwan, particularly that which advances the concept of the developmental state, gives context to Malaysia's and Singapore's development efforts. While there are important differences to the paths Malaysia and Singapore followed there are many similarities in the manner in which they pursued their respective industrialization strategies. The developmental state literature contrasts sharply with the neoliberal Washington Consensus theory of Asian economic development favoured by many economists and the World Bank (1993) and is a more accurate representation of the activist approach to guiding economic development pursued by many governments in the region.

The developmental state is a term that has been applied to describe the interventionist manner in which the governments of late industrializing East Asian nations, primarily Japan, South Korea and Taiwan, have guided their countries' economic development. Chalmers Johnson (1982) is credited with coining the term, if not the concept, in his study of what he called the Japanese miracle. Although he stated that it is 'not really a hard question' (17) to ask what the developmental state means, his answer is hardly succinct. Its meaning is best understood in comparison to other economic approaches. It stands in contrast to both Marxist-inspired command economies and neoclassical based market economics where the state plays a more supervisory, or regulatory, function as in the United States. Johnson argues that: 'The issue is not one of state intervention in the economy. All states intervene in their economies ...' (17). Rather, the main focus of the government in a developmental state is ensuring economic development. It plays an active role in determining the nature and form of the economy. Under neoclassical and neoliberal models, the state is more concerned with getting the macroeconomic basics, primarily prices, 'right' (World Bank 1993: 5) and allowing natural market forces to propel economic growth. Johnson's conception of the developmental state, or plan rational state, is again expressed by him by means of a comparison:

> In the plan-rational state, the government will give greatest precedence to industrial policy, that is, to a concern with the structure of domestic industry and with promoting the structure that enhances the nation's international competitiveness. The very existence of an industrial policy implies a strategic, or goal-oriented, approach to the economy. On the other hand, the market-rational state usually will not even have an industrial policy (or, at any rate, will not recognize it as such). Instead, both its domestic and foreign economic policy, including its trade policy, will stress rules and reciprocal concessions. (Johnson 1982: 19–20)

The concept of the developmental state built upon the work of Gerschenkron and greatly influenced subsequent scholarly writing on Asian development, but the precise meaning of the developmental state remained fluid. Meredith Woo-Cumings (1999) writing more than fifteen years after Johnson suggested that the developmental state was 'shorthand for the seamless web of political, bureaucratic, and moneyed influences that structures economic life in capitalist Northeast Asia' (1). Robert Wade (2004) portrayed the defining characteristics of the developmental state as combining to form a picture 'of a centralized state interacting with the private sector from a position of pre-eminence so as to secure development objectives...' (26). He concludes that as economic theories go the developmental state 'is not, however, much of a theory' (26). More recently, Daniel Breznitz (2007) has described the developmental state as providing 'a specific state structure that enables emerging economies to utilize a particular strategy for development' (14) while Joseph Wong's (2011) examination of Asian efforts to foster biotech industries argues that government action within the context of the developmental state was designed primarily to mitigate risk in the industrialization process (19), but the model is 'no longer viable in an era of science-based industries' (2).

Categorizing the precise nature of the developmental state is thus difficult. It could be argued that the developmental state can be viewed as a model for less economically developed countries in the same manner that lawyers us precedent agreements. Lawyers use precedents because there are commonalities to each acquisition, for example, but also differences. The precedent cannot be followed blindly. It must be carefully adapted to the unique characteristics and circumstances of each transaction. Similarly, the concept of the developmental state can be seen as informed by common principles that guide governments and often lead them to take similar actions, but the precise manner in which they act will vary between nations. In contrast, proponents of economic theories often take the position that the advocated theory should apply universally and can be used to explain countries' successes and failures. Whether the developmental state concept constitutes a comprehensive and coherent theory or whether it resembles a legal precedent likely does not matter. The development state literature is instructive in understanding the principles that underlay Singaporean and Malaysian industrial strategy and the manner in which their governments designed and implemented their growth policies. The developmental state may be better understood through an examination of some of its defining characteristics.

Economic development forms the government's overriding priority (Johnson 1982: 305) and it is achieved through direct intervention in the economy in a manner that seeks to guide growth. As such, it rejects important aspects of economic theories that advocate a substantially *laissez-faire* approach to the market. South Korean economic policy is described by Amsden (1989) as deliberately getting prices 'wrong' (39-45) in rebuttal to the World Bank report, *The East Asian Miracle*, (1993) that attributed the success of what it termed High Performing East Asian nations to their ability to get prices 'right'. That report was perceived by many critics as concluding that the economic growth enjoyed by those countries was due to neoliberal economic policies forming what was known as the Washington Consensus, despite substantial evidence to the contrary including a great deal of evidence found in that report. Amsden (1994) likened the report to Narcissus: '... all the Bank was capable of doing in its *Report* was seeing the image of its own "market-friendly" policies in East Asia's fortunes' (628). Similar, if not as vivid, criticisms were levelled against the report by Sanjaya Lall (1994) who called it a 'flawed work' (646) and Dwight Perkins (1994).

Commercial activity in the developmental state is carried out primarily by privately owned enterprises (Johnson 1982; Amsden 1989; Wade 2004) and can be distinguished from concepts of state capitalism where large scale domestic activity may be carried on by government controlled enterprises and where huge sovereign debt funds seek to further governments' goals through domestic and foreign investment (Economist 2012: 11–12) The government in the developmental state uses the coercive and cooperative tools available to it to exert pressure on private enterprise to act in the manner desired by government. These tools can range from highly targeted financial incentives and penalties to criminal sanction to the more cooperative formation of 'numerous, formal, and continuously operating forums for exchanging views, reviewing policies, obtaining feedback, and resolving differences...' (Johnson 1982; 318). Both Johnson and Wade (2004) emphasize the importance of the consultative function of such government created institutions in creating a symbiotic and self-reinforcing relationship between the government and the private sector whereby the country's economic goals and the means of achieving those goals are mutually determined, although not necessarily between equals.

In a developmental state, the government does not act through the elected politicians so much as through 'a small, inexpensive, but elite state bureaucracy staffed by the best managerial talent available in the system' (Johnson 1982: 315). The bureaucracy not only identifies the industries to be developed but determines the means by which those industries are to expand and, subsequently, by supervising competition (315). The 'best and the brightest' bureaucracy rules supreme in the development of economic policy. In Johnson's conception, the legislative and judicial branches of government are 'restricted to "safety valve" functions' (315). Their purpose is simply to oversee the bureaucracy and to 'restrain it when it has gone too far' (315), but otherwise they act to protect the bureaucracy from outside interest groups.

Of critical importance to the developmental state is the creation of institutions to formulate, implement and coordinate economic and industrial policy. In Japan, the function is performed by the Ministry of International Trade and Industry (MITI) which is described by Johnson (1982) as follows:

> MITI's experience also suggests the need not to be doctrinaire; functions can
> and should be added and subtracted as necessary. The key characteristics of
> MITI are its small size (the smallest of any of the economic ministries), its
> indirect control of government funds ... its 'think tank' functions, its vertical
> bureaus for the implementation of industrial policy at the micro level, and its
> internal democracy. (320)

Similar roles were played in South Korea by the Economic Planning Board (Amsden 1989), in the non-agricultural sector in Taiwan by a combination of the Council for Economic Planning and Development and the Industrial Development Bureau (Wade 2004) and in Singapore by the Economic Development Board (Schein 1996). Several government economic bodies in Malaysia, such as the Economic Planning Unit, the Ministry of International Trade and Industry, the Malaysian Industrial Development Agency and the Malaysia External Trade Development Corporation are concerned with much of the same subject matter, but none of these bodies nor the state bureaucracy perform the policy-making roles described by Johnson. Politicians rule in Malaysia.

Another crucial characteristic of the developmental state relates to the role of technology in late industrialization. Amsden credits the importation of technology, learning and 'catching up' as playing a particularly salient role in South Korean economic development as with all late industrializing countries. She views such countries as benefitting from what Gerschenkron (1962) called a 'backlog of technologies to draw upon' (Amsden 1989: 13). While earlier industrialization relied upon invention or innovation, late industrializers are able to 'borrow' technology and industrialize through a process of learning (1). Borrowing is used somewhat figuratively as the technology is not returned. Historically, it was more likely to be acquired by learners through a variety of individual means.

> If they are to be at all successful at learning, they visit international expositions, attend conferences and lectures, read technical journals, hire experienced workers, visit overseas plants, engage foreign technical assistants, consult machinery suppliers, and buy, borrow, beg and steal foreign designs. (20)

The process, however, had evolved from when South Korea had begun to industrialize and technology transfer became more likely to be accomplished through corporate channels. As corporate assets became more intangible and proprietary technology became more critical to competitiveness, as discussed in Chapter 3, it became more closely guarded. South Korea resorted primarily to licensing and technical assistance programs, eschewing FDI (20).

Johnson makes similar points to Amsden. Technology transfer was crucial to Japan's development efforts and all arrangements by which technology was acquired were closely monitored by, and subject to the approval of, MITI (Johnson 1982: 16). Indeed, almost all the technology needed for Japan's industrial growth was imported at prices that 'were slight compared to what such technology would cost today, if it could be bought at any price' (16). It is thus questionable whether the same methods of technology acquisition used by Japan and Taiwan would be available to those now seeking to industrialize. FDI may be the most practical method of acquiring technology for less economically developed countries.

Malaysia's and Singapore's strategies also bear resemblance to Peter Evans' (1995) conception of embedded autonomy as well as Wade's (2004) governed market theory, both of which are derived from the developmental state literature, and which provide further insights into the process by which East Asian governments carried out their policies. Evans (1995) perceived state bureaucracies as embedded in 'a deep network of social ties that enable political elites to negotiate goals, policies, and implementation strategies with business actors' (Campbell 1998: 103). Wade describes in detail the manner in which those governments were able to guide industrial action and improve economic performance. In contrast to the relationship described in the developmental state literature and its derivatives, the leverage Asian governments enjoy over highly mobile MNCs and the relationships between state bureaucrats and senior MNC management is very different than with local firms whose growth was protected in greater or lesser measure from competition.

Why Malaysia and Singapore?   Malaysia and Singapore are not less economically developed countries today, but they once were. Nothing was inevitable about their success. They do not float on vast oil reserves, although petroleum has become increasingly important to the Malaysian economy. The countries serve as a compelling focus for study for several reasons having shared a common and closely intertwined history, including being the same country from 1963–1965. Both have enjoyed prosperity since going their separate ways, but Singapore has clearly become more affluent than Malaysia. While the countries undoubtedly differ in terms of size, resources and the ethnic distribution of their populations, it will be argued that despite political considerations which sometimes forced their governments to realign their social and economic priorities, a closer look at the countries shows that their divergent rates of growth subsequent to their split in 1965 can be attributed more to the manner in which they implemented their policies and laws and built their institutions than to their different geographic and demographic characteristics or the growth strategies they pursued.

Wade (1992) claimed that over the preceding twenty years the economic growth literature was 'big enough to fill a small airplane hangar' although, in his opinion, only a somewhat smaller subset was 'economically literate' (270). Compared to Japan, South Korea and Taiwan, relatively little has been written about Malaysia and Singapore. Economically, they are smaller countries and neither is currently of major strategic importance. Certainly, neither benefitted from the billions of dollars poured into other economies in the region by the United States for military and geopolitical reasons. The study of Singapore, in particular, has been spurned by many developmental state scholars. Amsden (1989) dismisses Singapore as a country to which her paradigm of late industrialization cannot apply because it, like Hong Kong, did not begin from 'the agrarian or raw material base that is typically taken to be the starting point of industrial transformation' (4). Similarly, Wade (2004) asserts that Singapore and Hong Kong 'are city states and not to be treated as economic countries' (xv).[2] Amsden abstains from exploring the pre-requisite need of an agrarian or raw material base and Wade fails to offer any explanation of why Singapore is not a country for economic purposes. Neither provides any evidence to substantiate their statements.

Much has been written about the causes of growth elsewhere in the region. Since Amsden and Wade, the literature has expanded further of which some has been focused upon Malaysia and Singapore. Huff (1995) has discussed Singapore from a developmental state perspective. Writers such as Garry Rodan, Rajah Rasiah, Khoo Boo Teik and Jomo K.S. have produced an important body of work examining the political economy of the region. Nevertheless, the political economy of Southeast Asia remains comparatively unexplored next to Northeast Asia. There is likely far more that remains to be discovered about economic growth in Southeast Asia.

Malaysia and Singapore may also have more in common with, and can provide more salient lessons for, less economically developed countries elsewhere in Asia and Africa than can South Korea and Taiwan. Korea and Taiwan were occupied by Japan for decades ending only with the defeat of Japan in August 1945. Like most

---

2 Singapore's population is approximately 4.7 million. It is 10 per cent or less smaller than Finland, the United Arab Emirates, Turkmenistan and the Central African Republic and 10 per cent or less larger than Norway, Ireland, Bosnia and Herzegovena, Georgia, Costa Rica, Croatia, Moldova, New Zealand and the Republic of the Congo. https://www.cia.gov/library/publications/the-world-factbook/rankorder/2119rank.html Physically, Singapore is larger than countries such as Saint Lucia, Barbados and Malta. https://www.cia.gov/library/publications/the-world-factbook/rankorder/2147rank.html.

of Africa and the rest of Asia, Malaysia and Singapore were colonized by European powers; Great Britain in their cases. The legacy of European colonization upon legal and economic institutional structures was likely different from Japanese occupation. Prior to their independence, most manufacturing and heavy industry in Malaysia and Singapore had been British owned. After their independence both Malaysia and Singapore relied heavily, and in the case of Singapore almost exclusively, on FDI to industrialize. This was not the situation in any of Japan, South Korea or Taiwan. They protected and built upon their existing bases and created a wide range of vibrant enterprises. Outside of the former Soviet Union, most of the less economically developed countries that gained their independence after World War II are former European colonies.

Less economically developed countries today are attempting to transform their economies in a time of increasing global economic integration where cheap labour is losing its appeal and the need to integrate ICT usage into their economies is growing. It is highly unlikely that they will be able to acquire the technology they need to industrialize through the same techniques used by Japan, South Korea or Taiwan. They, like Malaysia and Singapore, will likely be much more reliant upon FDI. The manner in which Malaysia, particularly Penang, and Singapore were able to attract FDI initially and how their economies evolved in order to continue to attract FDI that utilized increasingly sophisticated technology, hold particularly relevant lessons for poorer countries.

Finally, it should be emphasized that the case studies of Malaysia and Singapore are not intended as comprehensive explanations of their economic growth or as illustrative of the manner in which the developmental state literature can be applied to their industrialization efforts, as informative as that literature proves. The purpose is to allow a greater understanding of the role of institutions as a mediating factor in the relationship between ICT usage and growth and to provide actionable advice to the governments of less economically developed countries and others concerned with economic development who must decide which institutions are important and determine how to build them. The case studies examine one aspect of their economic growth, namely, the institution building efforts by these countries in the three other areas that have been identified as mediating the relationship between ICT usage and economic growth: infrastructure; investment; and human capital. In many respects, the economic growth of Malaysia and Singapore is the story of how they built the institutions that allowed them to bridge the Digital Divide, although that term was not in use when they emerged from colonial rule in the late 1950s and early 1960s. Their wealth was built incrementally, through careful planning, meticulous attention to detail and strong implementation facilitated by well-constructed institutions. The most important lessons may derive from the manner in which they implemented their decisions rather than the specific decisions they made.

If economic growth is the aspiration and the pursuit of a given economic theory is the strategy to achieve growth, then institution building is about the implementation of that strategy. The case study of Singapore is presented in

Chapter 6 and that of Malaysia in Chapter 7. Chapter 8 examines the lessons that can be derived from the case studies and Chapter 9 offers some concluding remarks.

PART I
ICT and Institutions

Chapter 1
ICT in Context

Changing Views about Development

Concern for international economic development emerged in the aftermath of
World War II as the exhausted European powers quickly realized that they could
no longer maintain their empires and that the independence of their former
colonies was only a matter of time. Decolonization would take place during a
period of conflicting motivations for governments as the desire for international
reconciliation vied with profound ideological cleavages. The impetus to seek
peaceful alternatives to war led, in part, to the creation of the United Nations and
the belief that all humans possess inherent rights found expression in the Universal
Declaration of Human Rights. Concurrently, the alliance to defeat Germany
dissolved; eventually replaced by confrontation between NATO and the Warsaw
Pact. Thus, driven by an odd mixture of idealism and the *realpolitik* of Cold War
competition for the allegiance, if not the affection, of newly independent and
unaligned states, East and West separately sought to foster economic development
primarily in Africa, Asia and Latin America.

The Marshall Plan, which provided the assistance that allowed Western
European governments to rebuild their cities and reconstruct their economies,
provided a compelling template for the West's efforts. It was presumed that the
same methods that brought dynamic growth to countries emerging from the
destruction of war would equally bring wealth to newly emerging nations that had
never known prosperity. The predominant belief in the 1950s and early 1960s was
that strict adherence to relatively straightforward economic prescriptions coupled
with the financial largesse of wealthy nations would shepherd the poor to sustained
economic growth. This view was epitomized by Walt Rostow who enunciated
five progressive stages of development from traditional society through 'take-off'
to one of mass consumption to which all countries could progress, if sufficiently
disciplined. Positive outcomes were not merely presumed, they were assured.
Rostow confidently asserted:

> These stages are not merely descriptive. They are not merely a way of
> generalizing certain factual situations about the sequence of development of
> modern societies. They have an inner logic and continuity. (Rostow 1960: 3)

A seemingly simple recipe of domestic savings and investment, supplemented
where necessary by foreign aid and investment, formed the cardinal elements of
then prevailing linear stages of development models. By respecting these rules

rigorously, states could expect their economies to follow a natural evolution that would allow them to progress from very simple economic structures to those that were much more complex and, by extension, affluent. A yellow brick road to greater wealth lay before emerging states. Unfortunately, just as Dorothy and her travel companions encountered unforeseen obstacles on their path to the Emerald City, economic development did not transpire as fluidly as envisaged.[1]

By the time recession hit the United States and other wealthy market economies in the late 1980s and early 1990s little had improved significantly over the intervening thirty years for many of the less fortunate nations. Outside of some spectacular Asian successes, three decades of development efforts failed to deliver sustained economic growth to most poor countries. Under ideal circumstances the well-intentioned macroeconomic approaches advocated by Rostow and his contemporaries would likely have proved insufficient catalysts of growth. The recession, however, caused the prospects for continued prosperity amongst relatively wealthy nations to become uncertain. Michael Porter observed, 'Whether prosperous or mired in poverty, nations, states, and regions all over the world were searching for ways of coping' (Porter 1990: xvi). It became widely acknowledged that the less economically developed could not expect the same positive outcomes by pursuing the development strategies that had benefited the more economically advantaged when the latter themselves could no longer assume continued prosperity.

Two separate forces emerged in the 1970s and converged in the 1980s to challenge accepted notions of economic growth. Technological innovation in telecommunications and computer power, function and affordability, constituted the first. The advent and rapid growth of ICT provided the means to access, manipulate and apply information instantly as well as to replicate that information infinitely and disseminate it inexpensively throughout the world. The second force, global economic integration, evolved as a result of the cumulative effect of macroeconomic and political events. Free markets prevailed over state-directed economies. Export-oriented growth strategies supplanted protectionist, import substitution policies and these, in turn, stimulated international trade liberalization accomplished through inter-governmental bodies as well as regional free trade arrangements such as the GATT, later to become the WTO, the European Union and NAFTA. Cheaper, faster transportation, highly mobile capital, the collapse of the Soviet Union and a greater openness to foreign investment added further fuel to the process.

---

1   *The Wizard of Oz* is a political allegory written subsequent to the 1896 American presidential election pitting William McKinley, supporter of the gold standard (his path being the yellow brick road) and William Jennings Bryan, leader of the free silver movement, who campaigned on the promise to improve the condition of the common man in the less economically prosperous areas of the United States. Hence, the book stands as an early contribution to economic development literature (Rockoff 1990).

Absent the movement towards trade liberalization, the impact of ICT, while profound, might have remained predominantly domestic in nature. Without the rapid technological advances in ICT, the consequences of economic integration might not have proved so disruptive to the structure of national economies. The simultaneous spread of both, however, amplified their individual effects and proved to be mutually catalytic. The spread of ICT permitted the pace of global economic integration to accelerate as distance became less relevant and borders proved increasingly permeable not just to goods and investment but to a deluge of information. Economic integration quickened the speed and scope of ICT innovation and its acceptance into all aspects of commercial and personal endeavour as well as facilitating its spread internationally.

From a corporate perspective, ICT and global economic integration not only permitted, but often demanded that, firms, particularly multinational corporations (MNCs), restructure and redistribute their operations. Cheaper transportation, communications and reduced trade barriers made it economically and operationally feasible for them to organize their various functions globally in the same manner as they had done domestically. If automotive components could be manufactured in Tennessee, turned into cars in Michigan, and sold throughout the United States, they could equally be sourced in Hungary, assembled in Germany and the finished vehicles marketed globally. Every element of the firm's value-added chain became susceptible to being carved up, reconfigured and geographically redistributed to take advantage of economies of scope and scale. The scattering of activities meant that each location became more highly specialized as its functions were integrated into the firm's international operations. Fewer foreign affiliates of companies were permitted to operate semi-autonomously reproducing, usually on a smaller scale, home country facilities and similar, if not identical, products for the local or regional market. A firm's business may have remained basically the same, but how it divided its activities and where it carried out different functions had become geographically dispersed.

The confluence of ICT and integration equally brought about a reassessment of the respective roles of governments and business in economic matters. Through ideology or necessity governments increasingly stepped back from direct ownership of commercial activities, ceding their place to the private sector, the health and vibrancy of which became the measure of a country's economic success. As borders swung open, imports threatened the domestic markets of local companies while providing them with opportunities to export. Traditional theories of international specialization of production based on the comparative advantage of nations slowly ceded to newer concepts of competitive advantage whereby dynamic agglomerations of complementary industries, clusters, were attracted to countries or regions within countries because of their unique attributes. Improved productivity became, and remains, the mantra of economic analysts as nations clamoured for Porter to review their competitiveness and growth strategies. John Dunning neatly summarized the respective challenges to business and government:

To business practitioners, research is revealing that, as the core competencies of firms become more knowledge-intensive, yet more mobile across space, so the choice of location in the production, organization and use of those assets is becoming a more critical competitive advantage. To the national or regional policy-makers the challenge is to offer, both to indigenous and foreign-owned firms, the spatially anchored resources and capabilities within their jurisdiction, which are perceived by these firms to be at least as attractive complements to their own ownership-specific advantages as those offered by other countries or regions. (Dunning 2000: 7)

ICT as a General Purpose Technology

The impact upon firms and governments of the changes brought about by the combination of ICT and global economic integration is merely symptomatic of a more profound change. Change, of course, is constant and 'economists have known for a long time that technical change is the single most important force driving the secular process of growth' (Bresnahan and Trajtenberg 1995: 83). Most such change, however, occurs incrementally and does not lead to a widespread belief that a new technology has precipitated a restructuring of the international economy. There is strong evidence, however, that ICT represents such a technology. This view's proponents argue forcefully that ICT differs in nature from other technological advances and that the opinion that ICT's adoption has brought about a new economy reflects the considered view of academic writers and international institutions such as the World Bank. Universal adoption of a particular technology alone would not be sufficient to support a conclusion that it had led to a new economy. It must also lead to economic growth; otherwise its impact would amount to little more than a reorganization of economic inputs. At issue during the recession of the early 1990s was not whether ICT was altering the nature of economies, but whether the ubiquitous infiltration of ICT into commercial activity would reinvigorate economic growth. Robert Solow (1987) noted in the late 1980s what has become known as the 'productivity paradox': 'We see computers everywhere but in the productivity statistics.'

Solow's observation struck a chord with development economists. It was far from certain at the time of his comment that ICT would prove to be a catalyst of economic growth. In response to his challenge, a number of prominent economists led by Paul David (1990) sought to understand better ICT's likely relationship to growth by examining more thoroughly the historical effect of previous transformative technologies on the structure of economies. David and others concluded that one could distinguish a very small number of modern innovations that could be classified as general purpose technologies (GPTs),[2] whose impact

---

2   The term derives from the work primarily done by David (1990) in the late 1980s responding to Solow's 'Productivity Paradox': David originally referred to general purpose

on economic structures set them apart from other technological advances. David argued that parallels could be drawn between the electric dynamo and the computer and that the profound economic changes stemming from ICT usage found their analogy in the process of electrification at the beginning of the twentieth century in the United States and England. Building on David's work, several definitions came to inform the discussion of GPTs. Bresnahan and Trajtenberg (1995) are cited by Jovanovic and Rousseau (2003) as describing GPTs as possessing the following characteristics:

1. Pervasiveness: The GPT should spread to most sectors.
2. Improvement: The GPT should get better over time and, hence, should keep lowering the costs of its users.
3. Innovation spawning: The GPT should make it easier to invent and produce new products or processes.

Lipsey, Bekar and Carlaw (1998), characterized GPTs as follows:

> i) wide scope for improvement and elaboration; ii) applicability across a broad range of uses; iii) potential for use in a wide variety of products and processes; iv) strong complementarities with existing or potential new technologies. GPTs play the role of 'enabling technologies', opening up new opportunities rather than offering complete solutions. They act as catalysts, inducing complementary innovations in other sectors. (as summarized by David and Wright 1999: 6)

While emphasizing different constituent aspects of GPTs both analyses clearly recognize common elements. These descriptions prove more complementary than conflicting and allow some latitude in determining whether a particular technological innovation constitutes a GPT. David, writing with Wright (1999) ten years after his original work, and Hanna (2003) preferred the latter formulation despite, as they pointed out, that it led Lipsey to identify a lengthy list of GPTs in their analysis 'from power delivery systems (waterwheel, steam, electricity, internal combustion) and transport innovations (railways and motor vehicles) to lasers and the internet' (David and Wright 1999: 6). David and Wright saw these individual innovations as subsidiary or tributary streams of technical development constituting discrete products flowing from a more basic GPT. Thus, while the Lipsey's formulation of GPT gained favour with David and Wright and Hanna, those authors agreed with both Jovanovic and Rousseau, who preferred the former definition, and Bresnahan and Trajtenberg, that one could identify only three modern industrial GPTs: the steam engine; electrification; and ICT.

---

engines but subsequent writers (Bresnahan and Trajtenberg (1995); Jovanovic and Rousseau (2003); Helpman (1998); Crafts (1997, 2001)) picking up on his theme preferred to speak of general purpose technologies, a term which David subsequently accepted (see David and Wright 1999).

Many technologies possess the characteristics of a GPT in some measure as Lipsey's list of such technologies demonstrates, but in their essence, the other economists emphasize, GPTs represent a change in substance more fundamental than simply an improved method of carrying on an activity. Over time, they not only permeate throughout societies, but they ultimately alter the economic structures of those societies. As Jovanovic and Rousseau argue, the term is 'reserved for changes that transform both households and the ways in which firms conduct business' (1995: 1). They can be distinguished from other technologies by their ability to create new opportunities rather than offer 'complete, final solutions' (Bresnahan and Trajtenberg 1995: 84) themselves. Bresnahan and Trajtenberg illustrate the point by drawing an analogy to the case of hybrid corn which they contend could be perceived 'as a GPT in the context of agriculture' (86). Its importance lay in its 'invention of a method of inventing' (Bresnahan and Trajtenberg 1995: 86) rather than for the quality of the corn it produced.

Unstated but underlying the proposed definitions, as Solow succinctly highlighted, rests the assumption that GPTs must eventually lead to greater productivity and economic growth. The process may be lengthy. GPTs are disruptive by their very nature; their utility initially uncertain. Ultimately, however, industry and households find it economically preferable to adopt the new technology rather than repair or enhance existing systems. Once adopted by some industry participants the new technology provides them with a sufficiently significant competitive advantage so as to compel other participants to make similar investments. At the household level, it leads not just to a marked improvement in one's standard of living, but it can alter how one organizes one's life.

It may take decades of refinement before the new technology percolates through a society displacing the existing means of carrying out daily activities and even then, the surrounding circumstances must be propitious to its general adoption. The significance of the wheel was likely not universally recognized immediately upon its invention. Once a 'tipping point' has been reached GPTs represent an economic Rubicon; there can be no turning back. The steam engine permitted the mechanization of production, stimulating the industrial revolution with its resultant division of labour. Electrification altered industrial and household structures anew. Its importance lay not only in the potentially universal provision of relatively inexpensive power, a significant advance in and of itself, but in its capacity to allow industries to reconfigure themselves in novel ways and carry on their activities more efficiently. The impact of electrification is such that without its widespread adoption economic progress constitutes an impossible dream for less economically developed countries. Large parts of the word continue to live without electricity. They are invariably labelled as 'mired in poverty'.

The Process of Electrification

As stated, David (1990) saw a strong parallel between the process of electrification in the United States and Great Britain and the spread of ICT later in the century. A brief look at the spread of electricity sheds light upon the disruptive, but ultimately powerful, economic impact of ICT. Decades passed between the time electricity could be commercially generated for widespread consumption and when its economic impact became evident. Although the dynamo had been invented as early as the 1830s, the first mass electrical generation facility in Niagara Falls, New York came on-line only in 1894. By 1910 electricity accounted for only 3 per cent of all residential lighting and less than 5 per cent of the horsepower capacity of factory mechanical drive in the United States (Crafts 1997).

The 1910s saw the balance tilt rapidly as major investments in electrical generation, substantial drops in electricity rates and the integration of power distribution and transmission facilities over expanded territories caused industry increasingly to switch to remotely generated electricity from alternative forms of individual factory-linked power generation. By the early 1920s, over a quarter-century after the opening of the Niagara Falls hydro-electric facility, electrification finally exceeded steam as a source of power. Like the collision of events that served as catalysts for the spread of ICT, the electrification process was further abetted, according to David, by 'the development of a general fixed capital formation boom in the expansionary climate of the 1920s' (1990: 357) coupled with an increase in the human capital educated in the use of the new technology as embodied in factory architects, electrical engineers and electricians required to harness the benefits of electrification. A non-technological event also provided a critical stimulus to the process of electrification in the 1910s. Prior to World War I, more than one million European immigrants annually arrived on American shores providing a vast pool of inexpensive labour. World War I and subsequent changes to American immigration legislation altered the equation. The end of mass European migration resulted in a sharp increase in the price of labour.

> Although this history was largely independent of electric power technology, it was the confluence of these two streams that gave the decade of the 1920s its truly extraordinary character. Both were facilitated by favorable macroeconomic conditions, including the high rate of investment in new plant and equipment; the new flexibility in plant location and design facilitated the reorganization of job assignments and labor systems as well as physical arrangements. (David and Wright 1999: 5)

The combined effect of these events allowed firms to reorganize their structures, figuratively and literally, shifting production from the 'group drive' system of clustered groups of complementary machines, originally dependent upon water and steam powered motors, to the 'unit drive' system whereby individual electric motors operated each piece of equipment and the introduction of the assembly line. While on the surface, this would appear to be nothing greater than the substitution of one form of electricity generation for another, it had more profound ramifications for factory design and production techniques.

> The advantages of the unit drive extended well beyond savings in fuel and in energy efficiency. They also made possible single-story, linear factory layouts, within which reconfiguration of machine placement permitted a flow of materials through the plant that was both more rapid and reliable ... Electrification saved fixed capital by eliminating heavy shafts and belting, a change that also allowed factory buildings themselves to be more lightly constructed, because they were more likely to be single-story structures whose walls no longer had to be braced to support the overhead transmission apparatus. The faster pace of material throughput amounted to an increase in the effective utilization of the capital stock. Further, the frequency of downtime was reduced by the modularity of the unit drive system and the flexibility of wiring; the entire plant no longer had to be shut down in order to make changes in one department or section of the factory. (David and Wright 1999: 4)

Electrification allowed for the creation of assembly lines and mass production thereby reducing unit costs, but also devaluing many artisanal skills. Only after the investment had been made to reconfigure factories and electricity had been widely adopted by business and was the stage set for productivity increases and economic growth.

Endogenous Growth Theory

Under neoclassical economic theories 'there is no intrinsic characteristic of economies that causes them to grow over extended periods of time' (Todaro and Smith 2009: 151). Economic growth is viewed primarily as a function of the domestic use of capital and labour productivity and external, or exogenous forces, such as technology, which are assumed to be the same for all nations. Changes in the rate of growth that are not directly attributable to capital or labour are bundled and ascribed to a third category, commonly known as total factor productivity (TFP), also referred to as multifactor productivity (MFP) by some authors. 'Output growth is then a weighted average of the growth rates of these two inputs, plus the residual term, TFP growth' (Temple 2002: 247).[3] TFP, however, represents far

---

3   Todaro and Smith (2009) define the residual as the 'Solow Residual'. There is some suggestion that TFP and the Solow Residual may not be precisely the same and that the Solow Residual is a measure of TFP growth (see 'Total Factor Productivity,' http:// economics.about.com/od/economicsglossary/g/tfp.htm). The literature referred to herein almost exclusively uses the terms TFP and MFP, and not the Solow Residual when describing growth that is not attributable to capital or labour productivity growth.

more than merely a pigeonhole into which growth of indeterminate attribution can be slotted. TFP growth suggests a more efficient utilization of resources. 'A rise in TFP indicates that more output can be achieved from given inputs or, in other words, that the production frontier has shifted' (Temple 2002: 248).

Electrification eventually brought dramatic TFP growth to the United States in the early twentieth century. The manufacturing sector, which had averaged 0.5 per cent TFP growth annually between 1899-1919, soared to 5.3 per cent from 1919–1929 (Crafts 1997) of which electrification's contribution amounted to an estimated 2.4 percentage points per year, close to half the increase (David and Wright 1999). The American experience of 'delayed and then accelerated TFP growth, associated with electrification' (David and Wright 1999: 8) was mirrored in Great Britain. Despite the pronounced differences in the American and British economies during the 1920s[4] David and Wright note that it is 'something of a surprise to find a remarkable number of qualitatively similar patterns in the British productivity data' (1999: 8–9). From 1924–1937, TFP grew at an average annual rate of 0.70 per cent throughout the British economy, compared to 0.45 per cent from 1873–1913. Among the explanations for such a surge in TFP in Great Britain 'we find that at the top of the list is electrification' (David and Wright 1999: 9).

While growth rates tend to be calculated using neoclassical models, the theoretical underpinning that helps to understand the impact of GPTs and their effect on economic growth in individual countries can be found in endogenous growth theory. Technological change is viewed in neoclassical growth theory as exogenous, or independent from national economies. It suggests that all countries have relatively equal access to the same technology. Todaro and Smith (2009), however, criticize neoclassical theory as failing to explain why the use of technology and its impact on economic growth vary widely.

> Though intuitively plausible, this approach has at least two insurmountable drawbacks. First, using the neoclassical framework, it is impossible to analyze the determinants of technological advance because it is completely independent of the decisions of economic agents. And second, the theory fails to explain large differences in residuals across countries with similar technologies. (Todaro and Smith 2009: 151)

Endogenous growth theory stands in contrast to neoclassical growth theory by viewing the varying national rates of technological change as due to domestic factors such as government policies, institutions and human capital development. The origins of endogenous growth theory are often traced to Schumpeter's (2008) analysis of the effect of technological change upon economic growth, which he termed 'Creative Destruction', and Arrow's (1962) examination of 'Learning By

---

4   The effect of electrification on other countries was not easily available. The authors rely primarily on the work of Mathews et al. (1982).

Doing' by which the acquisition of knowledge, or learning, through experience in problem-solving produces an impact upon productivity.

Schumpeter viewed capitalism as a constant process of industrial innovation whereby new methods of production superseded established methods, rendering them obsolete. The transition from old to new, however, is far from smooth.

> The opening up of new markets, foreign or domestic, and the organizational development from craft shop and factory to such concerns as U. S. Steel illustrate the same process of industrial mutation ... that incessantly revolutionizes the economic structure *from within*, incessantly destroying the old one, incessantly creating a new one. This process of Creative Destruction is the essential fact about capitalism. It is what capitalism consists in and what every capitalist concern has got to live in. (Schumpeter 2008: 83, emphasis original)

As Schumpeter underlined in a footnote to the above quotation, although the process of change is incessant, change itself does not proceed in a linear manner. The revolutions he referred to occur in 'discrete rushes', like waves, and can prove quite disruptive to firms, individual well-being and national economies as new industrial processes are adopted.

Arrow looked more closely at the process through which technological change occurs. He postulated that technological change is derived from knowledge and that knowledge is a product of learning by doing. Workers who repeat the same task tend to become more efficient and, hence, more productive. Citing earlier studies that had noted improvements in productivity in the construction of airframes and in iron-works without new capital investment, he concluded that such improved productivity could 'only be imputed to learning from experience' (Arrow 1962: 156). Consequently:

> I advance the hypothesis here that technical change in general can be ascribed to experience, that it is the very activity of production which gives rise to problems for which favorable responses are selected over time. (Arrow 1962: 156)

He thus challenged the neoclassical view which also considered knowledge to be an exogenous variable, suggesting that knowledge levels were influenced by domestic factors and should be economically modelled as an endogenous variable.

More recent work devoted to the expansion of endogenous growth theory builds upon the work of Schumpeter and Arrow. Romer (1990) created what Todaro and Smith (2009) cite as the 'seminal model'[5] of endogenous technological growth in 1990 which he built upon the belief that technological change 'lies at the heart of economic growth' and that it 'arises in large part because of the intentional actions taken by people who respond to incentives' (Romer 1990: S72).

---

5   Crafts (1997) is of the view that Grossman and Helpman developed the paradigmatic model of this kind.

Romer's model explains technological change as resting upon public and private investments in human capital and knowledge-intensive industries. In particular, his model suggests:

> ... an active role for public policy in promoting economic development through direct and indirect investments in human capital formation and the encouragement of foreign private investment in knowledge-intensive industries such as computer software and telecommunications. (Todaro and Smith 153)

Aghion and Howitt in their textbook, *Endogenous Growth Theory*, discuss the relationship between the innovative technological waves suggested by Schumpeter and the much more recent literature that examines the notion of GPTs and their impact on economic structures. They note that GPTs eventually raise productivity, but are also disruptive to economies. Citing the work of David (1990) and Lipsey and Bekar (1995) studying GPTs, Aghion and Howitt emphasize that GPTs may improve productivity and lead to growth over the long run, but:

> there is no reason to expect this process to proceed smoothly over time...[T]he initial effect ... may not be to raise output, productivity or employment but to reduce them. (1998: 244)

They suggest that the explanation for such a result may be found partly in the work of Helpman and Trajtenberg (1994) who argue that GPTs 'do not come ready to use off the shelf' (Aghion and Hewitt 1998: 245). GPTs require the development of costly intermediate goods. Firms will switch to the new GPT only when they view it as profitable to do so. National income may fall during the transition period as resources are taken out of productive activity and put into the development of the needed intermediate components. Endogenous growth theory thus tends to view technological change initially as potentially harmful to national economies before leading to growth. The manner in which countries cope with such change and adopt the new technology depends upon domestic factors, not outside forces. The onus thus lies upon government, businesses and individuals to incorporate technology, such as ICT, into their work and personal activities.

Chapter 2
ICT and Economic Growth

ICT and Productivity

Early, and in retrospect relatively simplistic, notions of economic development were challenged in the 1980s by the twin forces of global economic integration and the spread of ICT. It became evident by the end of the twentieth century that ICT was one of a few relatively rare technologies known as GPTs that reshaped economic structures. Its economically disruptive nature and the manner of its progress were consistent with Schumpeter's notion of Creative Destruction. At issue in the late 1980s, however, was whether the ubiquitous infiltration of ICT into commercial activity would reinvigorate economic growth. It was far from certain at the time of Solow's 'productivity paradox' comment that ICT would do so. Proximity to change, however, exacerbates the difficulty in definitively establishing the impact of that change on productivity and economic growth. The economic effects of, and the nature of the changes occasioned by, electrification prove more obvious now than they likely did in the midst of the Depression in the 1930s.

Early in the new millennium economic studies began to appear attempting to determine whether a relationship could be clearly established between ICT, increased productivity and economic growth.[1] Only by then had ample time passed to allow for sufficient data to be accumulated and analysed to permit conclusions to be drawn with any degree of confidence. The preponderance of the growing evidence revealed by these studies suggests strongly that ICT usage can be a catalyst of growth. The strongest evidence of the relationship derives from detailed examination of the rise of American productivity in the second half of the 1990s, followed by the performance of other economically advanced countries whose experiences reproduce many aspects of American performance although not as widely or uniformly. Subsequently, mounting evidence emerged of a relationship between ICT usage and economic growth in the Asian 'tiger economies' of South Korea, Taiwan, Hong Kong and Singapore.[2]

The following review of the literature does not seek to reconsider whether such studies were correct. International organizations such as UNCTAD, the ITU and the WEF annually examine the spread of technology and its impact, as discussed in the Introduction. Rather, the purpose is to discern what those studies have identified as the mediating factors in the relationship between ICT and growth.

---

1   See, for example, Pohjola (2002b), Oliner and Sichel (2000), Jorgenson (2001), and Temple (2002).

2   See Cowan for a contrary view.

The United States

The last decade of the twentieth century marked an economic turning point in the United States. The gloom and uncertainty of the late 1980s ceded to an unprecedented period of strong economic growth, reduced inflation, low unemployment and a rampaging bull stock market. 'The US expansion which came to an end in 2001 had lasted exactly 10 years, one of the longest unbroken expansions ever recorded by an industrial country' (Temple 2002: 241). Real GDP growth averaged slightly over 4.2 per cent annually while non-farm output increased at a rate of 4.8 per cent per annum. The comparable figures for 1991–95 were approximately 2.5 per cent and 2.8 per cent, respectively (Bureau of Economic Analysis 2010). Matti Pohjola (2002b) estimated ICT's contribution to American GDP growth in the 1990s at close to one percentage point. During those ten years ICT came to permeate American life. At the beginning of the decade, for example, relatively few Americans owned cell phones or personal computers. By its end, most did.[3] The ICT share of aggregate capital stock rose from nil in 1960 to 0.02 per cent by 1990 to over 0.08 per cent in 2000 while between 1995–2001 American non-farm worker productivity rose 2.4 per cent annually (Temple 2002).[4]

ICT potentially manifests its contribution to output and productivity growth through one or more of three channels.[5] The first is as an economic sector in itself through the production of ICT goods and the provision of ICT-related services thereby adding to the value-added generated within an economy. Technological progress in the ICT-producing sector results in new products and services becoming available at lower prices than previously available for the products they replace, thereby driving productivity growth in that sector. The second channel lies as an input to labour productivity in the form of ICT capital deepening.[6] It measures the increased productivity of each unit of labour in the economy through the greater use of ICT. The third channel, and possibly most important because of its potentially profound, long-term economic consequences, is the effect of ICT on TFP growth through the creation of 'new markets, new products and new ways of organizing how society operates' (Temple 2002: 5). It attempts to measure the impact of the incorporation of ICT into the general economy. TFP growth has been described as the measure of the 'flow-on effect of ICT production on efficiency and productivity gains to non-ICT related industries' (Clarke 2003: 12).

The first channel of ICT's contribution to output, the ICT producing sector, increased dramatically in the United States in the late 1990s. Productivity growth

---

3   Personal computers were in less than 20 per cent of households in 1990 but over 60 per cent by 2000 (Jovanovic and Rousseau 2003).

4   See also Oliner and Sichel (2000: 3), who estimate productivity rose nearly 2.5 per cent annually from 1995–99.

5   See, for example, Temple (2002) and Qiang and Pitt (2004).

6   Temple defines ICT capital as usually including 'computer hardware, and sometimes software and telecommunications equipment' (2002: 247).

from 1995–99 was nearly double the average pace of the preceding 25 years and ICT usage and improvements in ICT production accounted for close to two-thirds of that increase (Oliner and Sichel 2000). Labour productivity, the second channel, which grew an average of 1.26 per cent per annum from 1973–1990 jumped to an average annual rate of 2.11 per cent from 1995–1999 (Temple 2002). The third channel, generalized economic TFP accretion due to ICT, was not as universally acknowledged as the productivity gains made through the other two channels, but the consensus was that studies of the issue supported the view that ICT alone increased TFP by slightly over 'one-quarter of a percentage point per year' (Qiang and Pitt 2004: 8). Highlighting the ability of highly competitive American service companies to compete successfully in an increasingly competitive world, it was confidently asserted that:

> … correctly understood, there is a new e-conomy. In particular, there has been a substantial structural acceleration of [TFP] outside of the computer sector. And there is clear supportive evidence of an acceleration of productivity in service industries that are purchasing IT. (Baily and Lawrence 2001: 310)

Ten years after Solow questioned whether the computer age would lead to increased productivity, the American economy answered emphatically that it did.

Western Europe, Canada and Australia

The situation in wealthy nations apart from the United States proved mixed during the 1990s. There was initially little compelling evidence that the demonstrated relationships between ICT and productivity gains in the United States had been fully replicated elsewhere. Studies showed that production and use of ICT outside of the United States led to productivity gains but not in the same comprehensive manner or of the same magnitude as was the case of America. van Ark et al. (2003b) compared the output and productivity contribution of ICT in the European Union with that in the United States. They found investment patterns and declining ICT prices to be similar in both. ICT's contribution to labour productivity in the European Union, however, was approximately half the American rate in the early 1990s. By the late 1990s, its relative contribution to labour productivity was similar but in absolute terms the rate continued to be much lower. Moreover, in contrast to the United States, TFP growth slowed in the European Union in the late 1990s. The authors dismissed the argument that Europe was merely lagging behind the United States in TFP growth, finding 'no evidence for this catching-up process' (van Ark et al. 2003b: 4). Pohjola reached a similar conclusion. Casting his net more widely, he examined 42 countries (24 of which were classified as high income) for which ICT spending data was available. His analysis 'did not display significant returns to ICT investment in terms of productivity growth' (Pohjola 2002b: 394).

In a second study also published in 2003, van Ark, writing with different co-authors, examined labour productivity across 51 industries in 15 OECD countries in addition to the United States between 1990–2000. Looking more closely at labour productivity in individual industries, particularly those classified as heavy ICT-using industries such as securities and both retail and wholesale distribution, they determined that Europeans were investing heavily in ICT equipment and software at 17 per cent of total business investment, but in the United States, the amount was close to 30 per cent (van Ark et al. 2003a). The authors concluded that the growth in American productivity can be attributed to 'rapid technological change in the ICT producing industries and rapid ICT investment in other parts of the economy' (van Ark et al. 2003a: 3). In contrast, 'it appears that the slower diffusion of ICT is the principal factor in explaining the lower European productivity growth' (van Ark et al. 2003a: 2).

Regional aggregation, however, can mask individual country performance. Panel studies of grouped nations, even those with similar levels of wealth, can cause anomalous performances to be overlooked. Contrary to the studies grouping large numbers of countries, several contemporaneous but more narrowly focused studies began to find increasing evidence of relationships between ICT and productivity outside the United States such as in Finland (Jalava and Pohjola 2001), Australia (Cardarelli 2001), Japan (Qiang and Pitt 2004), France (Estavao and Levy 2000) and the United Kingdom (Kodres 2001).

The OECD published a series of studies in 2004 examining the connection between ICT and economic growth and firm level productivity in its member countries. These studies sought to determine more precisely whether ICT affected economic growth and, if so, under what conditions. They concluded:

> Thus far, only few OECD countries have clearly seen an upsurge in productivity growth in those sectors of the economy that have invested most in the technology, notably services sectors such a wholesale trade, financial services and business services. (Pilat 2004: 8)

According to the studies, ICT diffusion varied widely across the OECD countries with the United States, Canada, New Zealand, Australia, the Nordic countries and the Netherlands enjoying the highest rate of ICT uptake (Pilat and Devlin 2004). Differences in diffusion patterns were attributed to several factors, the most important being differences in direct acquisition costs of ICT, the ability of firms to absorb it and enabling factors such as 'the availability of know-how and qualified personnel, the scope for organizational change and the capability of a firm to innovate' (Pilat and Devlin 2004: 33). It was postulated that the largest users of ICT would show the largest economic impacts.

The evidence demonstrated that those countries did, in fact, show the largest productivity gains but in different ways. One study showed that capital deepening through ICT investment 'establishes the infrastructure for the use of ICT (the ICT networks) and provides productive equipment and software to businesses'[7] leading

---

7   As summarized by Pilat in the introduction to Ahmad et al. (2004).

to labour productivity growth and between '0.3 and 0.8 percentage points of growth in GDP' (Ahmad et al. 2004: 9). Another study determined that 'the contribution of ICT manufacturing to overall labour productivity growth has risen over the 1990s' (Ahmad et al. 2004: 89) in most OECD countries. Similarly, the smaller ICT producing services sector showed improvements in labour productivity. ICT-using sectors showed mixed results. Slightly over half the countries showed increased growth rates when comparing labour productivity rates between 1990–1995 and 1996–2000. The evidence of the impact of ICT on TFP growth outside the United States remained similarly inconclusive. The contribution of ICT using services to TFP growth at the aggregate level could only be confirmed in a handful of countries.[8] Only in Australia was there strong evidence at the sectoral level that ICT growth could lead to TFP growth (Pilat and Wolfl 2004).

Asia

The evidence regarding the impact of ICT upon economic and productivity growth in Asia for the same period is also mixed. In a 2002 article, Wong Poh Kam compared ICT diffusion rates in 11 East Asian countries with those in 25 OECD nations. He found significant disparities in ICT diffusion within the region that corresponded closely with income disparities. Japan and the tiger economies of South Korea, Hong Kong, Taiwan and Singapore showed levels of ICT adoption similar to those in the OECD. The ASEAN 4 (Indonesia, Malaysia, the Philippines and Thailand) as he termed them, struggled to catch up although Malaysia had noticeably distanced itself from the other three nations:

> … the Asian countries as a group indeed exhibit *lower* levels of ICT penetration than can be predicted from their level of economic development (as measured by GDP per capita) or their level of competitiveness (as measured by their world competitiveness index). (Wong 2002: 181, emphasis original)

Potentially more troubling to Wong was the fact that the disparities in ICT adoption rates between the tigers and the ASEAN 4 were greater than their disparities in per capita GDP. His research determined that the less developed Asian nations underperformed relative to their wealth (185). Wong's findings were further confirmed by Kraemer and Dedrick in 2002 who found that 'on average, Asian countries and companies are not using IT effectively to improve productivity or develop their economies' (2002: 33, italics omitted).

Carrying Wong's work forward, but on a wider scale, Qiang and Pitt (2004) found that the divide between Asian and non-Asian countries had widened further. Within Asia, they found that the gap was 'extremely large' and growing. Their study examined the United States, 12 economically developed European countries and ten economically developing Asian countries to assess the impact

---

8   Canada, Germany, Denmark, and Finland (Pilat and Wolfl 2004).

on economic growth due to capital deepening and increases in total factor productivity. Qiang and Pitt's analysis of the East Asian experience did little to suggest that the situation had changed since Wong's study. Despite being massive producers of ICT goods, very little adoption of ICT could be found. They echoed Wong's findings of a sizeable and growing digital divide not only between more economically developed countries and Asia but within Asia itself.

The disparities in ICT adoption were also puzzling because East Asian countries had captured a disproportionate share of global ICT production. Japan and the tigers had initially been large producers, but as they grew wealthier and their labour costs rose, production had shifted to the ASEAN 4 which had also attracted North American and European MNCs active in the sector. Whereas Japan and the tigers had used ICT production as a stepping stone to more technologically sophisticated industries and to intensifying ICT usage throughout their economies, such did not appear to be the case among the ASEAN 4. Instead, Wong noted, the Asian financial crisis of 1997–98 suggested the opposite. In an effort to encourage ICT production, their governments may have discouraged diffusion through excessive regulation and policy bias that protected the ICT manufacturing sector but inhibited the growth of high ICT using sectors such as the financial services industry (Wong 2002; Qiang and Pitt 2004). The regression analyses Wong ran showed that ICT production provided few or no positive spillover effects and that the Digital Divide in Asia, already high, risked becoming even higher in the future.

These studies demonstrated but could not identify the cause of the growing gaps within Asia and between Asian and non-Asian countries. Kraemer and Dedrick (2002) emphasized that they did not believe their findings were skewed due to there being more economically developing countries in their Asian sample than their non-Asian sample. In their view: 'It is most likely that the explanation lies elsewhere' (29).

When ICT Leads to Economic Growth

As the literature demonstrates, ICT usage can result in productivity gains and economic growth, but it does not do so in all circumstances. The American experience of the second half of the 1990s presents the most dramatic evidence of a causal relationship between ICT and growth. Widespread ICT usage and a strong ICT producing sector stimulated significant gains in both labour productivity and TFP leading to uncommonly robust economic growth rates. Contemporaneous studies of other countries or regions led to mixed results. Surveys of Western Europe and of OECD members, other than the United States, found little evidence that ICT usage consistently led to productivity gains. Others reached similar conclusions in pan-Asian studies (Wong 2002; Kraemer and Dedrick 2002; and Qing and Pitt 2004).

Was the American experience anomalous? In the early 2000s such might have been arguable. No definitive connection between ICT and economic growth could be more broadly substantiated. Relatively little time passed, however, before new, more narrowly focused studies provided evidence that the United States did not stand alone. Surveys of affluent nations concluded that ICT contributed significantly to growth in almost all the world's largest economies, the G-8 nations. Outside of the G-8 but still within the circle of wealthy nations, evidence was found of labour productivity and TFP gains in Finland and Australia. In 2004, the OECD studies produced a much more optimistic picture of the European relationship between ICT and growth. They found ICT-related productivity growth in several Scandinavian countries, Ireland and the Netherlands. Further afield, compelling evidence of a relationship between ICT and productivity growth in Japan and the four Asian tigers – Hong Kong, Singapore, South Korea and Taiwan – but very little elsewhere in the Asia-Pacific region.

The answer to the question of whether the American economic experience of the 1990s was anomalous may lie in a combination of factors found only there at that time. In the early 2000s such factors became increasingly present in other affluent countries, such as OECD members and the Asian tigers, stimulating productivity and economic growth there, too. In contrast, those factors either remained absent or not present in adequate degree in the less economically developed countries to allow for similar results. Of the many potential factors, four have been repeatedly cited in the literature as necessary to fashion the links between ICT and economic growth. The first is physical infrastructure. Countries need an appropriate quality and range of telecommunications services for computers and other hardware to attach to. Second, nations – governments, firms, individuals – must invest heavily in ICT hardware, software and services and continue to do so for sufficient time to allow ICT usage to diffuse throughout the economy. Third, ICT requires human capital. Investing massively in telecommunications infrastructure and ICT hardware and software alone will not lead to economic growth unless a country is able to produce an adequate pool of skilled workers to take advantage of ICT's opportunities. Fourth, a country's enabling environment, or its policies, laws institutions, must be conducive to the translation of ICT usage into economic growth.

Infrastructure

The usage of ICT requires basic physical infrastructure including, at a minimum, wired and wireless telephone lines and broadband internet capacity to disseminate data, voice and pictures quickly together with computers and telephones to access, receive and send such information. By the mid-1990s the literature suggests that a critical mass of infrastructure existed solely in the United States. Differences in levels of basic ICT infrastructure, however, only offer a partial explanation of why OECD countries lagged behind the United States. Fortunately for those wealthy countries, they had the means to invest heavily in infrastructure and could quickly catch up. In less economically developed countries lack of physical infrastructure often represents a serious impediment to the diffusion of ICT beyond mobile telephony. As Qiang and Pitt note:

Production of some ICT services and efficient ICT use rely heavily on a dependable infrastructural framework. However, most developing countries do not possess an adequate information and communications infrastructure…and consequently, service is limited and expensive. (Qiang and Pitt 2004: 16)

Table 2.1 compares elements of basic telecommunications infrastructure from 1995-2001, the years of the strongest American productivity and economic growth, between high income OECD countries and those classified as developing and least developed. It also provides comparisons for the same period by geographic region. The North American region comprises the United States and Canada, but given the relative size of the two countries' populations and economies, the American component dominates.[9] Although the number of personal computers, internet users, telephone mainlines and mobile phones increased through all income groups over the time examined, the absolute numbers grew much more in the OECD countries than elsewhere. By 2001 the number of PCs and internet users in the OECD was approximately tenfold greater than in those classified as developing countries and 100 times greater than in the least developed. Less dramatic, but significant nevertheless, the figures illuminate important differences in levels of ICT infrastructure between the United States and Western Europe, providing a partial explanation of the failure of Western European countries to demonstrate ICT-related growth concurrently with the United States. North American computer ownership exceeded Western European levels by approximately 55 per cent in 1995. Underscoring the surge in American investment during the 1990s, the American level was almost twice that of Western Europe in 2001 despite substantial Western European investment that allowed its per capita ownership in 2001 to surpass that of the United States in 1995. The internet figures show the explosion in its use in the late 1990s. The ratio between the United States and Western Europe in internet usage narrowed considerably between 1995 and 2001 from over 2:1 to roughly 4:3 but was still large in absolute terms. In turn, the ratio of personal computer ownership and internet usage between Western Europe and East Asia and the Pacific[10] remained fairly constant at approximately 2:1 while also expanding in absolute terms.

---

9   Canada was one of the few countries to show ICT-related productivity gains roughly within the same period as the United States but to not the same extent. For the purposes of discussion, the references to North America in Table 2.1 will be taken to be references to the United States.

10   The East Asian and the Pacific region includes several wealthy nations – Australia, New Zealand, Japan, South Korea, Taiwan, Hong Kong and Singapore – as well as many poor ones. This is a much more economically diverse region than Western Europe thereby undoubtedly overstating the gap between Western Europe and the wealthy nations while understating it with respect to the rest of the region.

Table 2.1 Information and communications infrastructure, 1995–2001 (per 1,000 inhabitants)

Country Groups	Personal Computers		Internet Users		Telephone Mainline		Mobile Phones	
	1995	2001	1995	2001	1990	2001	1995	2001
Income Breakdown								
High-income OECD	188	363	34	360	455	574	89	690
Developing Countries	14	34	2	37	52	104	4	94
Least developed	–	4	–	3	3	7	0	8
Regional Breakdown								
Northern America	273	623	68	467	555	660	108	382
Western Europe	174	325	30	345	445	572	84	747
East Asia and Pacific	82	158	14	177	148	222	36	278
Eastern Europe and Central Asia	26	81	5	65	130	232	4	199
Middle East and North Africa	28	62	1	61	89	147	16	163
Latin America and the Caribbean	17	49	1	63	66	145	9	142
Sub-Saharan Africa	–	12	–	9	9	19	1	30
South Asia	0	4	0	4	5	20	1	9

Source: Reproduced from Qiang and Pitt 2000: 17.

Notes: – = Data not available, 0 = less than half the unit shown, and the classifications are based on the definitions in the World Bank's Development Indicators Database. All countries with a population below one million are excluded. The group average was calculated when data for a least half the countries was available.

Table 2.2 Teledensity (fixed and mobile) per region

Region	1990	1996	2002
Sub-Saharan Africa	1.0	1.4	5.3
East Asia and the Pacific	5.5	11.6	38.1
Eastern Europe and Central Asia	12.8	17.3	38.9
Latin America and the Caribbean	6.4	11.5	36.7
Middle East and North Africa	4.7	8.3	22.4
South Asia	0.6	1.5	4.5
Developed Countries	46.5	64.1	120.1

Source: Reproduced from World Bank 2005: 9.

Table 2.2 shows the extent to which access to basic telecommunication grew. Comparing East Asia and the Pacific with Developed Countries the teledensity of the former septupled from 5.5 per cent of the population to 38.1 per cent while that in Developed Countries 'merely' doubled resulting in a ratio that shrunk from over 8:1 to slightly over 3:1. The absolute difference, however, in teledensity doubled from 41 per cent to 82 per cent. The absolute gap between those classified in the World Bank report as the Developed Countries and the rest of the world continued to increase. While significant strides in building infrastructure have been made, the shrinking of relative gaps should not obscure expanding absolute gaps.

Although access to basic telecommunications and teledensity showed noticeable improvement, basic telecommunications represents only the most rudimentary infrastructure. 'Regarding access to more advanced ICTs, the picture remains one of considerable growth, but also considerable gaps' (World Bank 2005: 11). Internet usage and web hosting in less economically developed countries, for example, continued to lag badly behind the wealthy nations despite high economic growth rates relative to the more prosperous. While the amount of internet bandwidth improved in the less affluent countries the World Bank estimated, for example, that available bandwidth between Africa and the United States was merely one-three hundredth that of available bandwidth between Europe and the United States despite trade representing 10 per cent of European-American trade. (12) The amount of available bandwidth is paltry not only in absolute terms, but: 'Globally, the number of broadband subscribers and international bandwidth in the developing world is far lower than its share of the world economy would suggest' (12). The World Bank noted that although telecommunications access was generally not regarded by firms as a major impediment to doing business, in several less economically developed countries it was ranked as the number one concern (23). Lack of basic infrastructure thus stands as the first reason ICT-related productivity gains cannot be found in many developing and least developed countries, to borrow the OECD's classifications.

ICT Investment

The second factor relates to investment in ICT products. The availability of basic infrastructure acts merely as a pre-requisite to utilizing ICT. Governments, businesses and households all need to invest in ICT in sufficient quantity and for sufficient time that its usage permeates throughout an economy. Bassanini and Scarpetta examined productivity growth patterns in several OECD countries in the 1980s and 1990s. Amongst their conclusions they found 'a positive link between changes in ICT expenditure and the acceleration of MFP growth across countries' (Bassanini and Scarpetta 2002: 342), although they noted that spending alone would not lead to productivity growth. Moreover, their study supported a 'slow-diffusion' theory which argues that the impact of ICT investment upon productivity is both cumulative and slow. Productivity gains become apparent only with the passage of time after adequate investment has been made throughout an economy. Similarly, Lee, Oh and Seo found that the discrepancies between economic growth rates within the OECD could be traced to the cumulative effect of ICT investment. They argued that 'the differences in growth rates will widen or shrink according to the amount of IT investment in each country' (Y. Lee et al. 2002: 2). Similar conclusions were reached by the OECD in its 2004 studies which found that the economic impact of ICT was 'clearly linked to the extent to which different ICT technologies have diffused across OECD economies.' It attributed the need for diffusion to ICT being a network technology. The more who use it, 'the more benefits it generates' (Pilat and Devlin 2004: 20).

Total non-residential investment in ICT equipment and software as a percentage of all investment reached almost 24 per cent in the United States by 2000 and approximately 17 per cent in Canada and Australia (both of which showed early productivity gains), far in excess of any other OECD countries (Bassanini and Scarpetta 2002). The OECD reported similar findings for 2001 concluding that the ICT share of non-residential gross fixed capital formation was 'particularly high in the United States, the United Kingdom, Sweden, the Netherlands, Canada and Australia [but] substantially lower' (Pilat and Devlin 2004: 20) elsewhere in Europe and Japan. Differences in economic growth rates across OECD nations were attributed in large measure to the fact that some countries started earlier and invested more in ICT than others. In both studies, the countries with the highest ICT investment rates showed the greatest productivity growth. Consequently, part of the explanation behind OECD nations lagging behind the United States may simply be that by the late 1990s, when the United States experienced its productivity surge, the use of ICT by businesses and household had not diffused through those countries to the same extent as it had in the United States.

Investment in ICT and time seem to have been the crucial elements that allowed OECD countries to begin to show ICT-related productivity growth. A debate rages, however, whether building ICT infrastructure and sufficient investment in ICT over time will provide similar results in less economically developed countries. The preponderance of the evidence, as the indices produced by the ITU, UNCTAD and the WEF discussed in the Introduction demonstrate, continue to support the view of Bridges.org, an international organization devoted to studying the Digital Divide. It concluded in an early comprehensive report published in 2002 that:

> All countries, even the poorest...[are] increasing their access to and use of ICT. But the 'information have' countries are increasing their access and use at such an exponential rate that, *in effect*, the divide between countries is actually growing. (Bridges.org, emphasis original)

Furthermore, the organization noted that as the saturation points for baseline technologies are reached in wealthy countries, they acquire more advanced technologies which Bridges.org argues only they, having the requisite skills and wealth, can afford to acquire and use allowing them to derive 'exponential benefits'.

A number of East Asian countries engaged in the manufacture of ICT products, notably Indonesia, Malaysia, the Philippines and Thailand, have failed to exhibit ICT-related productivity gains. Aware of ICT's importance those countries built upon their strong histories of electronic consumer goods manufacturing sectors to foster economic sectors focused upon ICT goods production. They hoped that doing so would spillover into high rates of diffusion and adoption which would in turn lead to productivity gains and economic growth. Such has not been the result. In his analysis of eleven Asian economies, Wong looked specifically at whether the spillover effects from ICT manufacturing activities would improve ICT diffusion in those countries and foster its use more broadly the overall economy of the countries concerned. He unequivocally concluded that high levels of ICT production did not generate spillover effects on diffusion.

> The results clearly show that there is no statistically significant correlation between competitiveness in electronics production and all the ICT diffusion indicators except secure e-commerce servers, electronics consumption/capita and ICT expenditure/capita in the sample of all countries. (Wong 2002: 184)

Those countries have benefitted from the jobs such assembly operations have created, but no more than a manufacturing boom in any other sector would have produced.

Bayoumi and Haacker, in an IMF Working Paper appropriately entitled 'It's Not What You Make, It's How You Use IT', suggest the size of the manufacturing sector does not matter with respect to productivity gains. They found that the benefits of ICT production are 'highly skewed to a small number of countries with large IT sectors relative to output' (Bayoumi and Haacker 2002: 4). The consistent fall of ICT prices has resulted in a 'constant deterioration of their terms of trade' (Bayoumi and Haacker 2002: 4) benefiting the consumers of ICT, particularly the United States as the largest, far more than the producers. They note that greater economic benefits accrue to large users of ICT such as Australia and New Zealand, not to the major manufacturers of products such as those in East Asia.

Human Capital

Although ICT manufacturing has failed to generate productivity gains in East Asia, there is no guarantee that had government resources instead been directed at stimulating ICT usage the results would have been significantly different. More than simple spending on ICT equipment is needed to profit from ICT. Even in OECD countries, Pohjola concluded, spending on ICT proved to be a 'poor explanatory factor of economic growth ... consequently, it cannot by itself be the solution to the world's development problems' (Pohjola 2002b: 392). More likely, he continued, ICT infrastructure and investment must be accompanied by 'human capital and appropriate government policies which enhance and amplify the effects of investments in ICT' (Pohjola 2002b: 393). Levels of human capital in other OECD countries and the four Asian tiger economies are far closer to those in the United States than other East Asian ICT manufacturing countries. In addition, as Bassanini and Scarpetta noted, countries showing the greatest productivity gains had not only invested in ICT but had simultaneously enhanced labour market skills. Consequently, once ICT investment levels rose sufficiently in OECD countries they had the human capital available to convert that investment into productivity gains. Human capital is thus the third factor mediating ICT and economic growth. The reason investment in ICT has not led to productivity gains in less economically developed countries is due in large measure to a lack of human capital.

In a comprehensive World Bank study of the relationships between economic growth, education and technology levels in Latin American countries by de Ferranti et al., the authors found that the single greatest contributor to the widening gap in income distribution between prosperous nations and Latin American nations 'is due not to concentration of factors of production, such as capital, but rather of knowledge' (de Ferranti et al. 2003: 1). They compared resource rich Latin American countries first with other natural resource abundant countries such as Australia, Canada and the Nordic European nations and second with the four East Asian tiger economies which do not possess great natural wealth but in the 1960s exhibited levels of economic development comparable to the Latin American countries. The authors found that significant gaps between Latin America and the Asian tigers in the relative levels of education and ICT penetration appeared in the 1980s and did not shrink in the 1990s (de Ferranti et al. 2003). The emphasis upon technology and education in both the resource rich OECD countries and the Asian tigers led to a third gap between them and Latin America – productivity. TFP growth in Latin America languished badly behind the other two regions from 1960–2000 falling deeply into negative territory in the 1980s before recovering weakly in the 1990s (de Ferranti et al. 2003).[11] As a result, Latin American countries remained behind while the Asian tigers joined the resource abundant

11   Annual average TFP growth rates for Latin America for the 1960s, 70s, 80s and 90s were1.16, 0.47, -1.60 and 0.47 respectively. Comparable rates for the Asian tigers were

nations cited in the study – Canada, Australia and the Nordic European countries – along with the rest of the OECD, as among the world's most prosperous nations.

> The central premise of the report is that skills and technology interact in important ways, and this relationship is a fundamental reason for the large observed differences in productivity and incomes across countries. Indeed, numerous studies have shown that differences in per capita income depend more on differences in total factor productivity (TFP) than on differences in primary factor accumulation. And this report argues that skills upgrading, technological change, and their interaction are major factors behind total factor productivity growth. (de Ferranti et al. 2003: 2)

Effective use of ICT requires skills that can only be acquired through instruction and mastered through repetition. Equipment can be purchased and installed relatively quickly but using it effectively cannot be rushed. As Wong argued:

> First, technological learning may require a long cumulative process of human capital development through incremental learning by doing. Consequently, new technologies cannot be diffused at a faster pace in the late-industrializing countries than in the advanced countries because of the *human capital bottleneck*. (Wong 2002: 168, emphasis added)

It takes time to develop the expertise and human capital required to take advantage of ICT. Assuming, for example, an oil-rich but less economically developed country were to create excellent ICT infrastructure and could afford all the equipment and software needed to develop its favoured economic sectors, without a sufficient number of skilled workers the investment could not be fully utilized. The lack of human capital is the biggest impediment to rapid catching-up. Mobile phone penetration rates may be higher in some less economically developed countries than in more prosperous ones, but one cannot extend the rapid shrinking of that gap to ICT usage more generally. As Qing and Pitt argue:

> However, despite the potential advantages of being a late-comer, some ICTs are not amenable to leapfrogging but require instead a stock of existing ICT capital… The requirements for technology adoption in terms of human capital also vary across the new technologies, which allows relatively easy leapfrogging in some areas, such as mobile telephony, while other technologies, such as effective use of certain software applications, require higher levels of human capital. (12)

The need for human capital in order to utilize ICT underscores the unprecedented nature of ICT. If nineteenth century mechanization can be taken to have substituted

---

1.32, 1.09, 0.83 and 1.83 while those for the natural resource abundant countries were 1.75, 1.12, 0.83 and 0.90.

for, and enhanced, human strength, ICT acts as an extension of the human brain. Hanna, an economist and advisor to the World Bank on 'e-development', in his study of ICT's implications for national development policies maintains that 'ICT has become a tool for amplifying brainpower and innovation' (2003b: 17) not a substitute. Whereas the 'mechanization of industrial process was profoundly deskilling' (Hanna 2003b: 19), ICT is skill intensive. Understood in this manner, it becomes clearer that ICT rests on two equal pillars: the bundle of telecommunications infrastructure, computer hardware and software; and human capital. ICT stands at the intersection of technology and knowledge. Countries cannot expect to enjoy economic growth by investing in one without the other. Investment in technology will not yield the desired economic results without a pool of skilled labour. Countries may well find that the greater expense and more sustained challenge will be to develop human capital than to purchase hardware and equipment. Citing the United States as an example, Kenny estimates that:

> ... only 10 per cent of the cost of computer ownership to a company is accounted for by the purchase of the physical equipment itself – the other 90 per cent is made up of factors such as training and support. Where human capital is rare, these non-physical costs use [sic] are likely to be an even more significant barrier to use. (Kenny 2002: 8)

Institutions and the Enabling Environment

The fourth factor linking ICT usage to productivity gains and economic growth has been described as the proper 'enabling environment for development' (Clarke 2003: 19). Falling primarily to government, the right environment requires a concerted and conscious effort to align a country's policies, laws and institutions to create the necessary conditions to allow for growth. The role of institutions cannot be analysed separately from the other three factors in attempting to understand the relationship between ICT and economic growth, but within their context. Policies, laws and institutions create the structures that allow the other three factors to function effectively. Infrastructure, investment and human capital can be examined individually. The role of institutions forms an integral part of the analysis of each.

It has been suggested by Wong that the inability of Asian ICT manufacturing countries to benefit from ICT may be a function of either poorly conceived government policies or the inability to implement good policies due to poor institutions, or a combination of such reasons. He postulated that the lack of positive spillovers from ICT manufacturing resulted from policies that focus too much upon production of ICT goods and not enough attention to its usage in other sectors. This led to:

> ... underdevelopment of services industries, especially financial services and other knowledge-based services which are ICT intensive. Accordingly, many Asian governments, through excessive domestic regulations in general and possible policy bias in favour of manufacturing in particular, may have deterred (or at least not encouraged) the widespread diffusion and adoption of ICT applications in many service sectors of the economy. (Wong 2002: 169)

Similarly, Qiang and Pitt suggest that Asian countries have emphasized production to the detriment of use:

> The region's preoccupation with promoting ICT production has resulted in a minimal allocation of resources to promote its use – the assumption appears to have been that ICT production would automatically lead to widespread use of it, but it has not. (Qiang and Pitt 2004: 11)

They cited India as an example of a country where the ICT sector may have 'crowded out ... other industries competing for highly-skilled labour and capital resources' (Qiang and Pitt 2004: 11).

Unfortunately, it is easier to point to misguided policies in retrospect than to identify prospectively a specific course of government action likely to succeed in fostering economic growth. Well-intentioned recommendations for government action can appear overly broad and simplistic. The first recommendation of the DOT Force report presented to the G-8 leaders in its proposed plan of action boldly asserted:

> As a powerful tool to pursue development goals, national eStrategies need to receive the highest level of national political commitment and meet the requirements of each country. These strategies, generated by the countries themselves, should be the result of a consultative process involving all relevant interested parties in the country, including the private sector and non-profit organizations. (DOT Force 2001: part three)

Others have attempted to be more specific, but again speak in general terms. Wong pointed to the need for 'relatively efficient factor and product markets, well-functioning financial and regulatory institutions, etc.' (Wong 2002: 168) while Qiang and Pitt (2004) emphasized trade openness as did Caselli and Coleman (2001), particularly manufacturing trade openness vis-à-vis the OECD and good property-rights protection. Baily and Lawrence (2001) have pointed to policies that foster competition and fiscal discipline allowing for low interest rates thereby encouraging higher levels of research and development and investment.

A consensus clearly exists among economists that a country's enabling environment comprised of its policies, laws and institutions play a crucial role in translating ICT usage into economic growth. Their customary precision, however, seems absent in giving clear definition to those terms. Prescriptions on the role of government and the actions they should take to harness ICT's potential range from the vague over-arching platitudes exemplified by the DOT Force recommendations to the narrowly focused suggestions put forward by Caselli and Coleman or Baily and Lawrence. Consequently, the question of which policies, laws and institutions serve to stimulate ICT usage and translate it into economic growth remains unanswered by those examining the relationship between ICT and growth, just as those engaged in the study of endogenous growth theory give institutions a central role in the process of technological change, but provide little further guidance to governments attempting to determine which institutions are important.

Todaro and Smith, as noted above, see endogenous growth theory as suggesting an 'active role' for public policy, the development of human capital and the 'encouragement of foreign investment in knowledge-intensive industries' (2009: 153). Similarly, Crafts, in his discussion of the development of endogenous growth theory, stresses that 'Institutions (and policymaking) can be placed right at the heart of the growth process in a rigorous way' (1997: 68). Unfortunately, as Aghion and Hewitt (1998) point out, endogenous growth theory identifies the key role played by institutions, but pays little attention to them. The Solow Residual, or TFP, they underline, does not explain the role of technological knowledge in the growth process so much as acknowledge technology's importance, thereby highlighting general ignorance about the residual's cause 'and evidence that it [the Solow Residual] "explains" a lot is just evidence that our ignorance is very large' (Aghion and Howitt 1998: 66). While endogenous growth models thus emphasize the role of governments in fostering growth and the central role played by institutions, they shed little light on which institutions are important and provide scant guidance to governments. Trebilcock and Prado argue:

> Among economic theories of development, endogenous growth theory is perhaps the one that has most explicitly acknowledged the role of institutions in promoting economic development. However, they do not provide any insight into how to improve them. (Trebilcock and Prado 2011: 13)

Given the relatively recent nature of ICT and the study of its impact on productivity and economic growth, this area represents a comparatively new academic discipline and it may simply be that insufficient time has elapsed to allow those studying the relationship to be more specific. Governments of less economically developed countries, however, require more than vague advice to create an 'enabling environment conducive to growth' or to improve their institutions. A much clearer understanding is needed of the meaning of policies, laws and institutions, the distinctions between them, which institutions are important, particularly those that facilitate the relationship between ICT and economic growth, and how to build them.

Chapter 3
FDI and ICT: Mutual Attraction

One Course of Action

For the governments of less economically developed countries that lack the money to build infrastructure or invest in ICT goods, educate their populations and build strong institutions, the challenge of fostering ICT usage is particularly daunting. Reliance by less affluent nations on cheap labour or natural resources alone, however, will no longer be likely to provide a solid basis for sustained economic growth. More optimistically, the new economy presents opportunities for countries without such natural endowments to achieve greater prosperity. If they can build on the advantages they possess, economic integration can provide easier access to international markets and open new possibilities for growth. To seize those opportunities, however, they must begin to incorporate ICT usage into their economies.

It is not sufficient simply to advise governments to foster ICT usage throughout their economies. ICT hardware and software are expensive and ICT applications adapted for business use tend to be privately owned. Many governments lack the means to purchase what they require. FDI provides a potential avenue for such countries to acquire some of the investment needed and it forms an integral part of many nations' industrial development strategies. Attracting FDI, however, is very competitive and the benefits it can bring are far from guaranteed. The governments of less economically developed countries need to understand how the 'new economy' has altered what investors seek and how to improve the likelihood that such investment will deliver the desired benefits. An examination of the factors that mediate the relationship between FDI and economic growth suggests that they overlap significantly with those that mediate the relationship between ICT and economic growth.

The Role of ICT in Attracting FDI

'Foreign direct investment' is a term that captures a wide range of transactions, usefully categorizing diverse investment activities, but potentially obscuring as much as it illuminates when interpreted in such a broad manner so as to suggest that all transactions caught within its ambit are the same.[1] The words 'foreign' and

---

1 FDI simply describes a wide variety of activities with basic common characteristics. Generally, a commercial enterprise, often referred to as a multinational enterprise, based in

'direct' merely describe the source of the investment and the manner in which it is made. 'Investment', whether domestic or foreign, remains a commonly understood but vague concept describing the commercial expenditure of money or other assets in the hope of securing a profit. The term 'foreign direct investment' sheds little light on the nature of an individual investment. FDI is not a fungible commodity where one investment can be substituted for any other with either contributing equally to economic growth. No two investments are identical or affect economic development equally. Although the number of such investments may be counted, and the money and other assets invested quantified, doing so will not measure their effect on economic growth.

With global economic integration and the ascendency of export oriented regimes over import substitution regimes, the attraction of foreign investment has come to constitute an integral part of almost all nations' development strategies. For less economically developed nations the impact of each foreign investment can prove greater than in prosperous countries due to the paucity of domestic funds and its magnified consequences on a small economy. It thus becomes extremely important for the governments of those countries to determine what they want from FDI, how to get it and, once they get it, how to make the most of it.

ICT from FDI

Governments seeking technology, particularly ICT, need to look for it in the places where it is created and owned. Scientific and technological innovation

---

one country invests capital, goods or intangible assets such as intellectual property in a commercial enterprise based in another country, known as the host country. In exchange, the MNC receives an equity interest in excess of ten percent of the domestic commercial enterprise, with the intention of holding that interest longer than one year and participating actively in its management. The investment may establish a new enterprise, commonly called a 'greenfield' investment, acquire part or all of an existing business, or create a new entity through the formation of a strategic alliance or joint venture in cooperation with a domestic partner. UNCTAD (2002), p. 291; International Monetary Fund, *Balance of Payments Manual* (Washington, D.C.: IMF, 1993); OECD, *Detailed Benchmark Definitions of Foreign Direct Investment* (Paris: OECD, 1996). International forms of cooperation that do not involve the acquisition of an equity stake and a role in management by the foreign investor do not fall within the definition of FDI and, thus, do not show up in FDI statistical data bases or form part of the empirical analyses concerning FDI based on such data. The inherent nature of such contractual relationships will provide challenges to their quantification. With the growth of outsourcing and non-equity joint ventures and strategic alliances, an important and growing trend identified by J.H. Dunning in 'The Advent of Alliance Capitalism' in *The New Globalism and Developing Countries* edited by J.H. Dunning and K.A. Hamdani (New York: United Nations University Press, 1997), particularly in research and development activities, traditional form of measuring FDI may need revision, but the inability to account fully for such international transactions should not affect the current analysis.

and utilization, particularly in ICT, are highly concentrated in wealthy countries and, within those countries, ownership of the rights to such technology, research, development and innovation take place not just within the private sector but within a sliver of it (JBIC Institute 2002: 56). Most commercial applications of ICT are owned by MNCs. In 1996, for example, when personal computer use was in the early stages of its rapid spread, over 90 per cent of all global research and development expenditures occurred within the G-7 countries. The United States alone accounted for 40 per cent of the total. The expenditures by merely 50 American firms amounted to nearly half of all industrial-based R&D (JBIC Institute 2002: 56). Governments and publicly funded institutions such as universities remain the largest centres of basic research, but commercial application of technology of the type required to promote economic development rests predominantly within the grasp of MNCs.

Until such time as MNCs believe their interests are best served by providing their proprietary ICT to others in a more benevolent manner, those seeking its use will be required to acquire it on a commercial basis. There appears, however, to be a growing reluctance among MNCs to sell ICT. As an increasing amount of their core assets become intangible and knowledge based (Dunning 1998: 3–4), MNCs wish to exercise ever tighter control over the use of their technology and are unwilling to part with it to third parties (Lall 1997: 51). Even where MNCs are prepared to sell advanced ICT, the cost of buying such technology can prove to be beyond the means of less economically developed countries, as Narula and Dunning emphasize (1998: 10). Given the often limited resources available to less economically developed countries and the importance to their economies of accessing the ICT needed to develop specific sectors, FDI 'may represent the most *efficient* option' (Narula and Dunning 1998: 10)[2] [emphasis original] available to them to acquire the ICT they need. As UNCTAD noted, 'FDI and technology transfer are increasingly interlinked' (UNCTAD 2004: 4). In order for the governments of less economically developed countries to obtain the ICT they need to upgrade their targeted economic sectors, they will likely need to seek recourse to FDI.

Fortunately for those governments, there is substantial evidence that FDI can be an effective tool in transferring ICT (Nunnenkamp 2004: 667–8; JBIC Institute 2002: 56; Lall 1997: 53). Borensztein et al. (1998) examine the role of FDI in the transfer of technology to host countries and its impact on economic growth by analysing FDI flows into 69 less economically developed countries from 1970–1989. Their findings support a positive stance on the importance of FDI as a means to transfer technology as well as establishing the crucial role human capital plays in its absorption.

> Our results suggest that FDI is in fact an important vehicle for the transfer of technology, contributing to growth in larger measure than domestic investment.

---

2   See also JBIC Institute: 57.

> Moreover, we find that there is a strong complementary effect between FDI and
> human capital, that is, the contribution of FDI to economic growth is enhanced
> by its interaction with the level of human capital in the host country. (Borensztein
> et al 1998: 117)

They disagree with those who have postulated that the transfer of technology
through FDI produces a negative impact on the ability of domestic technological
capacity to develop, as do Pack and Saggi (1997) who look specifically at whether
FDI 'crowds out' the domestic development of technology and conclude that
'empirical research has, in general, failed to provide support for this view. The
list of studies providing contrary evidence is long.' (86) These conclusions are
reinforced by Blomstrom et al. (1999) who further find that foreign-owned firms
tend to introduce technology more quickly than domestic firms and that the
competition they engender leads to more rapid adoption of innovation by both the
MNCs and domestic firms.

Targeting Investment

Having identified the desired contribution from FDI, governments cannot simply
open their countries' borders in the hope that what marches in will provide the
benefits sought or lead to economic growth. Governments looking to attract FDI
as part of a larger strategy to stimulate the growth of a specific economic sector
and encourage the creation of sustainable clusters of competitive advantage need
to understand that the connection between FDI and economic growth depends
upon the ability of the host to take advantage of 'spillovers' from FDI through
its 'absorptive capacity'. Benefits do not simply spillover nor do they become
absorbed by the host country's economy.

In order to understand what attracts investment, governments must look at
investment from the perspective of the MNC. Three factors underlying investors'
decisions have been identified, most notably by Dunning (2000), as key to
increasing the probability of attracting the desired FDI. First, governments need to
determine what motivates investors active in the particular economic sectors they
wish to expand and to identify specifically what those investors seek to obtain from
their foreign investments. Usually, such motivations are a combination of general
factors, such as access to markets or resources, industry-specific factors, common
to most participants engaged in the relevant field of endeavour, and firm-specific
factors, which are unique to the individual investor. Only general motivations will
be discussed as the relevant industry and firm-specific motivations will depend
upon the targeted economic sectors.

Second, foreign investors often enjoy several choices to pick from in
determining where to make their investments. The factors that determine where
they make their investments are generally called locational determinants.
Locational determinants are comprised of the assets and attributes found in a host
jurisdiction that attract foreign investors. The relevant locational determinants

will vary according to the motivations of the investor. Two possible investment sites will rarely offer identical advantages to an investor or suffer from the same drawbacks. The ability of governments of a prospective destination to increase the number of salient locational determinants available in their jurisdictions improves the chances that they will be successful in attracting the FDI that they seek.

Third, firms operating in the same market tend to form relationships with each other, commonly called linkages, for the purchase and sale of goods and services. Such linkages can provide the means for the assets and skills brought by the FDI to overflow the confines of an investment vehicle first into the 'linked' domestic firms and then more broadly into the economy. Linkages also provide benefits to investors. Where an MNC believes linkages can be formed in a country it enhances the likelihood of it investing there as the MNC may see greater opportunities for hiring skilled labour or management, efficiencies through relationships with local firms and greater opportunities for innovation.

Changing Motivations: FDI as a Seeker of ICT

Firms invest abroad because they can carry on business more profitably or efficiently than by remaining purely domestic in nature. Their general motivations normally fall within the ambit of four categories: market, resource, efficiency and strategic asset seeking (Dunning 2000). Although not every investment fits comfortably into a pigeon-hole, one or more of the four general motivations drive most investment decisions. Historically, MNCs sought primarily to exploit natural resources, manufacture their products inexpensively or sell their goods into new markets (Dunning 1996; 1998; 2002; Vernon 1996). For countries with few attractions for investors other than nature's bounty, sweat or many mouths, the good news is that firms are still so motivated, although sweat may be in the process of being phased out. Scarce primary resources will continue to attract considerable interest by MNCs as the world's population and consumption increase and traditional sources of raw materials deplete. Firms dependent upon such resources will be attracted to countries where such resources are abundant.

Large markets, too, draw foreign investment. China and India caught investors' attention well before their governments liberalized their economic policies, despite widespread poverty, merely because of the number of people living there. Once these markets opened, eager investors poured in, notwithstanding difficulties in doing business that may have dissuaded the same investors from smaller jurisdictions with fewer potential business challenges. The size of a local market, together with accessible nearby markets and the ability of the target market to support demand are the main requirements for market seeking FDI (Narula and Dunning 1998). Market and resource seeking FDI remain extremely important motivations of MNC investment.

Efficiency and strategic asset seeking investment motivations are newer and spring from the same global macroeconomic forces that cause governments to re-evaluate continually their economic development strategies and focus upon their areas of competitive advantage. At the firm level these forces compel MNCs to reassess their organization, operations and core competencies. Efficiency seeking FDI, while not supplanting market and resource seeking FDI, has grown in importance compared to them as a motivating factor for MNCs (Dunning 1996). Cheaper transportation, communications and reduced trade barriers make it economically and operationally feasible for MNCs to organize their various functions globally in the same manner as they have done domestically. Every element of the firm's value-added chain is susceptible to being carved up, reconfigured and geographically redistributed to take advantage of economies of scope and scale (Dunning 1996). This point was succinctly reiterated by Thomas Friedman (2012):

> These C.E.O.'s rarely talk about 'outsourcing' these days. Their world is now so integrated that there is no 'out' and no 'in' anymore. In their businesses, every product and many services now are imagined, designed, marketed and built through global supply chains that seek to access the best quality talent at the lowest cost, wherever it exists. They see more and more of their products today as 'Made in the World' not 'Made in America.'… Victor Fung, the chairman of Li & Fung, one of Hong Kong's oldest textile manufacturers, remarked to me last year that for many years his company operated on the rule: 'You sourced in Asia, and you sold in America and Europe.' Now, said Fung, the rule is: 'Source everywhere, manufacture everywhere, sell everywhere.' The whole notion of an 'export' is really disappearing.

The redistribution of activities means that each location has become more highly specialized as its functions are integrated into the firm's international operations. As a consequence, the geographical configuration of an MNC's individual activities itself has become an important competitive decision for firms (Dunning 1998).

While not explicitly seeking knowledge, the decision by an MNC of where each element of its production or operations will be located is made after a careful analysis of where it feels the activity can best be carried out. Locating a specialized economic activity in one place implies that greater expertise resides there than in another. Hence, it is not surprising that where MNCs seek similar specialized knowledge, agglomerations, or clusters, of firms in related endeavours often result (Narula and Dunning 1998). Specialized knowledge is considered to be a created asset, as opposed to one that naturally occurs such as resources. Efficiency seeking MNCs thus require 'a certain threshold of created assets' (Narula and Dunning 1998: 13) in places where they choose to establish a presence.

The strategic assets sought by FDI are often intangible consisting of the knowledge, information and expertise embedded in a firm's people, processes and organization. Unlike a piece of equipment which can be put to only one use at a time, knowledge 'can be put to multiple uses; often one kind of knowledge needs to be combined with several other kinds to produce a particular good or service.' (Dunning 2000: 9) The knowledge needed to adapt and innovate rarely belongs to one firm or is situated in one place. MNCs scour the globe for knowledge to complement and enhance their existing assets. The primary purpose of strategic asset seeking FDI is to acquire the resources or the skills that that the investor believes will make its products more attractive or otherwise improve its competitiveness. Unlike resource, market and efficiency driven FDI, where MNCs seek to create wealth or enhance profitability by exploiting their existing assets, strategic asset seeking FDI endeavours to secure or enhance future competitive advantage. Strategic asset seeking FDI is highly concentrated in the most economically advanced countries quite simply because that is where the most advanced knowledge resides (Dunning 2002).

Resource and market seeking FDI still search for resources and markets, but there are indications that cheap labour may be losing some of its appeal. Adaptation of knowledge, embodied in technology, has led to traditional distinctions between high tech and low tech industries breaking down as activities that were once labour intensive are no longer so. The migration seems one-way as productivity gains through the use of ICT prevents sectors from reverting to labour intensive means of production. Efficiency seeking FDI looks to redistribute globally an MNC's activities in many instances on the basis of specialization which implies knowledge. Strategic asset seeking FDI seeks knowledge by definition.

In all cases, except possibly purely market seeking FDI, the component parts of ICT, knowledge and technology, if not advanced ICT itself in the case of strategic asset motivated FDI, are becoming of greater importance to MNCs as they determine how best to structure their operations. The level of technology use in a country, the ability of local labour to use their systems and operations effectively and the technological sophistication of complementary systems used by domestic suppliers and buyers act as important considerations in MNC decision making. In this sense, FDI has become a seeker of ICT.

Locational Determinants: ICT as a Magnet for FDI

Relatively little of the extensive empirical research into the impact of FDI has segmented FDI by motivation and matched it to specific locational determinants. Most studies aggregate national FDI stocks and flows. It is thus difficult to ascertain with confidence the relative importance of individual locational determinants in attracting differently motivated FDI. With the growth of efficiency and strategic asset seeking FDI, it was postulated that traditional locational determinants had declined in importance and that resources and market size alone were no longer sufficient incentives for investment (Davis 2003; Dunning 2002; JBIC Institute 2002; Kokko 2002). Labour costs, physical and financial infrastructure, local capabilities, financial incentives (tax breaks, concessionary loans and grants), economic and political stability, regional trade agreements, international trade and monetary policy, technical and management skills, education, availability of local inputs, business environment, protection of property rights (tangible and intellectual) and a host of others were suggested and, to a lesser extent, tested as the new critical locational determinants.[3]

Peter Nunnenkamp, too, wondered whether the nature of locational determinants had changed with economic globalization leading him to address the topic in several articles concerned with the relationship between FDI and growth (Nunnenkamp 2001; 2002, 2003 and Spatz 2003a and b). He concurred with the empirical studies which had historically tied FDI to market size and economic growth. Given, however, the UNCTAD World Investment Reports (1996; 1998) and other studies that adopted Dunning's analysis of the shift in the motivations underlying FDI, he asked whether 'this is (and will be) still true with ongoing globalization' (Nunnenkamp 2001: 14). It was possible that the size of a country's market had decreased in importance as a locational determinant.

> The relevance of earlier findings on the determinants of FDI is debatable. The relative importance of traditional determinants may have declined in the process of economic globalization. The economic effects of FDI do not allow for easy generalizations. Empirical studies on the growth impact of FDI have come up with conflicting results. (Nunnenkamp 2001: 3)

Some studies suggested that things had changed. When high tariff barriers and import substitution were preferred national policies, countries that first switched to a low tariff, export oriented, foreign ownership friendly regime found they had attracted the attention of foreign investors (Balasubramanyam 2001: 4). de Mello (1997), for example, argued that a more welcoming liberal regime to FDI had become an important determinant. Countries, however, copy each other. An innovative practice ceases to be so when everyone does it. More countries than not have adopted open, export oriented policies dismantling old, protectionist barriers. These practices remain important, but they are no longer unique distinguishing features. Many of the 'new' critical locational determinants may have been just that for a short time. As more countries adopt the innovators' ways, they are no longer innovative. Locational determinants remain locational determinants only for so long as they provide one country with a competitive advantage over others. Consequently, four years after de Mello's study, Nunnenkamp's research led him to reach a different conclusion:

> TNCs tend to take more liberal FDI regimes for granted, and consider the convergence of FDI regimes to be the natural consequence of globalization. As a

---

3   Davis (2003); JBIC Institute (2002); Nunnenkamp (2002); Dunning (1998) and de Mello (1997) all contain reference to the large number of studies on various locational determinants. This chapter will concentrate only upon those for which there is recurring evidence of their relevance in the literature.

result, the liberalization of FDI regulations may be characterized by diminishing returns. Developing countries not taking part in the general move toward liberalization are likely to suffer negative effects of restrictive policies on FDI inflows. But a liberal FDI regime does little more than *enabling* TNCs to invest in a host country. It is a completely different question whether FDI will actually be forthcoming as a result of FDI liberalization. (2001:12) [emphasis original]

Financial incentives serve as another case in point. Tax breaks, concessionary loans, cash grants, below market value land, factory development parks and free trade zones were viewed in the 1980s as important locational determinants. As early as 1993, however, it was argued that most 'studies examining the effectiveness of investment incentives have concluded that they have little impact on the location of foreign direct investment' (Rolfe 1993: 336). Similar conclusions were reiterated by Taveres and Young (2005) who criticize incentive and concession regimes as 'crude, discriminatory and expensive'(4), benefiting foreign investors to the detriment of domestic industry. They potentially risk being 'a waste of resources in the long run' (4) and create the conditions for a race to the bottom. Cass, in his 2007 study of the financial incentives offered in the transition economies of Eastern Europe, questions whether, in light of generally falling tax rates, 'an elaborate apparatus of fiscal and financial incentives continues to be necessary' (Cass 2007: 111). As Rolfe points out, however, and Taveres and Young acknowledge, focused incentives, aimed at securing investment in specific economic sectors by individual countries may meet with success provided they respond to the particular needs or concerns of the MNCs in that economic sector. Countries may also be forced into providing incentives as a competitive measure to 'seal the deal' in the case of locational tournaments where the failure to do so could cause a potential investment to locate elsewhere. Financial incentives alone, however, are unlikely to attract FDI.

Nunnenkamp examines the role of markets as a locational determinant more thoroughly in a 2002 study. Looking to corroborate the belief that economic globalization had altered traditional FDI determinants, notwithstanding the concerns he had expressed about liberal investment regimes being taken for granted, he studies investment conditions in 28 less economically developed countries since the late 1980s. Comparing traditional and non-traditional factors he finds that traditional market seeking locational determinants were still 'dominant factors shaping the distribution of FDI' (35). In fact, he believes, those determinants may have even become stronger. His research, however, identifies two exceptions which recur as locational determinants regardless of motivation. The first is the penetration of knowledge in a country in the form of human capital and technology. The second is the quality of a country's institutions.

Human Capital and Technology

Noorbakhsh et al. (2001) examine the impact of human capital formation on FDI flows from 1980–94 in 36 less economically developed counties in Africa, Asia and Latin America. Looking at different measures of education levels as proxies for human capital formation, they conclude that 'efficient education systems may result in a labour force that is literate, numerate and skilled in the use of modern production facilities and techniques' (1596). Such systems allow a country to produce the 'managers, administrators, professional technicians, or sub-professional technical personnel' needed to fill the most important manpower need of foreign investors (Noorbakhsh et al. 2001: 1597). This led to the conclusion that in a changing global economy; 'human capital has become an important location-specific advantage of developing countries' (1603). It is important not just to attract FDI but it becomes increasingly important as countries become more economically developed (Narula 1996). Nunnenkamp's 2002 study supports the finding of the Noorbakhsh study (2001) arguing that 'the availability of local skills has become a relevant pull factor of FDI in the process of globalization' Nunnenkamp 2002: 35). He, too, concludes that better education and training are likely to attract higher FDI inflows (36).

In 1999 Kuemmerle tested Dunning's hypothesis that strategic asset seeking FDI was drawn to knowledge by examining the locational determinants of foreign research and development facilities established by 32 American-based MNCs in the electronics and pharmaceutical industries. Adopting an analysis similar to Dunning, he divides the motivations underlying those investments into those designed to augment the MNC's existing stock of knowledge, which he designates Home Base Augmenting (HBA), and those designed to exploit such knowledge, designated as Home Base Exploiting (HBE). His hypothesis is that attractive markets draw HBE-motivated investment while HBA-motivated investment is 'more probable if the size of a country's knowledge base *and* the quality of this knowledge base is high' (4, emphasis original). His analysis determines that such is the case. HBA-motivated investment rises with a country's commitment to R&D activities as well as with the target country's 'quality of the human resource pool and with the level of scientific achievement in relevant sciences' (18).[4] Commitment to R&D is measured as a function of public and private spending and the quality of human resources is a function of tertiary education in the host country compared to the home base.

A more recent study by Hejazi (2010) examining FDI flows into Canada confirms the benefits that FDI can bring and comes to a similar conclusion as Kuemmerle regarding the role of domestic R&D in attracting FDI. Hejazi finds that foreign firms operating in Canada 'import significant amounts of technology from their parent companies, and the benefits of these technologies spill over to domestic firms' (1). He concludes that:

---

4   Co and List 2004 came to similar conclusions.

There is a statistically significant positive link between Canadian R&D intensity and inward FDI originating in the United States, which implies that domestic R&D intensity is a complement to inward FDI rather than a substitute. (25)

Institutions

While the importance of a domestic enabling environment conducive to the conduct of business has long been acknowledged by development economists to be of critical importance to the attraction of FDI,[5] it is only relatively recently that they have focused more sharply upon what such an environment entails in practice and the critical role policies, laws and institutions play in shaping a country's economic environment. Very little of the empirical research into the importance of locational determinants has focused on institutions. de Mello (1997), for example, points to the quality of a country's institutions as important to attracting FDI. Unfortunately, he does not develop that theme and like much of the literature is vague in defining its constituent elements.

The institutional features of the recipient economy are important determinants of FDI, including the degree of political stability and government intervention in the economy; the existence of property rights legislation determining the legal rights of foreign firms and limitations on foreign ownership; the property and profit tax system, the extent and severity of bureaucratic procedures. (4)

In 2003, Nunnenkamp and Spatz (2003a) examined the impact of US-based FDI stocks in the manufacturing field on growth rates in less economically developed countries. Although their primary focus is the capacity of FDI to stimulate growth, they view their findings regarding institutions as equally applicable to the ability to attract FDI. The positive effects of institutions on the ability of FDI to stimulate economic growth are found in both technologically advanced and less advanced industries motivated by market seeking and efficiency seeking reasons. Moreover, countries with poor institutions tend not to receive FDI in manufacturing particularly where the motive is efficiency seeking. 'In other words, a threshold

---

5 'Most empirical studies on the locational determinants of fdi [sic] recognize that these are strongly dependent on ... (b) the economic and business environment of host, or potential host, countries' (Dunning 2002: 6). 'The ability to attract and benefit from R & D-related FDI depends to a large extent on the policy environment in the host country' (UNCTAD 2004: 11). 'The extant theoretical and empirical literature on determinants of FDI yields the following broad propositions ... 6. A stable and transparent policy framework towards FDI is attractive to potential investors. 7. Foreign firms place a premium on a distortion free economic and business environment' (Balasubramanyam 2001: 2). 'Clearly, there is a need for more constructive, rules-based measures that can help in creating the sound business environment that firms need to make long-term investments, including the development of local skills and technological capabilities' (JBIC Institute 2002: 112).

of institutional development is required to attract FDI **and** to benefit from higher subsequent growth.' (Nunnenkamp and Spatz 2003a: 33, emphasis original) Institutional development was defined as including such factors as 'the rule of law, the degree of corruption, the quality of public management, and the protection against property rights infringements and discretionary government inference' (Nunnenkamp and Spatz 2003a: 3).

In a study published in December 2008, shortly before his death, Dunning writing with Zhang, attempts to determine the impact of resources, capabilities and markets (collectively, RCM) compared to institutions on FDI flows, both inward and outward. Adopting the meaning ascribed to institutions by North (1990), RCM is defined as a country's physical environment while institutions 'provide the incentive structures to make up the human environment, and which set the rules of the game, for ... firms and other wealth creating entities' (Dunning and Zhang: 2). Dunning and Zhang's analysis concludes that institutions may exert a greater influence on inward FDI flows than RCM and that that influence grows stronger with the higher the stage of economic development a country enjoys (16–21). Although their findings are not as statistically robust as the authors had hoped, the study demonstrates the growing recognition of the role of institutions in attracting FDI and will hopefully signal the beginning of further empirical investigation specifically on the role of institutions as locational determinants.

Spreading FDI's Benefits: ICT and Absorptive Capacity

If a host country cannot extract benefit from FDI then, at best, the impact of the FDI will be neutral and, more likely, the long term consequences will prove negative. In the obvious case, this occurs when non-renewable resources are dissipated. There is also the lost opportunity cost. A deferral of growth effectively puts a country in a worse position than prior to the foreign investment as the passage of time widens the knowledge gap between it and other countries making it even more difficult to catch up. As Agosin and Mayer's (2000) study contrasting Latin and South America with Asia demonstrates, when the impact of foreign investment is not positive, it is more likely to be negative than neutral. They argue that the lack of absorptive capacity in Latin and South American economies left them unable to take advantage of the potential benefits of FDI. As a result, domestic investment was crowded out whereas in Asia, where there was sufficient absorptive capacity, domestic investment was stimulated.

Linkages

Absorptive capacity is critical to spreading FDI's potential benefits throughout the domestic economy. It depends upon the existence of linkages between MNC affiliates and domestic firms which depend, in turn, upon the level of a country's usage of technology, the skills of its workforce and the quality of its institutions

(Lall and Narula 2004: 452; Nunnenkamp 2004: 669). Linkages are the key to the creation of clusters and to 'a virtuous cycle of development' (Scott-Kennel and Enderwick 2005: 129). FDI's potential benefits are transmitted primarily through vertical linkages and horizontal linkages as well as through labour turnover such as when individuals gain experience and knowledge through work and then take that knowledge to firms that supply goods or services to, or buy them from, MNCs (JBIC Institute 2002: 57; Lall and Narula 2004: 457). These channels constitute the transmission lines from foreign investment into the domestic economy.

Vertical linkages can run both backward, to suppliers of inputs required by the MNC affiliate and forward, to purchasers of the MNC affiliate's products, usually other firms that require those products for their own economic purposes (Lall 1980). Backward linkages, the most common, occur where local suppliers upgrade their products to be compatible with those of the MNC affiliate, often with the latter's help which may include the provision of raw materials, specifications, guidance and, occasionally, machinery and capital to institute the necessary production modifications (JBIC Institute 2002: 54). The knowledge acquired can then be applied to other of the domestic firm's operations and products. Forward linkages are forged with local buyers who incorporate the MNC affiliate's products into their own. More technologically advanced, higher quality or less expensive goods produced by the MNC affiliate can lead to innovation and adaptation in downstream products allowing for new or improved products and greater domestic and export potential. Vertical linkages are more likely to be created where the MNC uses intermediate goods extensively (Rodriguez-Clare 1996) and when more autonomy is granted to the domestic affiliate (Chen 1996). Once established, linkages have been shown to be able to grow over time from the relatively negligible to the highly significant as Rasiah's study (1995) of small local machine tool manufacturing firms in Penang demonstrates.

Horizontal linkages come about when the domestic competitors of the MNC adapt their products and practices in response to the superior technology that has been introduced (JBIC 2002: 60). As the domestic firms become more effective competitors, they in turn, force the MNC affiliates to upgrade their products and processes in order to maintain their competitive advantages, thereby creating higher order spillovers. FDI may thus both 'expand the range of technologies available to local firms' (JBIC Institute 2002: 60) as well as increase local competition. Only once linkages have been established between the MNC affiliate and domestic firms can the potential benefits from FDI spread more widely through the economy. Again, technology, human capital and institutions have been shown to constitute the three key factors facilitating the diffusion of benefits.

Technology as a Mediating Factor

de Mello (1997) argues that host countries must meet a minimum threshold of technological development to benefit from FDI. Where this is not the case:

... the impact of FDI on the productive capacity of the recipient economy may be circumscribed to a particular industry, most often specialised in export processing activities with virtually no growth-generating spillovers to domestic firms. (21)

Without the level of technology within the host country having crossed the minimum threshold the imported technology has nothing to plug into. There is no domestic ability to use the innovation.

More recent studies have determined that not only must the host country have reached a minimum technological threshold but that the gap between the imported technology and the level of technology in the host country's firms must not be too great. The smaller the technological gap, the greater the host country's absorptive capacity proves to be (Dimelis 2005: 101; JBIC Institute 2002: 66; Lall and Narula 2004: 454). Where the technology gap between MNC affiliates and local suppliers is too great backward linkages, in particular, do not form. In an analysis of over 2500 manufacturing firms in Greece between 1992 and 1997, Dimelis (2005) analyses the question of whether spillover effects from FDI have a positive effect on productivity growth. She concludes that they do, but:

... only after controlling for the technological gap separating domestic and foreign firms. Moreover, the 'absorptive capacity' hypothesis is supported, implying that the FDI spillover is larger when the technological gap is small. (101)

Nunnenkamp and Spatz (2003a) come to the same conclusion in their examination of American originated FDI stocks in less economically developed countries in seven manufacturing sectors. They are concerned with whether FDI leads to economic growth and whether their results vary with differences in the motivation of the investments between resource, market and efficiency seeking FDI, as well as the influence of various host country characteristics such as secondary school enrolment (which they use as a proxy for human capital), GDP per capita, the quality of institutions and openness to trade. They conclude that positive effects of FDI on growth are 'anything but guaranteed' (38) until they control for host country characteristics. There they find that the technology gap between countries is relevant:

Finally we reject the hypothesis that a large technological gap between the host and home country of FDI fosters FDI-induced catching-up processes in developing countries. Rather, the interplay of host-country and industry characteristics suggests that positive growth effects of FDI are more likely when the technological gap is relatively small. (40)

Human Capital as a Mediating Factor

The second factor that has been demonstrated to increase absorptive capacity is human capital.[6] Technology does not spread on its own. The people who use, copy and adapt technology spread it. Without sufficient human capital, absorptive capacity is limited (Borensztein et al. 1998: 117). Borensztein et al.'s (1998) findings closely parallel those concerning the relationship between growth and ICT in measuring the impact of FDI on growth. Using male secondary school education as a proxy for human capital they conclude there is a strong complementary effect between FDI and human capital 'that is, the contribution of FDI to economic growth is enhanced by its level of interaction with the level of human capital in the host country' (117). Although not emphasized amongst their conclusions, they find that when countries have very low levels of human capital, being defined as the bottom third of the survey in terms of secondary school attainment, the impact of FDI on growth is negative (123–5). Consequently, they conclude that human capital exerts a strong influence on a country's ability to benefit from FDI, but only when it has reached a certain level of attainment.

Similar conclusions regarding the importance of human capital as an important component of absorptive capacity are reiterated in a series of OECD studies examining the relationship between human capital and FDI. Ritchie (2002) who focuses upon the development of intellectual capital formation in Southeast Asia notes that general education and training are key. Without them, 'it is virtually impossible to leverage MNCs for skills formation beyond the immediate needs of the firm.' (23) Blomstrom and Kokko (2002) also argue that host countries with high levels of human capital are likely to attract high levels of technology intensive FDI while those with lower levels attract smaller inflows; 'the host country's level of human capital determines how much FDI it can attract and whether local firms are able to absorb the potential spillover benefits' (10).

Institutions as a Mediating Factor

The third key element of absorptive capacity is the quality of the host country's institutions. Lall (2002) vigorously argues:

> As more low-wage economies compete for mobile resources, and as technical change erodes the competitive advantage of cheap unskilled labour, *the quality of local capabilities and institutions becomes the prime determinant of the ability to attract and use foreign resources*. (43, emphasis original)

Nunnenkamp and Spatz (2003a), as noted above, whose findings are reiterated by Nunnenkamp (2004) writing alone, examine the importance of the host

---

6   For a contrary view as to the relationship between human capital and growth see Easterly 2001: 71–84.

country's institutions in their analysis of the effects of American FDI stocks in less economically developed countries, one of the very few such empirical examinations. They find the strength of a less economically developed country's institutions causes a profound impact upon the ability of host countries both to attract and to take advantage of FDI. Its significance is particularly acute in the latter case, especially with regard to both efficiency-seeking and market-seeking FDI (Nunnenkamp 2004: 674). Somewhat vaguely, however, he describes institutional development as involving 'a wide range of fairly time-consuming reforms, including the protection of property rights, control of corruption and efficient administrative regulations' (674–5). Hence, his likely correct, but somewhat unenlightening, conclusion that two conditions must be met to achieve international development goals. 'First, developing countries must be attractive to foreign investors. Second, the host-country environment ... must be conducive to favourable FDI effects ...' (673).

Evidence that development economists have turned their focus to the importance of institutions, but are still grappling with its dimensions, may be found in Lall and Narula's (2004) introductory article to the Autumn 2004 issue of *The European Journal of Development Research* devoted entirely to what they term as the 'nascent debate' (447) regarding the 'systems' (455) approach to the interplay between MNCs, FDI and development. They view the domestic absorption of FDI's benefits as occurring within systems of innovation which depend upon the firm's operating environment. According to Lall and Narula, the operating environment extends beyond the firm's customers and suppliers to:

> ... the social and cultural context; the institutional and organisational framework; infrastructure; knowledge creating and diffusing institutions, *and so on*. This is the essence of the systems approach to technology. (456) [emphasis added].

They view institutions as founded in government policy, created where possible by governmental legislative action or fostered through other means where not, that 'defines the stock of knowledge in a given location' through the 'serendipitous intertwining' with economic actors thereby determining how a country develops economically (456). The authors conclude: 'The importance of building institutions cannot be overstated' (456). There are ample grounds to take issue with whether the debate is 'nascent' as well as whether the manner in which institutions interact with economic players is 'serendipitous' and it is not at all clear what 'on so on' means. Nevertheless, it is highly significant that Lall and Narula, two of the most influential and respected scholars in the field of development economics, conclude that nothing is more important than institutions.

Chapter 4
Institutions

Shifting the Focus

Given that the literature points so decisively to institutions as a mediating factor between ICT and growth, but does a fairly poor job of defining, identifying and empirically testing them, it is reasonable to question whether the hypothesis can be supported. Governments of less economically developed countries need better advice than vague generalities and unsubstantiated hypotheses if they hope to devise and implement policies that will promote economic growth. If pre-eminent economists do not clearly provide a better understanding of which institutions are important for economic growth together with suggestions about how to build them, it is difficult to see how governments can be expected to do so in the countries where they are most needed and where such expertise may not be readily available. This chapter will address two preliminary questions. First, does the term 'institutions' enjoy a commonly understood meaning that permits a taxonomy that can provide some guidance to governments of less economically developed countries about where to focus their development efforts? Second, is there sufficient empirical evidence to support the conclusion that institutions actually do matter to economic development?

If the answer to the two questions is 'yes', then why have economists not been able to provide practical advice about which institutions are important and how to build them? One reason is that the definition most commonly used suits the original purpose for which it was formulated, but it is unworkable for empirical purposes. A second reason is that institutions are not inherently an economic concept. The distinction is often made between informal and formal institutions, as will be discussed in greater detail. Informal institutions are more commonly the domain of sociologists concerned with the roles of culture and social capital in a society whereas formal institutions are more usually within the lawyers' and political scientists' field of expertise. The economic outcomes produced by the interaction of people due to the nature of institutions in a society may be within the normal range of economic inquiry, but the nature of institutions is not. A third reason is that if the definition of institutions is unworkable and the nature of institutions is not generally within the realm of economics, then the results of empirical analyses cannot be expected to produce actionable results. Clear advice can be given in response to studies that demonstrate the importance of open trade policies or improving human capital levels. Being told simply to build high-quality institutions will likely be met with the equivalent of a blank stare.

   The purpose of this chapter is not to suggest an alternative to the economic analysis of growth and it is definitely not to demean the importance of economists' work. It is to illustrate the need for other disciplines to participate more actively in the development conversation and to build a more inter-disciplinary approach to solving the mystery of growth. Countries are poor for a host of reasons that require different expertise to understand fully or to begin to address them. The arguments about the process of institution building in this chapter and the examination of specific institutions that help mediate the relationship between ICT and economic growth in Chapter 5, are meant to push the discussion from whether institutions are important to which are important and to shed some light upon how they might be built.

Do Institutions Matter?

Chapter 2 demonstrated that without the widespread adoption of ICT, economic development will remain an elusive dream for many less economically developed countries. Four factors have been repeatedly identified as mediating the relationship between ICT usage and economic growth: infrastructure, investment, human capital and institutions. Chapter 3 argued that the most efficient means for countries seeking ICT is through FDI. The literature examining the relationship between FDI and growth reveals that three factors recur as key to both attracting FDI and spreading its potential benefits: human capital; technology which today primarily means ICT; and institutions. The meaning and scope of infrastructure, investment, human capital and technology are relatively clearly understood. They can be analysed individually and measured reasonably accurately. Institutions are different. They cannot be understood independently from context in which they are evaluated. Effective criminal laws, for example, require institutions such as an efficient police force and an impartial court system. Many institutions, particularly in the economic and commercial realm, contribute to the formulation, enactment, implementation and enforcement of policies and laws while other institutions are not primarily concerned with laws, as is the case with those relating to health care or postal service. Institutions help create the enabling environment that allows a society to carry out its social, political and economic activities.

   Individually, one can normally understand an institution's functions. The idea of an enabling environment, however, can seem somewhat ethereal and the collective role of institutions in creating that enabling environment can thus appear equally nebulous. It can lead to difficulties in understanding institutions and, as a result, in quantifying their effectiveness, as the literatures examining the relationship between ICT and economic growth and FDI and economic growth make abundantly clear. An example may help explain how institutions form an enabling environment.

   Take the case of an individual who wishes to open a small business selling fresh produce. At the very least, the merchant will have to acquire his or her fruits and vegetables from farmers or, more likely from a wholesaler, given that one farmer is unlikely to produce the variety the merchant wishes to sell. Some of the produce is likely to be imported. Transportation and storage will be needed and premises secured with electricity and running water. The merchant may need financing of a long-term nature, such as for capital costs related to renting and fixturing the premises, and a short-term operating line of credit, as the timing of revenues and expenditures may not coincide. Employees will be hired whose pay, work hours, working conditions and vacation entitlement will have to be established. Disputes may arise with suppliers, customers, employees or the landlord that cannot be settled amicably between the parties. In a well-functioning enabling environment, the merchant's headaches should be of a commercial nature. Beneath the veneer of a basic commercial activity lies a web of institutions. At a minimum they include: customs; food safety; transportation; courts; police; banks; workplace health and safety; education; zoning; legislatures; municipal councils; sewage; water; electricity; and telecommunications. There are undoubtedly more. The matrix of institutions that allows each step of this relatively simple commercial venture to function efficiently should be effectively invisible to the merchant.

It is only when institutions do not collectively function to create an effective enabling environment that their importance becomes apparent, not only to the merchant, but more broadly to those studying the economy. As de Soto (1996) vividly described, the red tape involved in opening a business in Peru effectively not only strangled entrepreneurship, but was so incompetent that for two years, the myriad of officials involved in granting the various permits never realized the proposed business was a fictitious experiment designed precisely to show how poorly the system functioned. As a result, de Soto argued that too many businesses were pushed into the informal, or 'grey market', economy where transactions are normally personal, on a cash basis and economically inefficient. Financing is difficult to obtain and expensive when available. Enforcement mechanisms where disputes arise are handled outside the legal system. Business transactions tend not to extend beyond the immediate community. According to Farrell (2004) not only is it difficult to progress from the informal to the formal economy, but the negative economic consequences are pronounced.

> … informal companies become trapped in a self-reinforcing dynamic that confines them to subscale, inefficient, low-productivity work. Around the world, this research shows, they operate at just half the average productivity levels of formal companies in the same sectors and at a small fraction of the productivity of the best companies. (3)

The Meaning of Institutions

The New Institutional Economics

The manner in which the term 'institutions' is used in the ICT-growth and FDI-growth literatures can give the impression that it serves as a repository into which those examining the relationship place factors of a political, legal or social nature that prove difficult to isolate and quantify. In the absence of precision examples of the institutions considered to be of particular importance are offered. Suggestions range from the very broad, such as democracy, to the somewhat more focused, such as trade policy, to the very narrow, such as labour laws. Very few of these hypotheses have been empirically tested which is odd given that so much of the literature involves the empirical testing of other variables that influence economic growth.

Unlike their colleagues focused primarily upon ICT's relationship with economic growth, economists in the NIE field have devoted considerable effort to understanding institutions and their impact on development. The genesis of the NIE is credited to Ronald Coase whose 1937 article titled 'The Nature of the Firm' examined transaction costs and their effects upon markets and decision-making by firms. He identified how governance structures impose costs upon economic actors which influence the choices firms make about their activities, such as whether to make or buy a component used in the manufacture of a product and, if the latter, from whom, where and on what terms. The discipline of organizational economics grew out of this line of inquiry. The NIE, in turn, evolved out of the study of organizational economics and another of its off-shoots, organizational institutionalism. It was only in the 1970s that Oliver Williamson coined the term the 'New Institutional Economics' and identified it as a discrete branch of economic study.

The NIE's ambit covers a broad spectrum of academic endeavour. Rooted in neo-classical economics, the NIE argues that people form rules, or institutions, to govern their interaction in order to reduce transaction costs and to allow the market to function more efficiently. At the macro-economic level, the NIE focuses extensively upon the institutions that shape the manner in which markets and firms function and how they interact with the state and the legal system. At the micro-economic level, the concern is centred upon the structures that govern contractual relationships between firms (Menard and Shirley 2005). The discipline was originally focused upon the domestic economic activities of firms and how the societal rules that govern relationships determine their behaviour. As the United States was the epicentre of research, the focus was almost exclusively upon the American experience. Interest in international economic development and why some countries are wealthy while others are impoverished came later. In this respect, the work of Douglass North since the early 1990s has been most influential.

The NIE is not the only branch of economics concerned with institutions. Historical institutionalism stands in contrast to the NIE and provides the basis for the literature concerning the developmental state, discussed in the Introduction, which has guided much of the discussion that seeks to explain economic development in East Asia. It emphasizes state capacity and the existence of public institutions together with the creation of close, or 'embedded', relationships with business elites that allow for the effective implementation of government policy (Rodan 2006: 5; Evans 1995).

> Those theorists emphasise that the state (and its institutions) played a pivotal role among late-industrialising countries. This perspective is based on an appreciation of a common structural predicament facing late-industrialising economies, namely the need to amass large concentrations of investment capital and to make strategic inroads into established global markets. Such experiences have involved state officials in crucial, positive roles as developmental elites. In this account, markets are not abstract entities but are largely constructed by developmental elites. They make their calculations, however, within specific historical pathways defined by previous layers of institutions embedded in structures of social power and culture. (Rodan 2006: 5, references omitted)

As a result, the state is able to pursue national development objectives as opposed to the neo-classical view that societal prosperity will result from the private sector's pursuit of individual goals. The historical institutional literature may provide a better understanding of Asian economic development than a neo-classical analysis, but the NIE is the branch that has examined most carefully the meaning of institutions and that has had the greatest influence upon those trying to measure the quality of a country's institutions.

Despite no universally accepted definition of institutions having found favour, a common conception of the term's meaning has emerged.[1] Lall and Narula employ Endquist and Johnson's definition which highlights the 'common habits, routines, established practices, rules or laws that regulate the interaction between individuals and groups' (Lall and Narula 2004: 456). Rodrik prefers Lin and Nugent's description of institutions as:

> ... a set of humanly devised behavioral rules that govern and shape the interactions of human beings, in part by helping them to form expectations of what other people will do. (Lin and Nugent 1995: 2306–7)

The meaning of institutions advanced by North, however, has drawn the most adherents and, as such, the conception of institutions and their influence on economic growth is best described by using North's own words. To North, 'Institutions are the rules of the game in a society or, more formally, are the

---

1 Such was not always the case. In the 1970s and 1980s a number of definitions of 'institutions' were proposed with differences in meaning that went beyond being mere alternative formulations of the same concept. See Ostrom (1986).

humanly devised constraints that shape human interaction' (1990: 3). He emphasizes that they 'include any form of constraint that human beings devise' and they provide 'the framework within which human interaction takes place ... [being] ... perfectly analogous to the rules of the game in a competitive team sport' (1990: 4). Consequently:

> ... they structure incentives in human exchange, whether political, social, or economic. Institutional change shapes the way societies evolve through time and hence is the key to understanding historical change. (North 1990: 3)

As perceived by North, the scope of institutions and the role they play in determining economic growth could scarcely be greater. Institutions are defined to include everything that influences the way people act, individually or collectively, regardless of how that collectivity is constituted. They range from our most basic core values of what constitutes right and wrong to mundane matters such as how to set a table. Together those institutions form a fully integrated, coherent system governing human behaviour.

North divides the constraints on human interaction into formal and informal institutions. Informal institutions are 'typically unwritten codes of conduct that underlie and supplement formal rules' (North 1990: 4). They originate in socially transmitted norms which form part of a society's culture. The governing structures in family, social and even business relations are overwhelmingly defined not by legislation but by 'codes of conduct, norms of behavior, and conventions' (North 1990: 36). Informal constraints are resilient, often surviving abrupt changes in political power and, of critical importance to North's perception of the ability of less economically developed countries to become prosperous, they evolve so slowly that 'we have to stand back as historians to perceive them' (North 1990: 6). Such rules are humanly devised, North emphasizes: 'indeed, the growing literature of the new institutional economics makes abundantly clear that institutions must be explained in terms of the intentionality of humans' (North 2005: 42). They may, however, only rarely be the creation of conscious decisions. They can develop as a result of repeated interaction between groups and individuals thereby allowing such transactions to be conducted with a measure of certainty. Informal institutions form the foundation for a society's formal rules and set the parameters within which formal rules operate. Formal rules must be grounded in the informal.

Formal constraints include legal, economic and judicial rules and can be viewed as giving substance to concepts such as the rule of law, the recognition and protection of property rights and human freedoms. Forming a hierarchy, constitutions sit at the top of a country's formal rules establishing a framework for all other national laws and imposing limits on lawmaking in much the same manner as informal institutions circumscribe the scope of formal institutions. Statutes lie below constitutions followed progressively by increasingly specific constraints such as regulations, judicial decisions and individual contracts. Formal rules change more rapidly than informal rules and the lower down the hierarchy they are found, the more quickly they can change. North describes the difference between informal constraints and formal constraints as one of degree, not substance. Formal rules represent a unidirectional shift along a continuum away from informal constraints to deliberately crafted constraints, usually written. As economies grow in complexity, the number and scope of formal constraints grow commensurately.

Institutions provide stability and structure to human relations, but from an economic perspective, they may not be efficient in nature. A stable society does not necessarily imply a prosperous one. Established patterns may favour one ethnic, racial or religious group or region in a country over others. Certain groups, such as women, may be effectively marginalized economically. Commerce in some societies may tend to be carried out between people who know and trust each other and not with strangers as the court system may be slow and cumbersome, judges may not be impartial and seeking judicial redress in the event of a contractual dispute would constitute a breach of acceptable social conduct. Thus, in North's model, the nature of a country's institutions explains why some countries are prosperous and others are not. The negative outcomes that flow from a society's institutions persist as stubbornly as do the positive ones. He postulates that institutions represent the 'underlying determinant of the long-run performance of economies' (North 1990: 107), elaborating that 'Third World countries are poor because the institutional constraints define a set of payoffs to political/economic activity that do not encourage productive activity' (North 1990: 110). Using language that evidences the NIE's roots in Coase's seminal article, he reiterates the impact of governance structures upon contracting decisions by firms and maintains that the inability of such countries to develop cost-effective contract enforcement mechanisms 'is the most important source of both historical stagnation and contemporary underdevelopment in the Third World' (North 1990: 54). North (1990) suggests that only exceptional events, such as revolutions, can radically alter development trajectories. Others have advanced a concept of 'critical junctures' distinguishing between normal times and abnormal times which include revolutions and war, but which may also include less violent events such as economic or political crises as uniquely occurring opportunities for substantive institutional change (Acemoglu 2011). Otherwise, those societies find themselves trapped in a vicious circle. Poor countries have weak institutions and countries with weak institutions remain poor.

Although his views about the ability to transform informal institutions seem to have slightly moderated more recently, North (2005) paints a bleak, path dependent future for less economically developed countries. Path dependence is portrayed as a function of the relationship between institutions and organizations. If institutions form the rules of the game, individuals and organizations are the players. Informal institutions give rise to organizations which both reinforce those institutions and govern the basic political and economic structures in a country. The inherited institutional structure may prove highly resistant to change due to the society's core beliefs or because challenges to existing institutions threaten those benefitting from the status quo. Those structures, in turn, determine the country's formal rules. The interplay between informal institutions, formal institutions and organizations brings prosperity to some countries, but not others. In the case of many poor nations, path dependency can serve to perpetuate a system whereby economic development is restricted to privileged elites.

A slim ray of hope is offered by North. The manner in which organizations interact with each other and with the government can also prove to be the most important factor in institutional change. Organizations undoubtedly act to promote their self-interest, indeed the very reason for the organization's formation may be to do so, but the pursuit of their own self-interest may bring broader benefits. North cites the example of nineteenth century American economic history. The perceived benefit of a better educated workforce led groups that would profit most immediately to demand from government significant investment in 'formal education, on-the-job training, and applied research' (North 1990: 79).[2] Not only were economic organizations consequentially transformed but such investment also witnessed 'the growth of educational organizations with their own agendas and influence on the polity' (North 1990: 79) as well as a change in perceptions about education among voters and politicians. Organizations may thus:

> ... encourage the society to invest in the kinds of skills and knowledge that indirectly contribute to their profitability. Such investment will shape the long-run growth of skills and knowledge, which are the underlying determinants of economic growth. (North 1990: 79)

North, however, remains sceptical of organizations' ability to act as agents of significant reform. While they can cause institutions to change for the greater good of a society, they can also prove to be agents that impede reform. 'The viability, profitability, and indeed survival of the organizations of a society typically depend on the existing institutional matrix' (North 2005: 62). Organizations representing powerful vested interests can impede change and, in less economically developed countries, perpetuate generally inefficient institutional structures that, nevertheless, are effective in providing benefits to the members of those organizations. As a consequence, institutional reform tends to be incremental and is path dependent. The nature of a country's organizations may be a critical element in transforming a country's institutions and allowing it to break out of its cycle of poverty or in maintaining the status quo.

---

2   See, more generally, Goldin and Katz (2008) for a discussion of the transformative effect on economic growth occasioned by the broadening of public education in the nineteenth century.

Classifying Institutions

North (1990) divides 'humanly devised constraints' into informal and formal institutions, identifying a hierarchy between the two. Informal institutions lie above, surround and supplement formal constraints. They shape formal rules. Although increasing attention has been paid to the formation of informal institutions, they have not been subject to systematic classification in the NIE literature. More attention has been devoted to the study of the hierarchy of formal constraints; from constitutions to contracts, those closer to the apex circumscribing the ambit and operation of those nearer the base.

Building upon North's basic division of constraints into informal and formal institutions, others have sought to elaborate more detailed systems of classification. Johannes Jutting, in a report prepared for the OECD, describes two predominant schools of thought. The first divides institutions vertically, classifying them as being economic, political, legal or social in nature, each category consisting of a composite of both informal and formal rules and norms. Economic institutions deal with rules defining 'the production, allocation and distribution of goods and services' (Jutting 2003: 14). Political institutions reflect the structure and mechanics of government, such as election rules, political stability and governance. Legal institutions give structure to the judicial system and provide for the enforcement of property and contractual rights while social institutions are viewed as primarily governing the provision of health care, education and social security. Although such a system of classification helps understand the focus and scope of the relevant institutions, it does little to clarify their interaction.

The second method, elucidated by Williamson (2000), divides institutions into four horizontal levels of 'social analysis' reaching across each of the categories described by Jutting. The higher levels impose constraints on the lower levels while feedback mechanisms exist through which the lower levels influence the evolution of the higher levels. The highest level, Level One, corresponds to North's conception of informal institutions. Williamson sees the institutions at this level as forming the social structure of the society. 'This is where the norms, customs, mores, traditions, etc. are located' (Williamson 2000: 596). While North recognizes that informal constraints can be replaced with formal constraints as a society becomes more complex, the informal institutions classified by Williamson as Level One are viewed as beyond the reach of government action. Williamson agrees with North that these values change very slowly, although unlike North, Williamson puts a time frame on such change – centuries or millennia.

The remaining three levels seek to organize formal constraints. Williamson describes Level Two institutions as creating the enabling environment for the establishment of more developed formal rules. They are a society's 'first order choices' which are 'partly the product of evolutionary processes, but design opportunities are also imposed' (Williamson 2000: 598). National constitutions are found at this level and basic determinations are made regarding the forms of a country's political regime, judiciary and bureaucracy as well as certain laws reflecting broad principles, such as those that give expression to property rights. A country's legal system, particularly its ability to define property rights and arbitrate disputes, is considered a Level Two institution. Such formal institutions are perceived as changing over decades absent abrupt changes such as military coups.

Williamson likens Level Three institutions to rules relating to the play of the game. They comprise the institutions of governance which Williamson defines as the 'effort to craft *order*, thereby to mitigate *conflict* and realize *material gains*' (Williamson 2000: 599, emphasis original). Described by Williamson in economic terms as being concerned primarily with the management of transaction costs, Level Three institutions translate higher level norms and principles into more detailed rules governing everyday interactions between people and organizations. They can change over a period of a few years to a decade.

Level Four is concerned with institutions relating to the allocation of resources as well as employment and social security mechanisms. These institutions, which continuously adjust to prices and outputs:

> ... craft order and reshape incentives, thereby building the governance structure
> of a society and leading to the building of specific organizations like the local or
> national government, state agencies, NGOs, etc. (Jutting 2003: 13)

The tools of government to shape policy and foster economic development are found primarily amongst the institutions at Levels Two and Three. As Williamson (2000) states, 'Many public policy issues, moreover, turn jointly on the combined use of Level Two and Level Three reasoning' (608). It is at Levels Two and Three that governments can most greatly influence the economic development course of their countries provided, presumably, that a country's Level One institutions do not act as an impediment. Neither North nor Williamson clarifies fully the impact of Level One informal institutions upon a government's ability to manipulate the formal institutions found at Levels Two and Three. North argues that path dependence can dictate the range of choices available to governments. If a country's informal institutions are poor, there is little hope for the formal. Hence, the prevailing view of new institutional economists is that a country's institutional matrix determines its economic destiny and there is very little that can be done to alter that fate in a relatively short time.

Do Institutions Rule?

North (1990, 2005) enunciated the theoretical basis for the primacy of institutions as a determinant of international economic development, but he did not engage in an empirical evaluation of his hypothesis. That work, however, was not left unattended. In a 2000 study, Janine Aron comprehensively surveyed the empirical research compiled to then on the relationship between a country's institutions and its economic growth. Her review showed correlations between institutional variables and growth, but not necessarily causality, which she found run both ways 'from good institutions to growth and from improved growth to better institutions' (Aron 2000: 115). She took issue with those who argue institutions lead to growth. In her opinion, 'the growth literature is burdened by a range of serious problems with data, methodology, and identification' (Aron 2000: 100). The literature relies on measures, or indices, of perceptions of political or economic institutional quality developed by third parties, she noted, most notably the *Governance Matters* indicators published by the World Bank under the direction of Daniel Kaufmann.[3] The Kauffman indicators, which are often used to measure institutional quality, Aron notes, say 'nothing about how such institutions perform' (2000: 105). A more likely explanation of the impact of institutions on growth, in Aron's view, relates specifically to the quality of a country's property rights regime and the rule of law although she did not address the likelihood of a country possessing good institutions in those areas while other institutions are weak. Where property rights or the rule of law or both are poor or absent in a country, transaction and transformation costs tend to be much higher, thereby inhibiting growth. The lack of formal institutions may not be an impediment to growth where economic activities are relatively simple and confined to exchanges between members of the same cultural groups. Arguing in the same vein as Farrell (2004), Aron contends such structures must become more formal for more complex transactions to be undertaken between members of different groups.

> When institutions are poorly defined or there are few formal institutions, economic activities are restricted to interpersonal exchanges. In such cases, repeat activities and cultural homogeneity facilitate self-enforcement. Transaction costs may be low in such an environment, but transformation costs are high because the economy operates at a very low level of specialization … It is clear, however, that firms or agents in an environment of weak institutions cannot engage in complex, long-term, and multiple-contract exchanges with effective enforcement as they do in industrial economies. (Aron 2000: 104–5)

Writing three years later, Jutting (2003) found that the issues connected to the measurement of institutions issues raised by Aron remained unresolved. In

---

3 Kaufmann et al. (1999, 2002, 2005, 2007, 2009, 2010) began publishing governance data for the World Bank in 1997 and have been doing so roughly bi-annually since then. They combine the results obtained from their numerous sources to create six indices measuring political stability, the rule of law, the effectiveness of the civil service, corruption, the government selection process and the government's ability to formulate and implement policies protecting private sector development. They note in the subsequent June 2009 edition of their work that, as in previous editions, they rely heavily upon perceptions of governance but their use of an increasing number of sources 'from a diverse range of informed stakeholders' such as risk rating agencies, non-governmental organizations and aid agencies has reduced their margin of error over the years of their studies.

addition to the concerns that Aron identified about basing indices upon subjective perceptions, Jutting argued that the aggregation of a number of diverse factors to produce a single index that purports to measure a country's institutions obscures the relative importance of individual institutional elements. Echoing Aron's comments, although from a different perspective, he further emphasized that the use of surveyed perceptions as a basis for the indices may also be of questionable value in less economically developed countries as 'these evaluations focus mainly on aspects of formal institutions, whereas in most low-income countries informal institutions are of critical importance' (Jutting 2003: 21).

Undeterred by the institutional measurement concerns expressed by Aron and Jutting, Dani Rodrik is likely the most forceful proponent of the importance of institutions. He has endeavoured to demonstrate that institutions exert the greatest influence upon a country's development trajectory and that their influence is more profound than geography, as Jeffrey Sachs (2001) argues, or trade, as Jeffrey Frankel and David Romer (1999) believe, the two other most commonly cited 'deep determinants' of economic growth. Rodrik and his co-authors, in a 2004 article whose title states its conclusion, 'Institutions Rule', ran a series of regressions comparing the impacts of geography, trade integration and institutions on national incomes. Institutions are not defined in his study, but the quality of a country's institutions is measured using the then most current set of governance indicators developed by Kaufmann. Rodrik sought to overcome the testing deficiencies that he perceived in the work of those advocating the primacy of trade and geography. He did so by using three data sets covering between 64 and 137 countries to determine which of institutions, trade and geography demonstrates the greatest effect on income:

> ... we find that the quality of institutions trumps everything else. Once institutions are controlled for, integration has no direct effect on incomes, while geography has at best weak direct effects. Trade often enters the income regression with the 'wrong' (i.e., negative) sign, as do many of the geographical indicators. By contrast, our measure of property rights and the rule of law always enters with the correct sign, and is statistically significant, often with *t*-statistics that are very large. (Rodrik et al. 2004: 135)

In his view, the data showing the primacy of institutions was not only robust, but close to overwhelming.

In a speech shortly after the publication of 'Institutions Rule', Rodrik (2004a) reiterated that the empirical analysis demonstrates that good institutions are, in fact, causal of increased incomes particularly where poorer countries are able to strengthen their property rights regimes. Again, Rodrik does not define institutions, but it would appear that the institutions whose quality he claims 'trumps everything else' must be formal institutions, not informal institutions. He again uses Kaufmann's governance indicators as proxies to measure institutional quality, arguing that the strength of a country's property rights regime depends primarily upon the laws and regulations relating to property ownership, private contracts and their enforcement mechanisms.

Rodrik is not alone in his belief in the paramount role of institutions in promoting or retarding development. In a lengthy study published roughly contemporaneously with 'Institutions Rule' and with a title similarly foreshadowing its conclusions, 'Institutions as the Fundamental Cause of Long-Run Growth', Daron Acemoglu et al. (2004) point to institutions as the primary determinant of incomes. Acemoglu's study considers geography, institutions and culture as the three possible alternative prime determinants of prosperity and engages in a quantitative evaluation of their respective impacts on economic growth. Explicitly accepting North's definition of institutions he explores the relationship between political institutions (which he classified as being those that place checks on political power, ensure that political power is broadly based and that the rents power holders can realize are limited) and economic institutions (which are described as those that 'provide security of property rights and relatively equal access to economic resources to a broad cross-section of society') (Acemoglu et al. 2004). The quality of economic institutions is seen as dependent upon good political institutions. Acemoglu uses the International Country Risk Guide to measure a country's institutional quality. He finds that in addition to the overwhelming support for the theories that emphasize institutions as the defining factor in determining prosperity 'there is convincing empirical support for the hypothesis that differences in economic institutions, rather than geography or culture, *cause* differences in incomes per-capita' (Acemoglu et al. 2004: 16, emphasis original).

Not everyone, however, is convinced. Subsequent to 'Institutions Rule', several authors, noting the issues relating to measurement that Aron and Jutting identify, reiterate the questions posed about the proxies used by Rodrik and Acemoglu to determine institutional quality. The main thrust of their argument is that the flow of causality in those studies is in doubt. In their view, countries that are wealthy create better institutions whereas Rodrik and Acemoglu clearly believe that good institutions lead to economic growth. Glaeser et al. (2004), in an article titled 'Do Institutions Cause Growth?', in the same volume of the *Journal of Economic Growth* as 'Institutions Rule', challenge Rodrik's use of the Kaufmann indices to measure the effect of institutions on economic growth. Glaeser and his co-authors argue that those indices do not actually measure institutional quality as much as perceptions which are bound to be better in prosperous countries than in poor ones. 'These are clear *ex post* outcomes, highly correlated with the level of economic development, rather than political constraints, *per se*' (Glaeser et al. 2004: 276). The authors identify even more serious problems with Acemoglu et al.'s (2004) use of the International Country Risk Guide which measures respect for property rights through an evaluation of the likelihood of governmental expropriation. In their view, human capital constitutes a greater determinant of economic growth than institutions. They maintain that countries improve their economic fortunes through the accumulation of human and physical capital and that 'once they become richer, are increasingly likely to improve their institutions' (Glaeser et al.

2004: 298). Nevertheless, they emphasize that their work should not be taken to suggest that institutions are unimportant.

> That proposition is flatly contradicted by a great deal of available empirical evidence, including our own. Rather, our results suggest that the current measurement strategies have conceptual flaws, and that *researchers would do better focusing on actual laws, rules, and compliance procedures that could be manipulated by a policy maker to assess what works*. (Glaeser et al. 2004: 298, emphasis added)

Oddly, perhaps, Rodrik's interpretation of his findings leads him to roughly the same conclusion. Despite his identification of institutions as the most important of the determinants of prosperity, he recognizes that his findings do not provide significant direction to governments or others concerned with economic development.

> How much guidance do our results provide to policymakers who want to improve the performance of their economies? Not much at all. Sure, it is helpful to know that geography is not destiny, or that focusing on increasing the economy's links with world markets is unlikely to yield convergence. But the operational guidance that our central result on the primacy of institutional quality yields is extremely meager. (Rodrik et al. 2004: 136)

Glaeser and Rodrik both argue that the choices governments make about the policies they pursue and the actions they take to implement those policies are the most important factors for wealth creation.

To summarize, the literature that identifies institutions as a mediating factor in the relationship between ICT usage and economic growth can be supported. There is a widely accepted meaning of institutions that has been enunciated by several authors; the formulation by North being the most commonly cited. That definition has also led to attempts to classify institutions. North draws a distinction between informal (unwritten) and formal (written) institutions, while Williamson identifies a hierarchy of three levels of formal institutions. Extensive empirical analyses also find that good institutions not only cause economic growth, but they are *the* most important factor. Others express doubts about the strength of such findings, but they do not suggest institutions are unimportant. Unfortunately, that knowledge has not led to concrete advice being offered about which institutions are important or how to build them.

The NIE literature, by its very nature, puts the role of institutions front and centre in the development debate. A country's institutional structure is identified as the main reason some countries are prosperous while others are not. Employing a sports analogy, North argues that institutions are the rules of the game and organizations, its players, but unlike in most sporting events, it is the rules rather than the players that determine outcomes. While his work, and that of others, provides a compelling basis for understanding the nature of institutions, he does not provide practical guidance to those concerned with economic development, nor do he and other writers on institutional theory suggest that such is their goal. The NIE thus appears to offer a persuasive analytical model that has held up to empirical testing, but that leads to a dead end.

Glaeser, Acemoglu and Rodrik diverge from North. While accepting the importance, if not necessarily the primacy of institutions, they argue that their empirical work proves that the choices governments make about the policies they pursue and the actions they take to implement those policies are the most important factors for wealth creation. Glaeser et al. suggest that institutional economists would do better to focus their efforts on 'actual rules, rather than on conceptually ambiguous assessments of institutional outcomes' (2004: 298). Rodrik et al. (2004a) believe that governments, such as in China, that break with the past and choose to protect property rights will be successful in attracting investment and generating sustained economic gains. While well intentioned, their practical advice is sparse.

Both the ICT-growth and the FDI-growth literatures maintain that institutions are a critical factor in mediating those relationships, but the poor definition of institutions in those bodies of literature and the wide range of suggestions of which institutions are important to the relationships provide little concrete advice to governments and others concerned with economic development. Similarly, the NIE literature, which argues that a country's institutions determine its economic status, does little to clarify which institutions are important for growth, in general, or the fostering of ICT usage, in particular. Neither the theoretical nor the empirical literature, however, is able to identify key institutions or provide substantive insight into how to build good institutions. On the contrary, the NIE's path dependent description of economic development suggests that a government can do very little to influence its country's economic trajectory. The East Asian economic transformation would tend to contradict such a conclusion. Several countries in the region have built the institutions needed to incorporate ICT into their societies and bridge, or at least narrow, the Digital Divide. The East Asian experience is due to deliberate human endeavour led by activist governments. It provides hope and a model to nations still struggling to escape poverty. Their growth stands for the proposition that what governments do does matter.

The Disconnect Between Theory and Practice

North (1990) and Williamson (2000) assert, but do not test their assertion, that the continued poverty many nations endure is due to poor informal institutions that change at a glacial pace. If North and Williamson are correct, then a great deal of time, energy and money is being wasted by those working in the economic development field, whether for governments, international organizations, non-governmental organizations or in the academic community. Presumably, they do not accept North's and Williamson's conclusions of unalterable path dependency. They must believe that their efforts can improve the lives of the poor. Somebody's logic must be flawed.

Part of the answer to the 'it-should-not-happen, but-it-does' dichotomy of relatively rapid growth may be found in the definition of 'institutions'. The word 'institutions' is rarely used in common parlance or in the empirical literature in the same manner as it is used in the NIE theory. The focus of the empirical literature is normally upon government-created institutions, not the totality of 'humanly devised constraints that structure human interaction'. It is difficult to reconcile the near universal acceptance of NIE theory as an explanation of why some countries are poor while others are rich and its apparently equal rejection in the day-to-day practice of economic development.

Definitions and Proxies

North (1990) maintains that how individuals, firms and other organizations behave depends upon the rules of the society in which they live and operate. At an abstract level, it is likely correct that values, beliefs and attitudes together with a country's constitution, laws and the other written rules that regulate daily life express themselves as an integrated system that governs the manner in which economic transactions take place and how individuals interact with each other within the incentive structure so created. It retrospectively explains how a society's system of informal and formal rules deal with changing circumstances in accordance with established patterns of behaviour, or what is called path dependent behaviour, to maintain a social and economic equilibrium regardless of whether that equilibrium is efficient or equitable. Looking back one can see the logic, based in historical antecedents, of how societies have coped with a constantly changing world.

> This structure of human interaction determines who are the entrepreneurs whose choices matter and how such choices get implemented by the decision rules of that structure. Institutional constraints cumulate through time, and the culture of a society is the cumulative structure of rules and norms (and beliefs) that we inherit from the past that shape our present and influence our future. (North 2005: 6)

Looking prospectively, North's definition of institutions is unworkable. If institutions are taken to encompass all humanly devised constraints, then the empirical work that cites their importance to development risks becoming meaningless. By defining institutions so broadly it is effectively tautological that a country's institutions determine its current economic status. If institutions are given such a definition, then it is difficult to determine what, precisely, the empirical studies of institutions are attempting to quantify. How could they not find that, at the very least, institutions are important? The economic studies in the

ICT-growth literature that attempt to determine the specific institutional elements that foster economic development create the impression that a hodge-podge of public policies, statutes and enforcement mechanism are all key to economic growth because they all fall within North's definition of institutions. Far more precise tools are needed.

The ongoing analysis of the role of institutions in economic development requires the ability to break down the conception of institutions into its component parts. It is helpful to have such an expansive term to explain a current state of affairs in a country, but that same term does not provide the precision needed to determine how that state of affairs can be altered. Different definitions need to be used for the purposes of understanding the role of institutions at the retrospective conceptual level of the NIE and for the prospective analysis of the role of institutions in the process of economic development. Shirley (2008) rightly notes: 'Definitions may be tedious, but they are not trivial.'

In common parlance, institutions are normally used to describe government created bodies charged with performing specific tasks. As Trebilcock and Prado (2011) forcefully suggest in discussing North's definition:

> However, from a lawyer's perspective, it is an odd definition of institutions. Beyond a country's constitution, lawyers do not tend to think of institutions as the rules of the game. For example, the legally prescribed speed limit on a given highway is not considered an institution but rather a legal rule promulgated by one set of institutions, enforced by another, and in the event of disputes, adjudicated by yet another. Also, the distinction between institutions and organizations that North draws is idiosyncratic in that many of his forms of organizations, like political bodies (political parties, the senate, a city council, a regulatory agency), are typically conceived of by lawyers as institutions charged either with making, administering, or enforcing laws. Finally, by including informal constraints (cultural conventions, norms of behaviour, and self-imposed codes of conduct) in his definition of institutions, North's conception of institutions becomes so all-encompassing that it includes almost any factor that may influence human behaviour and hence risks losing any operational content. (27)

Without an operational definition it is not possible to measure institutional quality properly. One cannot be precise in the measurement of something that is ill-defined and it is especially difficult to do so with the most commonly used proxies.

The most frequently used proxies, the International Country Risk Guide and Kauffman's Governance Matters indices, measure institutional quality only indirectly, if at all. The International Country Risk Guide is intended principally for foreign firms and passive investors in assessing the risk of investing in different jurisdictions. It assesses each of political, financial and economic risk and creates a composite risk rating. Political risk is measured subjectively based on research and studies of twelve components such as government stability, internal conflict, corruption, military involvement in politics, religious and ethnic tensions and quality of the bureaucracy. Each of 12 components is assigned a score based a pre-determined number of points. Government stability, for example, is scored out of 12 while bureaucracy quality is the lowest, with four being the maximum number of eligible points. Financial and economic risk are objectively measured using criteria such as GDP per capita, GDP growth, inflation and government finances. Individual components are assigned a score on a pre-determined scale and the aggregate ranking is calculated arithmetically. Given that the private company creating the reports has been doing so since 1980 and its product range has grown significantly since then, its reports are undoubtedly a useful tool for the market for which they are intended. The publishers, however, do not purport to measure institutions although one might be able to infer something about a country's institutional quality from the risk analysis conducted.

The Governance Matters indices are the most frequently used proxy to gauge institutional quality. They attempt to measure several elements of government legitimacy and effectiveness, which collectively are taken to constitute the quality of a country's governance. Kaufmann defines governance as:

> ...the traditions and institutions by which authority in a country is exercised. This includes (a) the process by which governments are selected, monitored and replaced; (b) the capacity of the government to effectively formulate and implement sound policies; and (c) the respect of citizens and the state for the institutions that govern economic and social interactions among them. (Kaufmann 2010: 4)

Kaufmann constructs two measures for each of the three identified components of governance resulting in what are termed six dimensions of governance: (a)(i)voice and accountability; and (ii) political stability and the absence of violence; (b)(i) government effectiveness; and (ii) regulatory quality; and (c)(i) rule of law; and (ii) control of corruption.

The indices produced by Kaufmann are meticulously compiled from an increasingly large variety of objective statistical material and subjective sources such as survey data that measure participants' perceptions. They provide an effective periodic snapshot of the quality of a country's governance and whether it seems to be improving, regressing or remaining relatively static. Institutions are explicitly contemplated as a crucial component of good governance and it is worth noting that the word is used by Kaufmann to describe government created bodies, specifically those that 'govern economic and social interactions' in contradistinction to 'traditions'. Kaufmann's indices, however, are not a direct measure of a country's institutions. As a report cautions:

> ... each of the individual data sources we have provides an imperfect signal of some deep underlying notion of governance that is difficult to observe directly. (Kaufmann et al. 2007: 10)

Consequently, the work of those who use Kaufmann's indices as a proxy for institutional quality may be seen to be directly quantifying the importance of governance, but that of institutions only indirectly. Rodrik can be interpreted as taking Kaufmann's hypothesis that governance matters and conducting the empirical analysis necessary to show that governance, in fact, rules. Rodrik's contention that institutions rule is based on the derivative implication that good governance can only be achieved where there are good institutions. That may well be correct, but that conclusion depends on a process of deductive logic. Kaufmann's indices reveal very little about which institutions matter for each measured outcome. Like a Seurat painting, the factors that lead to good governance become more abstract the more closely they are examined.

The Complexity of Informal Institutions

Culture

One step in deconstructing institutions so that better analyses can be conducted would be to recognize informal institutions' complexities. There are many more informal constraints than formal ones, according to North. Informal institutions, however, are frequently treated as being homogeneous. Williamson categorizes all informal institutions as Level 1 institutions. Given their importance in determining formal institutions and economic conduct, it would seem that they would draw more attention. Often, however, they are ignored or explicitly shunted aside as the domain of others, such as sociologists, as Lall and Narula (2004) suggest. Formal institutions, of which there are fewer, are classified into a hierarchy of three levels of institutions by Williamson and their interaction intensely scrutinized by economists.

Lall and Narula's (2004) perception of informal institutions as the proper domain of other social scientists serves to underscore the need for a multidisciplinary approach to development. Culture plays a dominant role in the formation of informal institutions. Jutting argues that formal rules are 'embedded in a local setting influenced by historical trajectories and culture' (Jutting 2003: 32). The crucial role culture plays in economic development formed the central thesis in Harrison and Huntington's (2000) aptly titled book, *Culture Matters*. Landes may go further than most when he stated in his contribution to the book: 'If we learn anything from the history of economic development, it is that culture makes almost all the difference' (2000: 2). Others in the same volume, such as Grondona, Montaner and Etounga-Manguelle, are more moderate in their views, but they, too, place culture at the heart of the development narrative and responsible for the historical woes of Latin America and Africa. They identify culture as determinative of informal institutions that promote rent-seeking, maintain economic inefficiencies, perpetuate inequality or lead to stagnation. The governments of those countries are held hostage by culture and prevented from taking remedial action, assuming the political will to do so. Culture, however, can change.

The symposium whose papers produced *Culture Matters* spurred a research project involving 60 international professionals known as the Culture Matters Research Project. The results of that project were presented six years after *Culture Matters* by Harrison (2006), writing alone, in *The Central Liberal Truth*. The project recognized that if there are more informal institutions than formal institutions and if formal institutions can be classified into three levels, then it is likely that there are at least as many levels of informal institutions. Harrison (2006) cites the Universal Declaration of Human Rights as representing principles that are, in fact, universally accepted by all societies, if not all individuals. Such values form the core values of a society. They are the 'bedrock of culture' and change only very slowly. If it is correct that all societies share similar core values, then the reason some countries are poor while others are wealthy must be due to lower level informal institutions that govern how people interact. Accordingly, Harrison (2006) draws a distinction between core 'values' which remain stable over time and less entrenched 'attitudes' and 'beliefs' which can change more quickly. Changing those attitudes and beliefs in societies where they act to perpetuate poverty is portrayed by Harrison as the key to unlocking those societies' potential for economic growth.

If the attitudes and beliefs that perpetuate poverty are to be addressed, then a better understanding of why and how they can be changed is equally needed. There are several possibilities and only a small number are suggested here. The NIE literature portrays societies as being fairly homogeneous, but even where this is true along the lines traditionally used to classify groups such as ethnicity, race, language or religion, one can find important divisions between people that may act to transform prevailing attitudes relatively quickly. Demographic factors like gender, age, socio-economic status and geographic residence (urban or rural; prosperous or disadvantaged region) can prove to be catalysts of change. People divided by such demographic factors often hold different outlooks and values, particularly on economic matters. It is not uncommon for one generation's views to be different on many subjects from those of the previous generation. Outside influences such as television and, more recently, the internet allow citizens in almost all countries to learn how others live and how their societies are organized, thereby making it much more difficult for governments closely tied to privileged groups to perpetuate inequitable social and economic arrangements as the 2011 'Arab Spring' uprisings attest. The refrain 'the old ways are dying' seems ubiquitous. As Harrison (2006) notes, French Quebec, traditionally a fairly homogeneous society, at least racially, religiously and linguistically, has transformed in a relatively short time from one that was religious and conservative to one that is secular and liberal.

In reality, few countries are ethnically, racially, religiously or linguistically homogeneous and many are becoming more diverse. Each identifiable group within a country can be considered to form a discrete society and each may have its own norms and informal institutions for certain types of interaction while others are shared more widely throughout the country. There may be many differing informal institutions that govern similar interactions within and among social groups. Some informal institutions might prove more beneficial, or lead to fewer economic inefficiencies, for a broader range of a country's citizens, if generally adopted, than others. A country's formal institutions traditionally reflect the dominant group's informal institutions, but where power shifts or one group can influence another's attitudes, then formal institutions might be quickly modified. In a democracy, demographic shifts between groups can change the outcomes of elections, leading to rapid economic reform. Thus, it may be more accurate to refer to a country's *prevailing* informal institutions as being the ones that determine from time to time its formal institutions and chart the course of economic development. Porter (2000) described the struggle between opposing cultures in terms of productivity.

> In any nation, there will be differences among groups and individuals in the beliefs and attitudes they hold. One can also view economic development as partly shaped by the tug-of-war between productivity-enhancing aspects of economic culture in a nation and productivity-eroding aspects of culture. Especially heavy weight is attached to the beliefs and attitudes of government leaders and the business elites. (22)

It is, of course, possible that a change in a country's prevailing institutions would merely substitute one predatory group for another where power is sought simply as a means to access spoils, but identifying such a problem might be the first step to addressing it.[4]

A further explanation of relatively rapid economic development lies in distinguishing between societies and countries, a distinction that North makes but does not develop. North maintains that institutions are the rules that govern *societies*. The institutional rules of a society, he further argues, impact *economies*. The study of economic development, however, is primarily concerned with *countries*. Societies, economies and countries are not synonymous terms nor or do they necessarily correspond to congruent territories. Great domestic disparities often exist. Notwithstanding that wealth may not be evenly distributed throughout a country – per capita income, unemployment, and growth rates can vary from region to region – economists are able to analyse economies on a country by country basis. A country's economy in such circumstances can be said to coincide with its national borders notwithstanding that aggregated national economic indicators can serve to obscure important variations in economic performance between regions, classes or groups.

Societies are portrayed by North as being uniform in character throughout a country, but they are not. Most countries are made up of many societies. Such is the case not only in immigrant countries, such as the Americas, but in Africa,

---

4   See, for example, Wrong (2009) where the author describes the events in Kenya subsequent to the retirement of long-time President Daniel arap Moi.

too, where the colonial powers often drew arbitrary boundaries. Countries are often said to have a society, as certain principles and values may be shared widely across religious, linguistic, racial and demographic lines, but countries are also a composite of societies, being rarely homogeneous throughout. One may speak about American society, for example, but America is an extraordinarily diverse country with a vast number of smaller societies creating its national mosaic. In Canada, it is not unusual to speak of Quebec or even Newfoundland as being 'distinct' societies. A country's society is heterogeneous in a manner that is different from its economy. Consequently, relatively rapid economic development may be more easily explained by viewing countries as a composite of dynamic and competitive societies where attitudes and beliefs are constantly being challenged, rather than as a single static and homogeneous society, and where demographic shifts or the simple act of sufficient numbers of people changing their mind can lead to a change in a country's prevailing institutions.

Social Capital

Personal interaction, either individually or jointly through organizations, and the patterns of behaviour that emerge from such interaction form the basis of North's conception of informal institutions. Those patterns of behaviour generate economic consequences. People form groups in reaction to those consequences. The formation of groups and their societal impact, whether with positive or negative societal implications, is often called 'social capital'. Fukuyama (2001) defines social capital as 'an instantiated informal norm that promotes co-operation between two or more individuals.' (7) It is better understood through its manifestations.

Social capital is most visible through the collective connections people form through their active participation in clubs, associations or other groups. The aims of the group do not matter. They can be, for example, social, political, recreational or religious. The unifying characteristics are cooperation, reciprocity and trust between members (Putnam 2005: 19–22). Fukuyama (2001) describes the creation of a 'radius of trust' between members of the group (8–9). Those within that radius of trust are repeatedly treated in a manner that gives rise to expectations of future behaviour from other members of the group and may impose demands upon one's own actions. They involve 'mutual obligations' and 'foster sturdy norms of reciprocity' (Putnam 2005: 20). While such groups are not necessarily concerned with norm formation, Fukuyama's radius of trust represents a 'circle of trust among whom co-operative norms are operative' (2001: 8).

Potentially more important from a social, political and economic point of view is how members of one group interact with those in other groups. Relationships can be positive or negative and may vary depending on the defining characteristics of the other group. Those outside the 'radius of trust' may be distrusted, or worse. Both Fukuyama and Putnam use the Ku Klux Klan as an example of a group that treats some people outside the group very differently from those within.

Less dramatically, Fukuyama points to certain Latin American societies where a very small radius of trust reserves good behaviour for friends and family, but not outsiders. It can lead to a 'cultural foundation of corruption, which is often regarded as a legitimate way of looking after one's family' (2001:12).

Recognizing the possible negative aspects of social capital, Putnam (2005) draws a distinction between 'bonding' and 'bridging' groups which he describes as exclusive and inclusive, respectively (22). Bonding groups tend to reinforce 'exclusive identities and homogeneous groups' while bridging groups aim to cut across such cleavages and build relations with other groups (Putnam 2005: 22). Both have their purposes and are needed to develop social capital within a society. In this regard, the advice of Sen (2006) in *Identity and Violence* about the need to overcome individual single-identity based affiliation is particularly salient.

In theory, social capital reduces societal transaction costs and allows an economy to function more efficiently although it can also lead to rent-seeking or a sub-optimal diversion of resources as when powerful political groups exert pressure for public funds to be spent on their special interests. Putnam et al.'s (1993) examination of the differences in prosperity between northern and southern Italy is particularly revealing about the manner in which social capital can affect economic performance. In 1977, the Italian central government ceded a number of powers to its regions. Putnam's work argues that such devolution failed to overcome existing economic disparities which found their root in differences in social structures. In particular, these structures were seen as more horizontal in the North and more hierarchical in the South (Helliwell and Putnam 1995: 295). Bonding associations with too little trust of outsiders and fewer linkages to other groups were more prevalent in the South whereas greater trust and, consequently, more bridging groups were found in the North. These differences were reflected in the platforms of the officials elected and in the policies they implemented, thereby illustrating Douglass North's contention that informal institutions determine formal institutions and circumscribe a government's power. Such informal institutions result in path dependent behaviour that perpetuates existing economic outcomes. Re-examining his earlier conclusions in 1995, Putnam writing with Helliwell confirmed his initial findings:

> ... our conclusions are consistent with Putnam's finding of pervasive influence of longstanding regional differences in social institutions and with his survey results showing much more effective regional governments in those regions with initially higher levels of social capital. (1995: 304)

Understanding how social capital is created and how norms are formed and transmitted is important to understanding how they can be changed, particularly where they perpetuate poor national economic performance and poverty except for a small elite who may exercise political and economic control. That investigation is primarily within the realm of sociologists. As Fukuyama states: 'The economists' approach to understanding how social capital is generated is ultimately very limited' (2001: 16).

Social Constructivism

A brief look at the application of social constructivist theory to norm formulation in international relations (IR), specifically compliance with international law, may prove instructive in understanding how informal institutions may change relatively quickly. Traditional IR theories, and the international legal compliance theories derived therefrom, owe their roots to economic theory (Wendt 1992; 1994: 392). Very generally, they are based on the fictional, although not illogical, precept that states, like people, are rational actors motivated by self-interest. They seek first to survive and then to thrive through wealth maximization or attaining other desirable ends. State action is constrained by, or compelled as a reaction to, the actions of other states. Traditional IR and compliance theories rest on the assumption that states respond to, and their identities are formed as a consequence of, exogenous factors. As Jutta Brunnée and Stephen Toope (2002) conclude, 'underlying most theories of compliance is a belief that external factors such as interests, incentives and punishments motivate actors' (3).

Unlike traditional IR theory, constructivism traces its roots to sociology and human psychology. These disciplines attempt to understand human motivations, reactions and interaction. Constructivist IR theory draws upon Durkheim, Mead and Weber (Wendt 1994: 389; Ruggie 1998: 857–62). It tries to understand state action as being determined by endogenous factors. Behaviour is primarily governed by internalized norms. States comply with international law because they believe they should, not merely because they fear the potential consequences imposed by other states if they fail to do so. Employing language similar to that used to describe social capital, John Ruggie (1998) resists the notion that social IR constructivists seek to:

> ... directly apply or copy their insights or methods. It is their theoretical objectives that are of interest...because these efforts illuminate the contemporary constructivist project. Both Durkheim and Weber held that the critical ties that connect, bond, and bind individuals within social collectivities are shared ideational ties ... (861)

Similarly, Brunnée and Toope contend that 'the internal legitimacy of international law, its binding force and its compliance pull are all inextricably linked' (2002: 18). They look to domestic factors to explain compliance with international law.[5] In this regard, the approach taken by Harold Koh (1997; 1998)

---

5   Brunnée and Toope (2002) credit the work of Lon Fuller (1964), Gerald Fitzmaurice (1956) '... the law is not binding because it is enforced: it is enforced because it is already binding' (1) and Ian Brownlie (1981) '... the law is ... not external coercive and alien but

conforms closely to theirs. Koh argues that states comply with international law because they have internalized international legal norms. These and other norms, primarily social and political, relating to state conduct form part of a state's self-image or identity. It results in states demonstrating obedience to international law as opposed to 'grudging compliance.' (Koh 1997: 2603) Interaction with other states results in the 'interpretation or enunciation' of a norm leading to a rule that 'guides future interactions between the parties' and repeated interaction is viewed as helping to 'reconstitute the interests and even the identities of the participants' (Brunnée and Toope 2002: 19). Hence, horizontal processes between states lead to vertical domestic processes of legal norm integration into a state's identity. Norm assimilation and not enforcement or sanctions form the basis for domestic legal compliance.

Support for a constructivist approach to compliance with legal norms may be found in an unlikely place; the US invasion of Iraq. The reality may only be that almost all states comply with almost all international law almost all of the time, but their rhetoric is such that all states claim to be in compliance with all of international law all of the time. No state comes to mind as having declared that its actions were taken in deliberate contravention. The United States attempted to justify the Iraq war as being both in compliance with established international law (self-defence in the face of imminent threat) as well as on the basis of a claimed emerging norm of international law characterized as threat prevention. There may be widespread scepticism about the facts underlying the former grounds and the validity of the proposed emerging norm, but it demonstrates the American desire to be seen to be acting in conformity with international law. Why should the United States care? If any state could substantiate the realist school that only power and self-interest matter, then that state would be the United States. It could have said it was simply acting in America's best interests, yet it felt compelled to justify its actions as compliant with international law. The reason may rest in America's concept of its identity.

Michael Ignatieff (2005), and Ruggie (2005), amongst others, have addressed the paradox of American exceptionalism and exemptionalism. On the one hand, the United States has been at the forefront of the drive to establish and expand adherence to international law. On the other, it has often resisted formal acceptance of the norms it sought to spread. Ruggie (2005) has attempted to explain this phenomenon in constructivist terms. He has called 'America's sense of self as a nation', as including, 'the promise of an international order based on rules and institutions' (304). So strong and important is this sense of identity that even Henry Kissinger, whom Ruggie (1998) sees as the 'master practitioner of realist statecraft,' came to admit that 'a foreign policy strategy based merely on interest calculations is simply too unreliable'(858). Now, Kissinger:

---

internal, logically necessary and familiar' (1) as having provided the intellectual foundation for constructivist legal compliance theory (6; 21).

... looks for salvation to the 'idealism' that he spent his entire career mocking – but which is more properly described as the animating ideas and values that emerge out of America's own sense of self. (Ruggie 1998: 858)

Ruggie's analysis suggests that the American need to present its actions in Iraq as compliant with international law stems from its sense of self-identity and is not merely an attempt to mollify the international community. The United States conceives itself as a law-abiding nation. This principle has been internalized within the American psyche and it motivates American behaviour. There may be a measure of self-deception within the self-perception but such would not contradict a constructivist analysis of US actions.

The process Brunnée and Toope, Koh and Ruggie describe is the same as the one described by North. Domestic norm formation is seen as the basis of state conduct. Ruggie (1998) cites 'the critical ties that connect, bond and bind individuals'. Although they use different language, much of it overlaps with that used by North (1990) who describes informal institutions as being based on 'codes of conduct' (4; 36) and 'norms of behavior' (36) that govern how individuals, firms and, more broadly, society make economic choices. Constructivist IR theory seeks to understand how those same forces manifest themselves in a different field. Contrary to North, however, they make no claim that such norms evolve so slowly that they require 'historians to perceive them' (North 1990: 6) or that it can take centuries or millennia (Williamson 2000). While no timetable is put upon this process, it would appear to be measured in decades, suggesting that the informal institutions that govern economic behaviour are equally susceptible to relatively rapid change.

A Modified Approach

There are three things, at a minimum, that can be done to help facilitate a better understanding of the process by which countries, such as those in Asia, have achieved relatively rapid economic development. First, new definitions should be adopted for the prospective study of development. Proper definitions are essential to proper analysis. The definition of institutions used by North may be suitable for the theoretical work of the NIE that explains economic history, but it encapsulates far too many concepts to be of practical value as an analytical tool. If the definition of institutions is too broad, then the proxies used to measure them may be of limited value. No proxy can measure institutions as defined by North. By narrowing the scope of what one is trying to measure, more accurate proxies can be used or developed. Second, more case studies of development efforts, in general, and institution building, in particular, need to be produced. If institutions are not susceptible to the same methods of empirical analysis as are other economic determinants of growth, then the methods used by other social scientists, such as case studies, should be used to complement such analyses. Third, a greater focus should be placed upon the process by which institutions are built. It is likely that there is no ideal set of institutions that all less economically developed countries should strive to replicate or a sequence in which their institutions should be built. Each country must decide which institutions are most important for it to concentrate upon given its unique circumstances and level of development. Successful efforts at building institutions appear to follow a common pattern. The process by which they are built may prove most important to their success.

Definitions

Constraints, or institutions, can be formal or informal. Informal constraints, normally unwritten, are made up of 'codes of conduct, norms of behaviour, and conventions ... They come from socially transmitted information and are part of the heritage we call culture' (North 1990: 36–7). Williamson (2000) describes them as 'informal institutions'. 'Informal institutions', 'informal constraints' and 'informal norms' are taken to refer to the same concept and will be used synonymously. They stem from a society's values, beliefs and attitudes and greater study should be devoted to informal institutions as suggested by Harrison (2006). Informal institutions influence all levels of decision-making and the interpretation, implementation and enforcement of laws, but having concluded that formal institutions determine to a greater extent the ability of governments to stimulate economic growth, informal institutions will not be dealt with in further detail.

The meaning of formal constraints, normally written, will be restricted to those that result from the conscious decisions of bodies empowered to legislate, decree or otherwise make the rules governing conduct. They include constitutions, statutes, regulations, by-laws, and, in common law countries, court decisions. These formal constraints will be collectively referred to as 'laws' regardless of their precise nature.

The term 'public policy' will be used to describe the intentions or the strategies used by governments to attain their objectives. Public policy is the theory that underlies the course of action that governments pursue in order to implement their societal goals, including those concerning economic development. The enunciation of public policy is the exclusive domain of governments. References to a government's 'economic policy' or 'social policy' are usually short forms of referring to its public policy on such matters. Although public policy may be viewed as covering the actions governments undertake to implement their goals, including the enactment of laws, the term 'public policy' as used herein will not include laws. Public policy leads to the creation of laws. 'Public policy' is distinguished from the commonly used term 'policy' which is frequently used to describe the manner in which a law may be interpreted, implemented or enforced. A police force may have a policy of not arresting people for what it considers minor infractions. The daily activities of both governments and government bodies may also be guided by policies which, in theory, will be in conformity with public policy. Interpretation bulletins issued by tax authorities and policy statements released by securities regulators are examples of policies although not all policies are as formal. To avoid confusion, such policies will be called 'interpretive guidelines'.

Contrary to North, but in conformity with common usage, 'institutions' will be used differently and will refer to governments and quasi-governmental bodies and agencies charged with the formulation, interpretation, implementation or enforcement of public policy or laws.[6] North considers any group of people, including law making bodies such as the Senate and regulatory bodies, to be organizations. They, too, will be classified as institutions. The term 'institution' can also refer to the manner in which government bodies operate. Where consultation regularly takes place between a government body and an organization, such as between the ministry of justice and a bar association, such consultation is often considered 'institutionalized'. The term 'convention' will be used to describe such an established consultative practice.

Institutions can be classified into three categories according to their function. First, they can serve to help formulate public policy and propose the laws designed to implement it. They can be used by governments as advisory bodies to study the means to carry out their goals and to generate proposals suggesting alternative courses of action, setting priorities, developing time lines and forecasting budgets. In essence, they can provide a road map that allows government to understand what needs to be done to achieve its strategies and the steps involved. Such institutions may be general in nature, charged with considering broad public policy objectives or narrower questions related to specific issues, such as competition law or transportation policy. Their structure is less important than their function as a formulator and generator of public policy proposals and laws for the government's consideration.

The second tier of institutions consists of those bodies charged with taking decisions and enacting laws. They are the rule makers and can be found in the legislative, administrative and judicial branches of government. It is at this level that the government turns public policy into the laws that give effect to the former. Specialized government bodies can do likewise within the scope of their mandates and the powers delegated to them. Institutions at this level may issue interpretive guidelines elaborating the manner in which laws should be applied by those institutions responsible for implementing and enforcing them. These institutions include the Cabinet, legislatures, municipal councils, regulatory authorities and the courts.

A third level of institutions is responsible for interpreting, implementing and enforcing laws. These institutions include courts, the police, administrative tribunals and regulatory bodies and may prove to be the most important as they are frequently in direct contact with the public. The finest public policies and

---

6   For a similar view, see Prado and Trebilcock (2009: 349): 'For our purposes, we understand "institutions" to means those bodies (formal and informal) charged by a society with making, administering, enforcing or adjudicating its laws or policies.'

laws will not be effective to spur economic development if the institutions at this level do not or cannot carry out their functions for any reason, such as corruption, underfunding or a lack of sufficiently trained people. An effective competition regulator, for example, requires substantial funding and human resources to conduct investigations, analyse commercial activity and prosecute allegedly unlawful acts. Many less economically developed countries simply lack both the money and the qualified people to apply laws effectively. Consequently, those charged with designing public policy and enacting laws must be acutely aware of the limitations that institutions at this level face in implementing and enforcing those public policies and laws.

Public policies, laws and institutions do not operate in a vacuum. They function within a country's civil society and they influence the everyday conduct of affairs and interaction between individuals and organizations. 'Organizations' will mean all non-government affiliated groups of individuals bound to promote a common purpose or by a common identity. They include economic, religious, social and educational bodies, as North notes. Organizations provide feedback on the manner in which existing public policies and laws function and they advocate on behalf of their members to create new public policies and laws, or alter and maintain existing ones. The dialogue between organizations and institutions takes place, or should take place, at all three levels of institutions and the formation of organizations and consultative conventions should be encouraged by governments.[7]

Case Studies

As Rodrik acknowledges, knowing that institutions rule provides very little guidance to policymakers. This inability to provide practical advice has led some economists to question entirely the validity of large scale, cross-country, macroeconomic regression studies. Although Jessica Cohen and William Easterly do not specifically refer to the literature attempting to measure the impact of ICT or institutions on growth, they argue that the growth literature has produced 'endless claims for some new "key to growth" (regularly found to be "significant")' (2009: 3). They suggest that proponents of macroeconomic growth theories use such a vast range of variables that it is 'easy enough to arrive at significant results' that

---

7   An analogous process of interaction and change is described by Milhaupt and Pistor in what they call the 'demand for law'. They explain that law is not a neutral endowment, but is constantly shaped by human interaction and politics. 'We argue that whatever its original source, in order for law to perform any useful function in support of markets it must fit local conditions and thus must continuously evolve in tandem with economic, social, and political developments.' Laws may be developed domestically or transplanted from other systems. Transplanted laws will only be effective if they meet the local demand, not just of the local legal community, which they term a 'micro-fit', but if they are well integrated into the political economy of the host country, which they term a 'macro-fit' (Milhaupt and Pistor 2008: 22).

allows one to see 'patterns in randomness' (Cohen and Easterly 2009: 3). In their view, micro-policy analysis through small, individually controlled trials, known as randomized evaluations, provide a better means of determining 'the most effective method for delivering public goods such as education and vaccines' (Cohen and Easterly 2009: 1).[8] Such tests seek to evaluate the effectiveness of small, highly targeted development projects. These approaches are succinctly categorized by Cohen and Easterly as 'Thinking Big and Thinking Small' about development.

It may be that randomized evaluations can make a significant contribution to improving people's lives by determining whether individual development projects achieve their goals. The knowledge derived from such studies is undoubtedly valuable if it can be shown that certain types of small scale projects, such as providing mosquito nets to people in areas suffering from high rates of malaria or purifying well water in remote rural areas, are consistently effective in accomplishing their goals. The nature of such projects, however, is to treat the symptoms of poverty and economic failure. The development community must also be concerned with attacking the causes of poverty.

Large cross-country studies are concerned with discovering the root causes of why some countries are prosperous and others are not. The literature's conclusion, albeit somewhat imprecise, that institutions are critical to growth, provides compelling evidence in understanding the dynamics of economic development. At the same time, it must be acknowledged that such studies alone have not provided a sufficient practical understanding of how to improve the fortunes of the less prosperous. Rodrik, in his contribution to Cohen and Easterly's book, attempts to reconcile the opposing methodological schools of thought. Referring to the two methods of economic analysis – large scale, cross-sectional, panel regressions and small randomized evaluations – he argues:

> In the technical jargon, the research strategies I have described have different degrees of internal and external validity. Internal validity relates to the quality of causal identification: Has the study credibly demonstrated a causal link between the policy or treatment in question and the outcome of interest? External validity has to do with generalizability: Are these results valid also for the broader population for which the policy or treatment is being considered? Sound inference requires *both*.

> Randomized evaluations are strong on internal validity but produce results that can be contested on external validity grounds...By contrast, the standard econometric and qualitative approaches are weaker on internal validity—but conditional on credible identification, they have fewer problems of external validity. (Rodrik 2009: 34, emphasis original)

---

8   The benefits of randomized evaluations are also emphasized in Banerjee and Duflo (2011) and Karlan and Appel (2011).

A more fruitful approach to understanding the role of institutions in economic development may be to borrow from the methods used in other social sciences that have not adopted regressions and other methods of econometric measurement as their dominant analytical tool. There is a growing recognition of the value of detailed case studies as is suggested by Shirley (2008) and by Rodrik (2007), where he calls for both cross-country regressions and case studies.

> Econometricians are still hard at work looking for the growth-promoting effects of policies that countries in Latin America and elsewhere embraced enthusiastically a quarter century ago. I am not a purist when it comes to the kind of evidence that matters. In particular, I believe in the need for both cross-country regressions and detailed country studies. Any cross-country regression giving results are that [sic] not validated by case studies needs to be regarded with suspicion. But any policy conclusion that derives from a case study and flies in the face of cross-national evidence needs to be similarly scrutinized. Ultimately, we need both kinds of evidence to guide our views of how the world works. (Rodrik 2007: 4)

In his emphasis on the value of case studies, Rodrik echoes Crafts who ten years earlier undertook an examination of the historical evolution of endogenous growth models. He called on economists and economic historians to work together to understand better the political economy of growth through the use of 'an endogenous innovation framework' (Crafts 1997: 69). In his view, their common goals would be more likely to be achieved 'through a portfolio of detailed case studies of individual countries than through regressing growth rates against standard variables' (Crafts 1997: 69).

The purpose of case studies is not merely to see what has worked, or failed, elsewhere. Successful economic development efforts in one country cannot simply be copied by others. Too many country-specific factors are at play to permit this strategy to be successful, but a body of case studies allows for recurring themes or patterns to be discerned. In particular, it may be just as important, if not more so, to learn how public policy was developed and implemented than which specific public policies were pursued, laws enacted and institutions created. If a sufficient body of cases studies can be produced that specifically attempts to address which institutions are important to growth and how to build them coupled with the large scale cross-country regressions and other forms of econometric analyses to verify the universality of their application, greater progress may be made towards understanding how poor countries may become more prosperous.

Process

Policy makers need actionable advice about which institutions to build and how to build them. The choice of which institutions are most important for a country's economic development depends upon which sectors its government believes present the best opportunities for expansion. Each country has to determine which sectors those may be. By encouraging those sectors to become more efficient and productive they can hopefully serve as drivers of growth in associated fields. There is no ideal or universal set of institutions governments must first build nor is there evidence that a particular sequence of institutions building must be followed.

Prosperous countries enjoy a range of institutions that they have developed over decades, if not centuries, covering the expanse of government action. Poorer countries will likely create similar institutional matrices over time if, and as, they grow wealthier provided they share similar social, political and economic values. How each country chooses to formalize those principles will vary from country to country and other countries' courses of action can serve as valuable precedents, but simply advising a less economically developed country to replicate a wealthy country's institutions is unhelpful. Institutions cannot be copied from one country and successfully grafted onto another.

Countries must build their institutions, often from scratch. Building institutions is more than a mechanical process. Precise mandates, organization charts and job descriptions alone will not result in an effective institution. Too often, governments are simply advised that institution building is important and that they should build the institutions that will facilitate economic growth. In a 2005 report published by the G-20 titled *Institution Building in the Financial Sector* the report's authors emphasize the link between appropriate institutions and economic performance. As the title of the report suggests, they examine the institution building efforts of the G-20 members in the financial sector to determine the keys to success. The first of its main conclusions is:

> Building the appropriate institutional framework is a cumulative effort that takes a long time and that must be adapted to changing circumstances. Policymakers should not neglect building high-quality institutions, since they are indispensable for rapid and sustained growth. (G-20 2005: xii)

No doubt, the advice is well-intentioned and its conclusions are correct, but such platitudes provide no operational help. The report then refers more specifically to the need for central bank independence, a well-functioning legal system, strong and efficient payment systems and deregulation as part of the institution building process. The efforts of the G-20 countries in the studied sphere are thoroughly reviewed in the report, without providing actionable suggestions to policymakers.

As repeatedly stated, the reason institutions are emphasized in the economic development literature is that they form an integral part of the enabling environment needed to allow business activities to be carried out effectively and efficiently thereby leading to economic growth. Good institutions help to overcome the structural inefficiencies inherent in any society, but the governments creating them may not always know the specific challenges impeding effective implementation and enforcement. The people who best understand the problems are those active on a regular basis in sectors whose activities will be most affected by the institutions. Depending on the sector, they may include businesspeople, investors, lawyers, academics, civil servants, teachers, students, consumers or members of the general public. Although not necessarily everybody, an interested stakeholder could be anybody. Good institutions thus grow out of widespread consultation and communication between individuals, groups and government on an on-going basis. A good institution is one that accomplishes the purpose for which it was created. Creating institutions that accomplish the purpose for which they were created is not a matter of luck. Their creation depends, in large measure upon the consultative process which governments choose to follow. That process appears to be a key component of institutional change at both the most abstract and the most tangible levels.

Woodrow Powell has studied the process of institution building and institutional change within the context of the branch of economics known as organizational institutionalism. Organizational institutionalism applies what Greenwood et al. (2008) call an institutional perspective to the questions: 'How and why do organizations behave as they do, and with what consequences?' With its roots in the study of the behavioural theory of the firm, similar to the NIE, organizational institutionalism emerged as a discrete subject of study in the late 1970s and early 1980s. In the view of the editors, 'the idea that captured the imagination was that organizations are influenced by their *institutional context*, i.e. by widespread social understandings' (Greenwood et al. 2008: 3, emphasis original). The institutional context was defined by Meyer and Rowan in 1983, in terms exceptionally similar to those employed by North in 1990, as 'the rules, norms, and ideologies of the wider society' (Meyer and Rowan 1983: 84). Institutions are thus understood in the same manner as the NIE.

One branch of organizational institutionalism is concerned with institutional creation and evolution. Powell has been at the forefront of what he describes as the 'microfoundations' of organizational institutional theory. He argues that change comes to a society's norms and values through the interaction of individuals, particularly those whom he terms 'policy entrepreneurs'. Policy entrepreneurs play a disproportionately influential role compared to most individuals in advancing new ideas, of their own or of others, and causing them to be adopted more widely. Those thought leaders are able to induce others to cooperate with their vision through reliance on a 'repertoire of tactics, including the use of legitimate authority, agenda setting, and brokering' (Hwang and Powell 2005: 191). Essentially, their power is the ability to persuade others.

The micro-level approach to macro-level institutional changes relies strongly upon avenues of repeated discourse between and among individuals and organizations to build and alter social norms. In this respect, it closely resembles the process of building social capital described by Putnam and Fukuyama. The interaction builds consensus and acceptance of evolving institutions. Writing with Jeanette Colyvas, Powell maintains that: 'Institutions are sustained, altered, and extinguished as they are enacted by individuals in concrete social situations' (Powell and Colyvas 2008: 276). Ideas and their transmission to others lie at the fulcrum of this process as they allow for innovation and adaptation. New ideas are taken from one environment and transposed into another. Changing informal institutions is viewed as a process dependent on the work of individuals acting both on their own and in collaboration with others. This process acts as a catalyst for the relatively rapid change of informal institutions and, consequently, formal institutions.

In an entirely different context than the one contemplated by Powell, Caroline Mascarell, in a project review published in 2007 by the World Bank, described the same process in her evaluation of community development projects in Macedonia (MCDP) and, in particular, the institution building aspects associated with the project. With a total budget of US$8.7 million spread across over 200 micro-projects, the MCDP attempted to provide sustainable poverty reduction solutions in a highly challenging environment. The economy of Macedonia had come close to collapse in the aftermath of the breakup of Yugoslavia. Ethnic tensions and unemployment levels were high. Within this context, the central government attempted to decentralize and delegate services to municipalities that lacked the capacity to assume them.

> Extensive efforts were made under the MCDP to make beneficiaries aware of their potential role in the project and seek their active involvement. Thus, the Project created demand for participation. Second, the project kept its focus on service delivery. It understood that making people feel that government paid attention to their needs and could contribute to their lives was the key to success. (Mascarell 2007: 2)

Mascarell describes in detail the extensive consultative process that was undertaken among members of the affected communities. Terms such as 'capacity building', 'engagement'. 'communication', 'community outreach' and 'participation' are prominent in her report. In order to foster involvement, a community implementation committee (CIC) was created in each municipality that included 'representatives of schools, health care programs, nursing homes, NGOs, the mayor, city counselors, directors of public enterprises and the like' (Mascarell 2007: 12). Proposals for micro-projects within the municipality were presented to the CIC which would then meet at least three times over three months to determine which projects to pursue. That determination involved further extensive community participation.

> There was one general meeting in which citizens from different localities participated, after which people in smaller localities discussed their needs and made a list of their own priorities. In a second general meeting, each community within the municipality had to argue why their priorities were more pressing for the municipality than the priorities of other communities. Finally, in a third general meeting, they had to take a final vote and generate a list of five

infrastructure projects and three social services projects for submission as their proposed projects. (Mascarell 2007: 13)

According to Mascarell, the micro-projects proved a success with high levels of satisfaction being noted in response to their goals including improved living conditions, better social integration, the quality of the works, sustainability and transparency of the process. Mascarell stresses that the consultative process among all interested stakeholders played a critical role in building institutions at the local level and to the success of the outcomes. Local residents were empowered and made to feel that they had a vested interest in the success of the project. In her view, the MCDP demonstrates that:

> ...it is possible to install practices of good governance by local example that spiral up from communities through the layers of subnational governments to the national government and back down again—thus providing the basis for multi-layered consensus-building that is fully participatory and mutually reinforcing. (Mascarell 2007: 32)

The consultative process described by Powell and Mascarell can be applied to building and transforming institutions as the discussion of the Finnish experience in education reform in Chapter 5 and the case studies of Singapore (Chapter 6) and Malaysia (Chapter 7) further demonstrate. Effective and on-going communication with all interested parties, such as the civil service, members of the government, individuals and organizations is crucial. The composition of the interested parties, or stakeholders, will undoubtedly vary from issue to issue. Such widespread consultation allows for the generation of new ideas, the examination of proposed policies and laws, and the evaluation of the effectiveness of their implementation and enforcement through continuous feedback to assist in determining where modification may be required.

By listening to a multiplicity of voices, institutions can develop a better understanding of the impact of existing laws and the potential impact of a suggested course of action, thereby resulting in better designed public policy, laws and interpretive guidelines that are more likely to achieve their intended purposes. The opportunity afforded organizations to provide input into the institutional matrix can result in lower implementation and enforcement costs of public policies and laws through greater voluntary compliance. By encouraging the formation of social capital through a diverse range of organizations such as those based on commercial interests, professional activity, recreational pastime or political philosophy, in addition to traditional groupings based on race, ethnicity, religion or gender, governments can potentially accelerate growth by altering the existing self-perpetuating relationships between institutions and organizations where such structures are inefficient. There will always be groups with stronger voices than others and political considerations will always influence those in power, but on balance a vibrant consultative process will result in better public policies, laws, institutions and outcomes.

Summary

North's broad conception of institutions captures the manner by which constraints, regardless of their source, govern conduct and explains why some countries are prosperous and others impoverished. His discussion of path dependency illuminates how a society's institutions, particularly informal institutions, lead to enduring poverty in some countries and may continue to do so as manyinformal institutions change only exceedingly slowly. Notwithstanding North's pessimism, several countries have shown that substantial economic transformation is possible within a matter of decades.

The reason that countries' prospects can change relatively quickly is because informal institutions are not as homogeneous or rigid as North suggests. Harrison has described hierarchies of informal institutions – values, beliefs and attitudes – in a manner analogous to Williamson's taxonomy of formal institutions. The highest level institutions, or a society's core values, are viewed as the most difficult to change, but those values also appear to be common to all societies. If all societies share similar core values, but their economic outcomes are different, then the causes of those economic disparities must find their genesis in lower level attitudes and beliefs, which change more rapidly. A greater understanding of the manner in which such attitudes and beliefs change will provide an important insight into how to foster economic development.

The definition of institutions used by North is useful when used for retrospective purposes, but not when it is used prospectively. If one accepts that governments and others concerned with economic growth can influence development paths, then the definition of institutions that serves to elucidate why some countries are rich and others poor needs to be altered to allow for better analysis of the factors that can affect economic development. Precise definitions, widely adopted, would greatly aid the ability to focus upon and analyse the discrete elements of a country's institutional matrix. Accordingly, if the definition of institutions is too vague, then the proxies employed to measure them must be used with caution. The most common proxy, the Governance Matters indices, is of enormous value in measuring changes to the quality of a country's governance over time, but the extent to which they can be said to measure institutions is uncertain.

Even with improved proxies, the very nature of institutions makes it challenging to quantify their quality and effectiveness. It may be more fruitful to complement the use of empirical studies with the means used more frequently by other social scientists, case studies, to better understand the role of institutions in creating a country's enabling environment. A substantial body of case studies can help to uncover recurring themes that will provide improved guidance about which institutions are important for growth and how to build them. A growing body of evidence emphasizes the consultative process as a common and key ingredient in building institutions suggesting that the manner by which institutions are built is the most important factor in determining their success.

Chapter 5

Which Institutions?

Stating the Obvious?

Much of the academic literature on development is concerned with big ideas. To what extent should a government guide the economy or should market forces prevail? Should economic reform be rapid or gradual? What is the key to fostering growth? These are important questions that need to be addressed. Their discussion can make fascinating reading. Too much of the literature, however, can resemble an intellectual jousting match where economic theories about are debated, but little of pragmatic value is offered to the governments of less economically developed countries. These governments have to make choices and determine how to implement their decisions. Daily. The discussion of the importance of institutions cannot remain simply a theoretical exercise. It must lead to practical solutions.

This chapter seeks to shift the discussion from 'Whether Institutions?' to 'Which Institutions?' Compared to the theoretical literature, practical advice can seem mundane and pedantic. There is likely no one right answer to 'Which Institutions?' The range of institutions needed to create an effective enabling environment for development is wide, but if one accepts that ICT usage is essential for sustained economic development and that three factors in addition to institutions have been demonstrated to mediate the relationship between ICT usage and economic growth – telecommunications infrastructure; investment in ICT; and human capital – then one place for governments to begin their institution building efforts could be with the institutions that have been identified as salient to building infrastructure, encouraging investment in ICT and developing human capital. This chapter is not intended as the definitive institutional assembly manual. Others will undoubtedly be quick to point out its shortcomings. Hopefully, they will venture their own opinions about which institutions are important and how to build them. Then, at least, the debate will have shifted.

Telecommunications Infrastructure and Regulation

Infrastructure and Economic Growth

In a 2001 study, one of the first to consider specifically the role of telecommunications infrastructure in the spread of ICT and its relationship to growth, Roller and Waverman examine the experience of 21 OECD countries between 1970 and 1990. They contend that it:

...is clear that the effect of telecommunication and information technology infrastructure on productivity and economic growth are potentially very different from that of other types of infrastructures. (Roller and Waverman 2001: 911)

Other infrastructure, such as roads, may depreciate in value over time and become less efficient with greater use, as when traffic jams occur or cracks or potholes develop. In contrast, network externalities cause the value of ICT infrastructure to increase as more people use that infrastructure for a variety of purposes (Roller and Waverman 2001). Roller and Waverman's modelling led them to conclude that there is a 'causal relationship between telecommunications infrastructure and aggregate output' (2001: 921). They further suggest that there may be increasing returns to telecommunications investment, the impact of which is only felt after a critical mass of telecommunications infrastructure exists.[1] Although they did not examine the role of institutions in the relationship, others have done so.

Levy and Spiller (1994) consider the impact of institutions on telecommunications regulatory structures and economic performance in five countries – Argentina, Chile, Jamaica, the Philippines and the United Kingdom. Drawing heavily upon the NIE literature their objective is to determine how the economic performance of the telecommunications sector is affected by the manner in which political institutions interact with the regulatory process thereby increasing or decreasing the risk of administrative expropriation or manipulation. The restraint of arbitrary action is identified as the key factor in producing a positive outcome. If an effective regulatory system can restrain such action in the telecommunications sector, the sector will grow, notwithstanding continuing challenges in an otherwise 'problematic environment':

> We argue that the credibility and effectiveness of a regulatory framework – and hence its ability to facilitate private investment – varies with a country's political and social institutions. Further, we argue that performance can be satisfactory with a wide range of regulatory procedures, as long as three complementary mechanisms restraining arbitrary administrative action are all in place: (a) substantive restraints on the discretion of the regulator, (b) formal or informal constraints on changing the regulatory system, and (c) institutions that enforce the above formal – substantive or procedural – constraints. Our evidence suggests that regulatory commitment can indeed be developed in what appear to be problematic environments... (Levy and Spiller 1994: 202)

---

1 The authors contend that such a critical mass is obtained at the 40 per cent penetration level which is the norm in OECD countries. The ITU (2009) determines telecommunications infrastructure penetration as a function of the number of main lines per 10,000 inhabitants. A main line is defined as 'a telephone line connecting the subscriber's terminal equipment to the switched public network and which has a dedicated port in the telephone exchange equipment.' Roller and Waverman (2001) and Henisz and Zelner (2001) adopt this definition.

Henisz and Zelner (2001), in a study covering 147 countries between 1960 and 1994, published shortly before that of Roller and Waverman (2001), attempt to determine how differences in constraints on political discretion affect rates of telecommunication infrastructure deployment. They conclude that 'stronger constraints on executive discretion should lead to more rapid infrastructure deployment' (Henisz and Zelner 2001: 124). Their reasoning is based in large part on the argument of Levy and Spiller that the 'economies of scale in and massive consumption of telecommunications services create an inherent political interest in telecom...pricing' (Henisz and Zelner 2001: 127) which may lead to expropriation of telecommunications infrastructure assets or rent-seeking in an effort to obtain a share of telecommunications services revenues. Telecommunications deployment depends on institutional safeguards to limit that risk (Henisz and Zelner 2001: 127).

More recent studies narrowed their focus further, pointing directly at the role of telecommunications law and the function of an independent regulatory institution as critical to addressing the issue of government credibility. In 2003, Gutierrez examined 22 Latin American and Caribbean countries from 1980–1997 to determine the effect of a specialized telecommunications regulator on sector performance. He finds that countries with 'a better regulatory framework will have greater network deployment' (Gutierrez 2003: 279) as measured by the number of main lines per 100 inhabitants. Independent regulators improve government credibility by reducing expropriation risk and that of opportunistic behaviour. Other important factors include the opening of the market to competition and 'the free entry of private investors in basic telecommunications services' (Gutierrez 2003: 279). Gual and Trillas, in 2006, construct their own indices to measure regulatory independence and entry barriers in 37 countries that vary economically and geographically. They, too, find that the existence of an independent regulator may help expand infrastructure investment and counteract the negative effects of a relatively weak perception of the rule of law (Gual and Trillas 2006).

In a 2007 examination of regulation in the telecommunications sector, Maiorano and Stern look closely at the impact of telecommunications infrastructure on income growth and the role of institutions. They try to 'separate the impact of regulation from the potential indirect effects due to country institutions' (Maiorano and Stern 2007: 2). The authors examine 30 low and middle income countries and conclude that the evidence:

> ... confirms the positive effect of regulatory institutions on telecommunications penetration and also highlights the contribution of a more widespread telecommunications infrastructure to higher levels of GDP per capita at least for mobile telecom services. (Maiorano and Stern 2007: 3)

What Infrastructure?

The studies provide substantial support for the view that telecommunications infrastructure can be linked to economic growth where strong laws and an independent regulator are in place, but the literature does not address the type of telecommunications infrastructure that should be built or where it should be built in order to spread most effectively the use and access of ICT. Given its highly capital intensive nature and the years it may take to build, telecommunications infrastructure constitutes 'sunk' assets that cannot be easily sold, moved or reused (Stern 2007). Deciding what to build and where to build it involves complex choices for governments, particularly if their financial capabilities and human capital resources are modest.

Prior to deciding what and where to build, governments should determine what economic goals they hope to accomplish through building such infrastructure. As unequivocal as the literature is that emphasizes the importance of an independent telecommunications regulator, the regulator should not be expected to make such decisions. What gets built depends on the development policy the government wishes to pursue. It decides, for example, whether it is preferable to provide wireless broadband capacity in urban areas as opposed to what is commonly called 'plain old telephone service' in remote regions where previously there was none.

A decision that the type of infrastructure to be built first should be based on a calculation of where that infrastructure will generate the greatest immediate economic return has its appeal, and may be the correct decision, but it may also serve to perpetuate or reinforce structural inefficiencies within an economy that allow an already relatively prosperous region or group to become more so, thereby increasing existing disparities. Thus, the questions of who receives the economic benefit of infrastructure construction and the scope of the economic growth it will potentially stimulate need to be addressed by the government and the institutions and organizations that provide input into the decision-making process. They are questions of economic planning and priorities more than telecommunications policy alone. Consequently, the institutions that formulate economic policy in consultation with those that implement telecommunications policy, should be the institutions charged primarily with determining what infrastructure should be built and where. As Hanna notes, this is not a task solely for governments and institutions; the participation of organizations is critical. Governments need to work closely with the private sector to 'identify target market opportunities; match specific niches to comparative advantage, systematically assess current constraints and jointly devise the policies and programs' (Hanna 2003b: 30) needed to exploit those opportunities.

The strategic process of how best to utilize ICT to stimulate economic growth and the consequent decision of what to build and where may be a collaborative process between economic planning institutions, government ministries, the private sector and individuals and organizations with a vested interest in such decision, but the literature emphasizes that the execution of the strategy should be left to an independent regulator. The quality of that regulator thus becomes exceedingly important. Where regulatory shortcomings can be blamed for a failure to provide the telecommunications services necessary to support increased adoption of ICT at the firm and individual level, investment in the sector will assuredly be sub-optimal and economic growth stifled. Hence, the constitutive elements of successful regulation bear closer examination.

The Telecommunications Regulator

The ICT Regulation Toolkit (the 'ITU Toolkit') is an on-line resource developed and regularly updated by the ITU and *info*Dev designed to provide guidance to governments and regulators (www.ictregulationtoolkit.org). It is referred to in detail because of the quality and depth with which it addresses the practical challenges confronting effective regulation and because many of the recommendations regarding structure and operations apply equally to all institutions. The model telecommunications regulator presented in the ITU Toolkit is an idealized goal, the achievement of which requires financial and human resources that are beyond the current means of many less economically developed countries. Nevertheless, the underlying principles of transparency, impartiality and fairness can and should be respected from the beginning. The scope of the regulator's mandate and its ability to undertake some of the suggested actions can be expanded as resources permit.

The main purpose of telecommunications regulation is to help a country to 'attract sufficient and sustainable investment to satisfy existing demand, expand supply and introduce new services' (ITU Toolkit, Module 1, 2.4). Regulation of the telecommunications industry may be carried on by the government directly, but given governments' historical participation in the sector, the large amounts of capital involved in telecommunications projects and fear of inappropriate government behaviour, most countries have created an independent regulator.[2]

A truly independent regulator ensures non-discrimination, both in practice and perception, in carrying out the regulatory function. Stern cites three 'meta-principles' developed by the World Bank as underlying the regulatory process:

Credibility – Investors must have confidence that the regulatory system will honor its commitments.

Legitimacy – Consumers must be convinced that the regulatory system will protect them from the exercise of monopoly power, whether through high prices, poor service, or both.

2   An independent telecommunications regulator is also required under the Reference Paper for best practices under the WTO Basic Telecommunication Agreement (1997). A total of 82 WTO members of the 108 parties to that Agreement have committed to the Reference Paper. See also Trebilcock and Howse (2005).

> *Transparency* – The regulatory system must operate transparently so that investors and consumers know the 'rules of the game'. (Stern 2007: 4)

The manner in which the regulator is established is the first test of its credibility. The nature and scope of its powers should be clearly defined in its enabling legislation. Such legislation should state the ambit of the regulator's powers, establish its authority to regulate the industry and ensure its ability to carry out its mandate without interference. In carrying out its functions, the regulator's authority needs be delineated from that of other authorities, such as the ministry in charge of telecommunications or other institutions concerned with competition. Its actions must be subject to such governmental oversight and judicial review as are necessary to ensure that it stays within its authority and does not engage in the arbitrary or discriminatory behaviour that its independence is supposed to protect against. The regulator must also be shielded from 'capture' by industry, particularly former monopoly, operators. WTO rules require that the regulator be established independently from operators (ITU Toolkit, Module 6, 5.1.1).

In order to function independently, the regulator requires the human resources and funds necessary to carry out its mandate. Top management should be qualified professionals with security of tenure to guard against outside influence or premature removal from office, which should only be permitted in clearly enunciated cases of misconduct. The staggering of terms can also help prevent politically motivated wholesale dismissals of management. The regulator should be permitted to endeavour to be self-financing though the imposition of licensing fees, contributions from operating revenues and fines where its rules have been breached.

Once established, the most important duties of the regulator, depending on the government's priorities, may include: (a) implementing the authorization framework to maximize investment opportunities and the establishment of new ICT businesses; (b) regulating competition to provide effective enforcement of fair and equitable market principles; (c) interconnecting networks and facilities; and (d) implementing universal service mechanisms (ITU Toolkit). Authorization is the term applied to the process by which the regulator grants a license or other legal instrument to a service provider or network operator to carry on its business in the telecommunications market. It is the means by which competition is introduced or intensified in a market sector. The legal documents attached to an authorization set out the rights and obligations of the recipient. The terms and conditions attaching to an authorization can attempt to deal with such unfair practices that a participant, particularly a former monopolist might engage in, such as predatory pricing, tied-selling and high interconnection rates, on an *ex ante* basis. Interconnection is the manner in which different networks, such as those using wireless and land line technology, connect with each other to allow service users to communicate seamlessly with each other regardless of their geographical location, service provider or the means by which the communication is transmitted. Such networks are often considered essential facilities:

... the regulation of the terms and conditions under which competing firms have access to essential inputs provided by rivals has become the single biggest issue facing regulators of public utility industries. (OECD 2004: 7)

At least as important as the precise functions of a telecommunications regulator is the manner in which it carries out those functions. Three aspects of good regulation recur regardless of the function being carried out: transparency; public consultation; and the ability to enforce decisions. Transparency provides the regulator and by extension, the regulatory process with credibility. An open authorization process gives service providers and the public confidence that decisions will be made fairly and without bias or discrimination (Eberhard 2007). It reinforces the regulator's independence, as it makes undue government or industry influence more difficult to exercise (Guermazi and Satola 2004). By reducing the opportunity of government or industry participants to engage in improper activity, transparency fosters the expansion of both ICT infrastructure and ICT services (ITU Toolkit, Module 3, 6.1). It also leads to predictability where regulatory decisions are consistent with each other. Predictability allows consumers and service providers to develop an understanding of the manner in which the regulatory system works and to govern their behaviour accordingly. 'Transparency measures provide a common understanding of the "rules of the game" and how they are applied' (Eberhard 2007: 5).

Underlying transparency are publicity and public scrutiny. All laws governing the regulator, particularly those provisions regarding its powers, should be in the public domain so that there is no uncertainty as to whether the regulator or some other body enjoys the power to rule on a given matter. It is common practice for telecommunications regulators to publish guides to the authorization process including procedures to be followed, qualification criteria, selection criteria and fees. The principles applied in rule-making together with the regulator's rules and policies should be put on the public record. Where the regulator intends to authorize a service, for example, it should publically issue a request for applications. In many countries, applications are available for public review with a proviso for maintaining the confidentiality of proprietary technical or financial information which could be detrimental to the applicant's competitive position. Hearings would normally be open to the public and all decisions, accompanied by reasons would also be released in a timely manner as would any agreements between the regulator and interested parties. The means of dispute resolution as well as rights to, and grounds for, appeals and judicial review of regulatory decisions should be publicized in a clear manner so as to be easily understood by the public and service providers. The manner in which the regulator's personnel is selected, particularly top management, should also be a matter of public record to ensure such personnel are unbiased and hold the necessary qualifications for their positions (Eberhard 2007; ITU Toolkit, Module 3, 6.1).

Public consultation permits the regulator to gain valuable information and feedback as well as knowledge and ensure that its review of an issue has been as thorough as possible. It fosters transparency and provides the regulator with credibility with interested parties and the public (ITU Toolkit, Module 6, 7.2.1). Regulators enjoy a host of options for public consultation and the form it takes in any particular case will vary with the nature of the issue, the range of people affected and the potential market impact. Often, the laws governing the regulator will set forth the circumstances and manner by which the regulator will undertake public consultation or it may develop its own policies. The most common form of consultation is by written submission as it allows for detailed, and sometimes voluminous, arguments and evidence to be submitted and studied. Public hearing may be used in certain instances as can public 'town hall' style meetings to allow members of the public without the expertise or resources to prepare detailed written submission to voice their concerns about identified issues. Other options include individual meetings with interested parties, workshops, opinion surveys and on-line bulletin boards. In Hong Kong specialized committees have sometimes been formed with members drawn from the regulator's staff and outside experts to study an issue (ITU Toolkit, Module 6, 7.2.1).

The telecommunications regulator must have the means to enforce its rules and decisions. Its powers, however, are not absolute and are restrained by a system of checks and balances. Its decisions are normally open to judicial or other independent, impartial review to ensure that its own rules of procedure have been respected and appeal, although this may be permitted in more limited circumstances. Decisions are usually subject to review where there is concern that due process was not followed or appeal. Care must be taken to ensure that the regulator's credibility is not compromised and such review or appeals are not subject to manipulation by the government or other stakeholders. Appeals may in some jurisdictions be restricted to questions of law, as in New Zealand, or otherwise limited in scope particularly where technical matter are involved as the regulator is presumed to have greater expertise in the field than a court (ITU Toolkit, Module 6, 7.4.2). Where an appeal is successful, a court may order a new hearing by the regulator, rather than substitute its finding, where the matter is of a technical nature. More generally, the normal functioning of the regulator is subject to government or legislative oversight through, at minimum, annual reports (ITU Toolkit, Module 6, 5.1.3).

The regulator must be able to conduct investigations, enter into settlement agreements and impose fines or other penalties such as suspending an authorization, for violation of its decisions, license conditions or applicable laws. The ITU Toolkit describes four hallmarks of an effective enforcement system. It must be fast 'to reduce uncertainty in the market and deter future violations'; firm in imposing meaningful penalties; fair by basing its decisions on objective tests and ensuring that all decisions be made public; and flexible by allowing for a variety of means beyond litigation, such as alternative dispute resolution, 'to ensure that the severity of the punishment matches the severity of the violation' (ITU Toolkit, Module 6, 7.4.2). It further argues that where those standards are achieved, voluntary compliance tends to be enhanced.

Enforcement procedures should be clearly written and published as part of the law governing the regulator, the regulator's rules or as provisions of the licences it grants or a combination thereof. Due process needs to be observed as the alleged offender must be given notice of the offence in sufficient detail that it may prepare a response and have a reasonable amount of time to file such a response. Where there is a formal hearing, the regulator must adhere to the usual rules regarding fair hearings and due process. The regulator's decision should be written with reasons and put on the public record.

The described manner in which the independent telecommunications regulator should function represents a goal to which countries can aspire. Building such institutions takes time, money and expertise. Botswana, for example, undertook relatively little public consultation when it first created an independent regulator, but increased it as funds became available and sector knowledge was built (ITU Toolkit Module 6, 7.2). Most importantly governments should not lose sight of the underlying fact that the purpose in creating an independent regulator is both to inhibit inappropriate action such as favouritism and rent-seeking and to create the public perception of fairness and openness. It is thus preferable to do less, but do it well than to postpone reform due to the inability to create the ideal from the beginning.

Stimulating Investment

The second factor shown to mediate the relationship between ICT and economic growth is investment in ICT equipment, machinery and software. Greater investment in ICT can contribute to commercial and industrial efficiency, bringing productivity increases and economic growth. The process of capital deepening, however, is expensive and on-going. Despite the consistent and significant drop in the price of computing power, technology budgets tend not to shrink as firms constantly need to upgrade their hardware and software in order to remain competitive. ICT products become obsolete much more quickly than most other capital assets.

The initial adoption and constant need to upgrade ICT may prove challenging in countries where financial resources are scarce. ICT adoption, like mechanization, can also result in job losses, and societal and political pressures on governments to maintain jobs may be particularly acute in less economically developed countries where unemployment is high and social programs for the unemployed few. Nevertheless, countries face very little choice over the long term. Protectionist policies and reliance on cheap labour have not proven a successful recipe for economic prosperity. While the 'writing may be on the wall' for those lagging in ICT adoption, potential users may be unwilling to invest until they see tangible evidence that their economic well-being is jeopardized. Before being spurred into action by fears for their continued economic survival they need more immediate, tangible incentives to invest. Government can help provide the incentives needed for initial and sustained ICT investment. The universe of potential incentives to foster ICT usage and access is likely limited only by the human imagination, but as few governments enjoy reputations for innovation, certain incentive programs tend to be followed by governments seeking to increase ICT investment.

Financial Incentives

Incentives aimed at stimulating ICT investment may be direct or indirect. Direct incentives relate specifically to the use of ICT and serve to encourage investment. They can be financial in nature, such as subsidies, grants and tax measures or non-financial, such as laws that protect intellectual property rights in software code or that provide for the digital signature of contracts. Indirect measures act collectively to improve the enabling environment for firms to expand their ICT investments. Certain indirect reforms, while not on their face aimed at promoting ICT investment, produce a disproportionately significant impact on the adoption of ICT than elsewhere in the economy. They include reforms to labour laws that restrict the ability of firms to reduce their workforces thereby obviating potential productivity benefits from ICT usage or banking laws that allow lending only on the security of traditional assets such as accounts receivable, inventory, equipment and land. Both direct and indirect incentives aimed specifically at ICT will be discussed further.

In order to stimulate ICT investment, governments must first view ICT goods and services as important inputs needed to increase productivity and stimulate economic growth and not as luxury goods. As very few less economically developed countries have ICT producing sectors to protect, higher than usual sales taxes that are imposed on luxury items and import duties should be eliminated or drastically reduced as such duties and taxes unduly impede ICT investment by artificially raising costs. While the government may undoubtedly forego some revenue, lowering the cost of ICT products to industrial, commercial and individual users should increase consumption and represents a relatively simple action to implement.

Financial grants and subsidies offer the most common direct means of encouraging ICT investment. Such mechanisms tend to be aimed at individuals and small and medium enterprises on the assumption that larger firms have already recognized the need and have the means to invest in ICT. Grants are characterized by the direct transfer of money to the end user for the purpose of spending those funds on ICT equipment, software or services. They are relatively rare given that the direct costs involved are often beyond the means of less economically developed countries. Nevertheless, in the early 2000s Morocco made funds available to individuals for the purchase of a personal computer together with free internet service for one year. Combined with its earlier efforts to reform the telecommunications sector, the government's actions pushed Morocco from a laggard in internet usage to the North African leader within a few years although, as the World Bank (2004) noted, Morocco failed to sustain its reforms.

Subsidies prove more common than grants. Subsidies usually involve the expenditure of government funds to cover the cost of building telecommunications infrastructure or the provision of ICT services. The purpose is normally to underwrite, in part, the cost associated with the provision of telecommunications services at commercially sustainable rates. Projects that do not fulfil such criteria or that will require on-going financial assistance should likely not be subsidized. Subsidies are often directed at promoting ICT usage among lower income families or extending service to remote geographical areas where distances and smaller populations tend to make the infrastructure investment uneconomical for the private sector (Frieden 2005). Innovative approaches to the problem have been implemented in Kazakhstan and Ireland which have provided financial aid and discounts on telecommunications bills for low income families as well as in Chile which has subsidized rural public telephone calls (Wellenius 2006). The Canadian government has paid up to 50 per cent of the eligible costs to develop broadband service in communities in the high Arctic that can demonstrate adequate service demand and sustainability (Frieden 2005). In Egypt, the government has subsidized dial-up internet users by allowing individuals with computers to access the internet for the cost of a local telephone call without having to subscribe to an internet service provider (Wellenius 2006).

The decision to provide grants and subsidies is a matter of policy to be determined by the government in consultation with its economic planning institutions and telecommunications regulator. Their implementation and administration is usually left to the telecommunications regulator. The grants and subsidies must be provided and administered in a transparent manner without favouritism and in accordance with clearly published rules and criteria with the funds flowing directly to the intended beneficiaries (Wellenius 2006). In order to prevent abuse, all interested parties, not just the grant or subsidy provider, should have a financial stake in the commercial viability of the services being subsidized. Service providers should be expected to put up their own funds and customers should be prepared to pay for services 'at least as much as is needed to meet operating and maintenance costs' (Wellenius 2006: 49).

Financing subsidies represents a challenge for less economically developed countries. Several countries have established telecommunications development funds which are generated by a levy imposed upon service providers as part of the terms of their authorizations to finance in part the provision of telecommunication services to remote areas (ITU Toolkit). The levy represents one per cent of gross operating revenues in Peru and Uganda and two per cent in Nicaragua and the Dominican Republic (Wellenius 2006). Wellenius (2006) argues, however, that it may be preferable to fund such subsidies from an efficiency and equity perspective from general tax revenues, as is done in Chile and Nepal. He also notes that such subsidies have a mixed record of success and, with the spread of commercial mobile telephone service at the expense of fixed line service, several South American counties have altered the scope of services subsidized from basic telephone service to enhanced services, such as the internet (Wellenius 2006). The success of grants and subsidies depends greatly upon the manner in which the goals are clearly identified and the programme administered.

Governments wishing to stimulate ICT adoption and usage, specifically research and development and the acquisition of machinery and equipment more commonly employ tax relief than grants and subsidies (Fraunhofer Institute 2004; Brinkley and Lee 2007). Although the latter are more directly targeted and, potentially, more effective than tax relief, tax relief proves more popular than grants and subsidies because it does not involve out-of-pocket payments by governments and the costs involved in establishing a subsidy or grant programme, identifying beneficiaries, administering and monitoring a programme are higher than altering tax rates.

Tax relief normally takes one of two forms: tax credits on taxable income; and relatively high rates of depreciation on ICT machinery and equipment purchase compared to that allowed for spending on other capital goods. In a 2004 study comparing tax incentives in Canada with those in 15 other OECD countries plus China and India, Warda noted that 'depreciation is the main channel for stimulating the investment in ICT at the firm level' (2005: 5). Rates vary both within and across the countries examined depending upon the equipment in question. Generally, annual depreciation rates of 30–40 per cent were considered the norm although there was some variation. Depreciation rates in India were in the 60–80 per cent range and, as a temporary measure to spur ICT investment, the United Kingdom permitted 100 per cent of equipment to be written off in the year of acquisition (Warda 2005).

Tax credits have proved more widespread in the case of stimulating specific corporate activities. The growing recognition of the importance of human capital in the adoption of ICT equipment and machinery has led to 'a global trend to gear the tax incentives to corporate training that would assimilate a greater rate of ICT adoption' (Warda 2005: 5). As at the time of the study, six of the OECD countries examined offered tax credits specifically for ICT skills training programs ranging from 10 per cent of eligible expenditures in France to 35 per cent in Spain. Austria allowed expenses of up to 2,000 Euros per employee per year while Japan granted credits that vary according to the intensity of the training programme and the size of the company. The smaller the company, the greater the tax credits that it can potentially claim (Warda 2005). Such tax credits, however, tended not to be specifically aimed at ICT and are available for a much broader range of scientific endeavours.

Whether grants, subsidies, tax policy or some combination thereof should be used to achieve a government's public policy goals is a matter of choice. The manner in which that choice should be implemented should be determined through consultation among the government, the economic planning institutions and the institutions that will be charged with implementing that policy as well as interested parties and, possibly, the wider public. Where subsidies are chosen, the telecommunications regulator will normally be involved in the decision to ensure that the formulators of the policy are aware of the feasibility of implementing the policy, the costs involved and resources required to implement the policy and whether the policy, if implemented, is likely to achieve the intended goals. As always, the rules should be easily available to the public, subject to public consultation and transparently implemented. The necessary laws, whether new legislation, regulations under existing states, or other rules determined by the tax authority or telecommunications regulator, acting within its delegated mandate, should be clear, unambiguous, published and easily accessible by interested parties.

Non-Financial Measures

Several non-financial measures aimed primarily at encouraging ICT usage and investment have emerged as economic structures have altered. Countries may need to update their laws to recognize the increasing use of the internet to communicate and transact business. The traditional rules relating to the admissibility of documents in court proceedings, for example, should be revised to permit email correspondence and to recognize the conclusion of binding contracts over the internet given the decreasing frequency with which parties to an agreement place their signatures on the same piece of paper. Laws specially designed to deal with the purchase and sale of goods and services over the internet, e-commerce, need to be adopted.[3] Rules protecting the privacy of internet users, providing security from fraud for financial transactions and minimizing the misappropriation of financial information, are required to provide firms and individuals alike the confidence to transact electronically (OECD 2002, 2003). E-government, which includes the provision of government services, information about government programs and rules and the filing of documents, can also act as an important stimulus to ICT adoption as government 'shows the way' to the private sector (OECD 2002, 2003, Clarke 2003, Kaitila et al. 2006).

Three indirect, non-financial areas of reform, while important to traditional forms of economic development, prove to be particularly important to the growth of ICT. The first is the protection of intellectual property rights. Unlike specifically ICT-focused laws such as those relating to digital signatures, rules relating to the protection of intellectual property are not new, but as firms' assets become increasingly intangible (Dunning 2000), the need to protect such assets from misappropriation is perceived to have grown commensurately. Consequently, intellectual property laws may have to be updated and stringently enforced to safeguard ownership rights.

There is disagreement about whether less economically developed countries should extend protection to intellectual property rights as is the norm in most wealthy nations and, if so, to what extent. Protection of intellectual property rights is generally viewed as an incentive to innovate as such protection provides an economic benefit to the innovator through the payment of royalties or other forms of what economists call monopoly rents. Intellectual property protection, however, may also serve to slow the diffusion of technology throughout a society where its

---

3   See, for example, Wang (1999) for an extensive list of such cyber-laws.

use or imitation might bring significant economic benefits (Trebilcock and Howse 2005). Subject to any international trade obligations or treaties to which it is party, each country must weigh the costs and benefits of enacting legislation to protect intellectual property rights and, more importantly, vigorously enforcing such legislation.

In making its decision, a country will need to determine whether it is more likely to grow economically through innovative activities or through imitation and adaptation. For many less economically developed countries their growth, at least initially, is more likely to come from imitation and adaptation than from innovation. Deardorff (1990) has made the argument that extending protection throughout the world to one aspect of intellectual property rights, patents, can result in a reduction of global welfare. As patent protection 'has the effect of transferring income from consumers in the protected market to monopoly investors/producers' (505) and as most monopolists reside in wealthy countries, the effect is to transfer welfare from the poor to the rich. Consequently, Deardorff recommends that poor nations be exempt from providing patent protection in order to provide greater global income equality.

It may be helpful to make a distinction in the ICT sector between the protection of the intellectual property connected with mass consumer goods and the intellectual property belonging to manufacturers that is only of interest to the relatively small number of firms currently competing with those manufacturers or those who could do so relatively easily if they acquired the intellectual property, as might be the case where a group of employees left a manufacturer to open a competing operation 'across the street'. In terms of maximizing its country's welfare, it might be in the economic interest of governments wishing to spread the use of ICT to turn a blind eye towards inexpensive bootleg versions of widely used software as the price of the authentic product might be beyond the means of too many of its citizens.

Poor intellectual property protection in countries seeking to obtain ICT through FDI might inhibit MNCs owning important intellectual property from investing in such countries. Trebilcock and Howse (2005) have called the empirical support for the view that FDI flows to a country will be hurt by poor intellectual property protection 'sketchy and anecdotal' (388). Others, however, have stressed the importance of intellectual property rights protection. The OECD (2005) notes that effective intellectual property rights protection 'is often essential to enable a firm to raise finance, to access new markets and to protect existing market positions' (26) and Clarke (2003) has argued that such protection is 'paramount to ICT investment' (25). Empirical studies by Nunnenkamp and Spatz (2003a) and Branstetter et al. (2007) also identify intellectual property rights protection as important to attracting FDI.

The second area relates to labour protection. While ICT usage can improve productivity and stimulate economic growth, it can come at the expense of jobs, at least initially. Governments that promote ICT investment run the risk of greater unemployment. Job creation is almost universally viewed as one of governments' most important tasks. The apparently conflicting priorities of job creation and the promotion of ICT usage can present particular challenges in countries where alternative employment is difficult to find and social safety nets limited or non-existent. There is no simple short-term solution to the potential disruption caused by ICT investment. Over the long-run, however, there is no feasible alternative if one accepts the need to foster ICT usage and access. In order to maintain high employment, some governments have enacted laws that inhibit the outsourcing of ICT-related functions or that make the dismissal of employees difficult for employers or that encourage the employment of far more people than needed, particularly in state-owned enterprises. Such laws inhibit ICT investment by impeding a firm's ability to reduce costs as a result of investment in ICT. As the OECD notes:

> Such regulations may also impede reorganization or competition between firms
> and thus affect investment. If firms cannot adjust their workforce or organization
> in a way that allows them to exploit the capabilities of ICT, they may decide to
> limit investment or relocate their activities. (2003: 13)

The OECD suggests that employee groups, employers and governments work together to ensure 'a virtuous circle' (2003: 19) of organizational change, training and skills promotion, and ICT introduction in order to alleviate some of the social disruption caused by the introduction of ICT.

ICT is capital intensive and starting a business in the ICT-producing sector or adopting ICT for innovative production techniques in more traditional industries can be highly risky. In order to make such investments and take such risks, adequate financing must be available to established firms and entrepreneurs. The third area is reform of the financial sector to allow for the formation of adequate capital to finance investment and risk taking. Kiessling in a 2007 study argued that financial institutions 'matter most during the initial introduction of the technology in a country' and that they are 'most important for countries with an already low level of available credit' but are of less importance in countries where their quality 'has passed above a certain level' (4). Asset-based lending has ceded in large measure to newer forms of angel and venture capital, private equity and easier access to public capital markets in order to finance businesses unable to provide traditional tangible forms of security for loans (Clarke 2003, OECD 2005). While government likely should not provide the financing for individual companies and attempt to 'pick winners', it is up to governments to ensure that company, banking and securities laws and the institutions that oversee these sectors keep pace with changing forms of finance. Kaitila et al. argued that the reform of the Finnish financial system through the 1980s and 1990s was instrumental in the evolution of Finland 'from a resource-driven to knowledge-based economy' (2006: 27). In contrast, Chidamber, in a 2002 study of ICT usage in Vietnam, maintained that the failure to upgrade financial markets in that country has been an impediment to ICT adoption.

The responsibility for fulfilling the need for adequate telecommunications infrastructure to facilitate the expansion of ICT usage and access lies incumbent almost exclusively upon the telecommunications regulator. The institutions involved in stimulating investment in ICT – tax authorities, securities regulators, patent offices – are far more diverse. Unlike the telecommunications regulator whose primary focus is ICT-related, ICT investment is only part of these other institutions' mandates. No one institution is charged with stimulating investment in ICT or implementing the enabling environment necessary for ICT investment. In countries where institutions operate on restricted budgets with limited professional personnel, there may be other priorities to which scarce resources must be devoted. They cannot be reasonably expected to determine individually the relevant policies to stimulate ICT investment or to coordinate with other affected institutions. The obligation to formulate a comprehensive and coordinated ICT investment policy ultimately falls upon a country's government. Governments have responded in a number of ways to the need to turn a broad policy to foster ICT usage and access into a plan of action.

Developing ICT Policy

Some countries create task forces or specialized study groups to examine discrete issues and then delegate their implementation to the relevant ministries and institutions as Canada did with its plan to deliver broadband services throughout the country (Frieden 2005). Such *ad hoc* approaches to specific issues tend to find favour in countries that already enjoy relatively high levels of ICT penetration and large civil services with the human and financial resources to coordinate and implement policy. Other countries pursue a more comprehensive approach. In 1993, the Finnish Parliament created a 'Committee of the Future', which Kaitila et al. (2006) described as unique. The committee was originally created on a temporary basis to respond to, and examine methods to implement, policies submitted by the government concerning Finland's economic future. Composed of Members of Parliament from all parties, the Committee of the Future was made permanent in 2000. While not devoted solely to ICT, the Committee 'conducts assessments of technological development and the effects on society of technology' (Committee of the Future) and examines 'issues pertaining to future development factors and development models' (Kaitila et al. 2006: 32) acting as an advisory body to the government.

Other governments have created institutions specifically charged with the development of ICT policy and its coordination with the relevant ministries and other government bodies with mixed results. They serve as a fulcrum, identifying issues that need to be addressed in order to fulfill a country's ICT policy, consulting with interested parties and organizations and dealing with the relevant government ministries. Specialized units have been created in some countries, such as in Bolivia, Venezuela and the Dominican Republic, within their ministries of telecommunications or science and technology, to deal with

ICT issues. Being located inside a ministry may, however, render them less effective in their dealing with other ministries than an independent body, as individual ministries may resist cooperation as they defend their 'turf'. Some less economically developed countries that have moved towards middle income status have created independent institutions, usually responsible to a minister or the cabinet, as is the case of Mauritius which established the National Computer Board to, in part, 'make policy and legal recommendations, analyze the trend in ICT technologies, promote the use of state-of-the-art technologies and carry out R&D in ICT' (National Computer Board). The Thai National Electronics and Computer Technology Center (NECTEC) was created in 1986, and became an independent agency in 1991.

> Its main responsibilities are to undertake, support, and promote the development of electronic, computing, telecommunication, and information technologies through research and development activities. NECTEC also disseminates and transfers such technologies for contribution to the economic growth and social development in the country, following the National Economic and Social Development Plan. (National Electronics and Computer Technology Center)

To summarize, government action to stimulate ICT investment can be divided into direct and indirect actions. Direct actions can be financial and non-financial in nature. Direct financial actions require government to spend money, normally through targeted grants and subsidies, or forego income by lowering or eliminating import duties on ICT products, providing tax credits for ICT-related training and increasing tax depreciation rates in recognition of the rapid obsolescence of ICT machinery and equipment. Non-financial direct actions involve the enactment of new rules or the modification of existing ones. Their substance is directly related to ICT. Such non-financial direct actions include revisions to intellectual property laws to protect the increasingly intangible nature of proprietary corporate assets as well as laws to facilitate e-commerce and contract formation where all communication between the parties to a transaction is electronic. Indirect actions are those that are primarily related to non-ICT activities, but have a disproportionate impact upon ICT investment compared to other fields of endeavour. Labour and banking law reform are examples of the indirect actions governments may need to undertake.

The institutional implications of stimulating ICT investment are more complicated than with the building of ICT infrastructure where the telecommunications regulator is the primary responsible institution. Implementation of actions to stimulate ICT investment affects diverse institutions such as tax authorities, patent and trade-mark offices, financial services regulators and labour boards. While ICT infrastructure and the provision of telecommunications services may be the predominant mandate of the telecommunications regulator, ICT investment is likely only one of many responsibilities of the other institutions. Fostering ICT investment, however, requires a coordinated approach by government. Many countries, particularly the less economically developed with low levels of ICT penetration and lacking the institutional strength of the more affluent, have created specialized bodies responsible for the development of policy, subject to government oversight, to stimulate the usage of and access to ICT, including ICT investment, and coordination with the relevant ministries and other institutions. The composition, scope and powers of such institutions vary widely, but their increasing popularity suggests a growing recognition of the importance of a coordinated ICT policy.

Human Capital

Meaning and Quantification Challenges

Human capital is the third factor mediating the relationship between ICT and economic growth. The term describes an economic concept dating back at least to Adam Smith. He classified human ability as an aspect of fixed capital comprised of:

> ... the acquired and useful abilities of all the inhabitants or members of the society. The acquisition of such talents, by the maintenance of the acquirer during his education, study, or apprenticeship, always costs a real expense which is a capital fixed and realized, as it were, in his person. (Smith 2008: Book 2, Chapter 1)

A country's human capital encompasses its inhabitants' collective skills and abilities howsoever attained. Countries wishing to increase their stock of human capital should seek to promote its accumulation through the three means identified by Smith: formal schooling (education); workplace training (apprenticeship and on-the-job learning); and individual learning (study). Of the three means of increasing human capital, however, World Bank (2002, 2003, 2005) studies emphasize the importance of formal education. The provision of a solid primary education to its citizens by government remains an important pre-requisite to economic growth, but such education is no longer sufficient. The World Bank studies argue that the quantity and quality of secondary education has become the key ingredient in taking advantage of ICT.

Formal education also represents the aspect of human capital formation most directly within the control of government. The manner in which education is provided, the extent to which schooling is compulsory and the content of the curriculum may vary from country to country, but government bears primary responsibility for making and implementing those decisions. The development of human capital is largely determined by a country's government. Government can exert influence on workplace training, mainly through grants and tax policies that provide financial incentives to companies, but it is up to individual firms to determine the training to be provided. Government's ability to influence individual learning is weaker still. Formal education will thus be focused upon, workplace training will be discussed briefly and individual learning will not be examined.

In its studies, the World Bank (2005) contends that the demand for educated workers now exceeds supply. It argues forcefully that technology, skills, wages and economic prosperity are inextricably linked. This determination echoes the findings of de Ferranti et al. in their comprehensive examination of the relationship between technology, education and economic growth published in 2003: 'The central message of this report is that the interaction between technology and skill is critical in determining growth, productivity and the distribution of earnings' (49). Without a base of skilled workers, countries will find it increasingly difficult to introduce new technology into existing domestic businesses, attract FDI or develop the absorptive capacity to benefit from the potential spillovers from FDI (de Ferranti et al. 2003: 63, 67).[4]

The challenge for governments is to determine how to improve the skill level, or stock of human capital, in their countries. Human capital differs fundamentally from infrastructure and investment. Given enough money, as a number of oil rich states have demonstrated, telecommunications infrastructure and ICT machinery, equipment and software can be built or bought in a relatively short time. Human capital, however, cannot be so purchased, although those states have been able to rent it. Most less economically developed countries do not enjoy that option. Human capital takes time to develop. Countries lacking in human capital face a 'bottleneck' that can prevent them from benefitting from ICT usage or 'leapfrogging' their economic status from poor to wealthy (Wong 2002; de Ferranti et al. 2003).

Secondary Education

The basic literacy and mathematics skills acquired in primary school are no longer sufficient for most employment or to encourage business investment either from domestic or foreign sources. Prosperity in an increasingly integrated international economy demands workers with more education.

> In today's world, acquisition of the enabling skills and competencies necessary for civic participation and economic success depends on access to good secondary education...Secondary education plays a key articulating role between primary schooling, tertiary education, and the labor market. The specific dynamics of this articulation is crucial because it determines future educational and job opportunities for young people. Secondary education can become a bottleneck constraining the expansion of educational attainment and opportunity, or, conversely, it can open a set of pathways and alternative channels for students' advancement. (World Bank 2005: 36)

---

4   See also Lall (2001).

The purpose of secondary education is broad; training youth not just for the workplace, but to be active and successful participants in their societies. Education systems that teach reasoning together with strong math, science, literary and communication skills (oral and written) produce graduates who are better able to adapt to labour markets and rapidly changing economic structures than those without such skills. Tertiary education, too, is extremely important, particularly for nations that wish to compete at the frontiers of innovation. Secondary education, however, appears to be the key to 'staying competitive for countries at an intermediate level of industrial development and with export-oriented activities' (World Bank 2005: 34). There is evidence that in countries where access to secondary education remains limited or the distribution of education is inequitable the result does not merely impede economic development but exerts a 'strong and robust negative effect on growth' (World Bank 2005: 33).

Vocational Training

Vocational, or workplace, training is different from vocational education. The former is carried out by employers for their employees, usually in the workplace, while the latter takes place in a classroom, normally as part of the public education system or at a facility accredited by the government. Although workplace training is not the direct responsibility of governments, they play a role in fostering its provision, most commonly through the provision of financial incentives. de Ferranti et al. (2003) maintains that workplace training provides the link between formal education, which may be vocational, and the application of technology in the workplace and that government policy towards workplace training should strive to link its broader education policies with its technology and economic development policies, terming the relationship between them as 'symbiotic'. Employers seek employees who can be easily trained rather that those with specific skills, but are not as able to adapt to new technology, and better educated workers are also far more likely to receive workplace training than those whose educations are perceived as deficient. As a consequence, de Ferranti et al. argues in favour of:

> ... an increased emphasis on providing learning rather than vocation-specific skills in schools, and a shift away from publicly sponsored vocational education in schools or industry-level vocational training institutes to well-designed training incentives to firms. (2003: 109–10)

A pool of workers with secondary education is thus increasingly necessary for firms to invest and provide workplace training and such education improves an individual worker's chances of receiving that training.

The best course for governments, in addition to providing quality secondary education, may be to provide financial incentives to employers to provide employees with training in the specific skills needed for their jobs. The use of tax credits was discussed briefly in the section discussing investment in ICT. Three other mechanisms have found broad application. The first, a payroll levy-grant system is common in Latin America as well as in East Asia. A small percentage of a company's payroll is paid into an independently administered, segregated fund from which grants are made to participating companies for employee training programs. To be effective, as de Ferranti notes, industry should control the fund to prevent its use by government for other purposes and to limit political interference. Such funds can be divided by industry sector and payments sometimes can be matched with government grants. National Training Councils have proven useful in parts of Latin America. Such councils function in a similar manner but are usually government created and administered by representatives of government, business, unions and members of the public. Funds may be secured from payroll levies, the government or raised through membership dues and course fees. Third, a number of countries have established matching grant schemes whereby funds spent by companies on approved training programs are matched by government grants.

Economic Stagnation – Latin American Weakness

To demonstrate the need to develop a strong public education system that produces an 'adequate amount and mix of skilled workers' de Ferranti et al. (2003) examine the poor economic performance between 1960–2000 of the nations of Central America, South America and the Caribbean (collectively, 'Latin America') compared to the success of several East Asian countries (the 'Asian tigers')[5] and nations that were categorized as natural resource abundant.[6] The Asian tigers were selected because their level of economic development was similar to most Latin American countries in 1960 while the resource abundant countries were found to be a relevant comparison because 'many countries in Latin America have a comparative advantage in natural resources' (de Ferranti et al. 2003: 23). Among the resource-abundant countries, Finland's experience proves particularly enlightening as its GDP per capita and educational attainment closely resembled the levels of some Latin American countries in 1960.

The main reason human capital increased in the Asian tigers and Finland was because of massive reforms to their education systems that began in the 1960s. In every country in Latin America, the Asian tigers and Finland in 1960, over three-quarters of the population had no more than primary schooling. Latin America held an advantage in the provision of primary education over the Asian tigers in 1960 and trailed Finland by only slightly over one year. The mean years of schooling was 4.1 in Latin America, where it did not exceed five in any country, and below

---

5   de Ferranti et al. (2003) refers specifically to Hong Kong, Malaysia, Singapore and South Korea, although it is more common to include Taiwan, not Malaysia, amongst the four.

6   de Ferranti et al. (2003) refers specifically to Australia, Canada, Finland, New Zealand, Norway and Sweden.

3.5 in the Asian tigers (de Ferranti et al. 2003).[7] In Singapore, Malaysia and South Korea, over 60 per cent of the population had received no formal education at all. Finland enjoyed a relatively high mean of 5.4 years. By 2000, de Ferranti calculates, the average Latin American had 5.8 years of education compared to 9.7 years in the Asian tigers and over ten years in both South Korea and Finland. In Latin America, Mexico and Peru were the only countries where the average number of years of schooling increased by four or more over the 40-year period:

> ...in some countries, such as Mexico, one of the region's star performers in terms of skill upgrading, the mean and distribution of education attainment in 2000 were similar to Korea *two decades earlier*, while in others, such as Colombia, which had done comparatively little skill upgrading, the mean and distribution in 2000 were similar to those in Korea *three decades earlier*. (de Ferranti et al 2003: 79, emphasis original)

As these figures suggest, if primary school lasts six years, Latin American countries did not generally face an educational deficit at the primary level by 2000. Basic literacy needs were being met. At the secondary level, however, where more advanced skills are taught, 'the region has a *massive* deficit in secondary enrolment' (de Ferranti et al. 2003: 79, emphasis original). The deficit at the tertiary level is also large, but not as pronounced as at the secondary level, suggesting that those with secondary schooling in Latin America are slightly more likely to advance to tertiary education than their counterparts in the Asian tigers, but are less likely to do so than in Finland.

Increasing the stock of a country's human capital cannot be accomplished quickly. By definition, it takes fifteen years to provide nine years of schooling to a newborn, assuming primary school begins at age six. There are likely a wide range of approaches to the reform of a country's education system. de Ferranti, however, maintains that history demonstrates that the best way to do so is from the ground up.

> The most successful episodes of educational upgrading – the United States between 1850 and 1950, Korea and the Scandinavian countries since World War II – have all followed a pattern of bottom-up upgrading, first building up basic education, then secondary education and finally, university. (de Ferranti et al. 2003: 75)[8]

Typically, more people have only some primary education than some secondary and more people have some secondary education than some tertiary in less economically developed countries. When educational attainment is illustrated

---

7   It should be noted that de Ferranti et al. (2003) refers to the Asian tigers as Singapore, Malaysia, South Korea and Taiwan, not Hong Kong, for the purposes on these figures.

8   See also Goldin and Katz.

as a horizontal bar graph such a distribution resembles a pyramid. The shape of the illustration alters with changes to the distribution of education. A diamond shape represents the situation where more people have some secondary education than either primary alone or tertiary and an inverted pyramid occurs there those with some tertiary education form the largest group and those with only some primary education form the smallest. As an education system is built from the ground up, the pyramid develops a narrower base and wider middle and top level, ultimately coming to resemble inverted pyramids. de Ferranti (2003) notes that in 1960 virtually all the countries examined in the study had distributions of educational attainment that were broad-based pyramids in shape. The Asian tigers and Finland resembled more narrowly based pyramids by 1980, but most Latin American countries did not do so until 2000. By 2000, as two more highly educated generations aged and many of those with little education died, the illustrations of the distribution of educational attainment altered in the Asian tigers and Finland to resemble diamonds. Such a redistribution had not taken place in even one Latin American country.

de Ferranti (2003) attributes the different growth rates to the approaches to education taken by the governments concerned. He emphasizes that the Asian and Finnish success could not be attributed to the money spent on education alone, while admitting that 'public expenditure aggregates are notoriously difficult to compare' (de Ferranti et al. 2003: 83). Despite such difficulties, based on World Bank data, he determines that Latin American countries spent a greater fraction of GDP on education that the Asian tigers. He also concludes that the absolute amount spent per capita is not the decisive factor, given the high achievement on international tests of the Cubans in a country where great emphasis, but relatively little money, has been spent on the education system. More important than the amount invested in education is how the education system is structured and how the money is spent. The Asian tigers and Finland adopted the bottom-up approach cited by de Ferranti et al. (2003) while most Latin American countries followed a policy of 'slow, top-down upgrading' (78).

Education Reform – Finnish Strength

In their examination of the Finnish education system, Aho et al. (2006) claim that the Finnish economy in 1950 resembled that of Sweden in 1910. Little had changed by 1960. The economy was predominantly agricultural and natural resources driven. No doubt, Finnish society was, and still is, very different from those in Latin America. It is a small, relatively homogenous country that has grown slowly from approximately 4.4 million people in 1960 to 5.1 million in 2000 (Official Statistics of Finland). It has benefitted from European growth over same the time and, more recently, from Russian economic expansion after the collapse of communism. Nevertheless, the re-making of Finland's system of education from 1960 when education levels were similar to Latin America to being considered a model of a 'knowledge society' (Dahlman 2006) is remarkable. The educational reform process it followed is highly instructive and the lessons drawn from that process could prove beneficial to less economically developed countries.

Aho notes that a number of social, economic and political forces combined in the early 1960s to spur a broadly supported drive to reform the Finnish education system, a consensus that Aho considers essential to the reform process. Finland's accession to the European Free Trade Association in 1961 sent a strong message to Finnish politicians that: 'To be competitive, Finland had to substantially boost investments in education and research' (Aho et al. 2006: 33). At its core, the reform movement reiterated what Aho (2006) and Koski et al. (2006) describe as an egalitarian guiding tenet of Finnish education: 'Every child deserved a good basic education, and it was up to the government to provide it regardless of family income, social status, or place of residence' (Aho et al. 2006: 55). In response, the government instituted a comprehensive review of the education system that involved 'much committee work, experiments, pilot programs, input from the elementary school teacher's union and above all, vast political support and consensus' (Aho et al. 2006: 34) culminating in legislation enacted in 1968. The legislation thoroughly reformed the structure and administration of the system as well as the school curriculum. It also recognized that the reforms were unlikely to be successful unless teacher training was more rigorous and the reforms, including those most directly affecting teachers, achieved teacher 'buy-in' (Aho et al. 2006: 36).

The cardinal elements of the reform can be divided into substantive and process changes. The more substantive elements included: the length of compulsory education; revision of the content of the curriculum; restructuring the administration of the school system; and improved teacher training and qualifications. The procedural elements included: consultation with educators, administrators, parents, students and other interested parties; the creation or restructuring of numerous institutions related to education such as administrative district school boards not directly involved in teaching; the manner by which the reforms would be implemented; and the recognition of the need for continual monitoring and further reform.

Most likely the key element in the reform was the increase in the number of years of compulsory education from six to nine. Lower Secondary School became compulsory and its curriculum became closely integrated with that of primary schools. Parallel primary school systems were eliminated and the segregation of students towards different educational streams was postponed from age 11 or 12 until after the end of Lower Secondary School. The third level of schooling was divided between Upper Secondary Schools and Vocational Schools.[9] They each comprise an additional three years of schooling after Lower Secondary School, preparing students for tertiary education through universities or polytechnic

---

9   Since the initial reform, the distinction between Primary School and Lower Secondary School has been abolished and the schools have been replaced with nine year Comprehensive Schools.

institutes to continue their studies. As of 2011, there were 20 universities and 28 polytechnics in Finland (Official Statistics of Finland).

Educational decision making power was withdrawn from local authorities and consolidated education policy and planning was placed under the Ministry of Education thereby seeking to ensure that standards were at a similar high level throughout the country and not dependent upon the relative wealth of individual communities. Management of schools and implementation of the reforms were delegated to what became known as Provincial Education Departments thereby returning certain powers and discretion to authorities making them an integral part of the reform process (Aho et al. 2006).[10] Each municipality was responsible for drawing up a plan by which the reform would be implemented, subject to national oversight.

The changes to the education system did not take place in isolation from their broader social, economic and political setting. They were part of larger reform efforts aimed at shifting the Finnish economy away from its reliance on natural resources and agriculture. It was determined that doing so necessitated a far greater emphasis upon science, research and innovation throughout Finnish society. Three institutions, primarily oriented towards science and technology, stand out as playing a particularly important role in developing Finland's policies in those areas and ensuring that the education system responds to the needs of changing economic structures.[11] The broad consensus that supported educational

---

10   More recently power has been decentralized and more decision making authority has been delegated to the Provincial Education Departments.

11   The Academy of Finland traces its roots back to 1918, shortly after Finland's independence. It was reconstituted in 1948 and again revamped in 1970 as part of the economic and education restructuring and is focused upon science policy, acting as a funding agency for basic scientific research dispensing approximately 15 per cent of all government research money (Dahlman 2006). Citing universities as its 'most important partner in its mission to advance scientific research' as well as 'participating actively in the public debate on science policy' (Academy of Finland) its relationship to the education system is reinforced by the fact that it falls under the Ministry of Education.

The Technical Research Centre of Finland (VTT), under the Ministry of Employment and the Economy, was created in 1942 and reorganized near the end of 1971. Restructured again in 1994, it acts as an umbrella organization for six specialized research institutes. It is a non-profit organization focused upon applied research and innovation. In contrast to the Academy of Finland which funds basic scientific research, VTT's staff of over 2,700 is focused upon providing technical applied research solutions to its mostly private sector customers in a wide range of scientific endeavour. Despite the commercial focus of its work, VTT (2007) emphasizes that the 'firmly established link between ourselves and the global world of higher learning is absolutely essential.' The VTT is regularly consulted by the Ministry of Education about scientific education policy.

Founded in 1983, the National Technology Institute (TEKES) acts as an agency for government funding of technical innovation to industry, research institutes and universities. Unlike VTT, TEKES is not focused upon product-driven applied research and is more academically oriented. 'Research grants typically are allocated via technology programs planned in collaboration with firms and research institutes' (Dahlman 2006: 104, emphasis

reform thus served as a catalyst for other structural and institutional reform. The results of the process speak for themselves.

Latin America and Finland make for a particularly stark contrast between 1960–2000 because of their similar starting points and the structure of their economies. It is not suggested that less economically developed countries should mimic Finland's reforms or that if they attempted to do so that they would achieve the same results. The Finnish example does provide, however, an important model of how to improve a country's stock of human capital, from which other countries can take many lessons. The process Finland followed exemplifies how the relationship between the institutions concerned with public policy, enacting laws and implementing and enforcing those laws can work together and how they interact with interested individuals and organizations. Reform of the Finnish education system began in earnest in the early 1960s with, as Aho (2006) describes, large scale consultation by legislators of all stakeholders and policymakers inside the Ministry of Education and outside, such as with at the institutions referred to above. The reform process 'sparked criticism and debate' (Aho et al. 2006: 1), but through sustained consultation consensus was achieved setting the groundwork for successful implementation.

The education reforms acted as a catalyst for wide scale institutional change in Finland. As discussed, the Ministry of Education was reorganized, existing institutions were restructured and new ones were created. Importantly, many of the key Finnish institutions are not solely, or even primarily, concerned with education. They are focused upon economic development, science and technology. Their input into the educational decision making process allows for the expression of a variety of perspectives and underscores the need for education policy to be informed by economic development policy to increase the likelihood of a successful outcome. Of equal importance to the success of the reforms was the role played by individuals and organizations. Input was received from all stakeholders at the policy formulation, legislative and implementation stages as well as subsequently as part of the continual monitoring and modification process in response to ongoing challenges and continually changing circumstances.

North argues that the key to institutional change and the way to break path dependency is through the power of organizations. Finland has shown that, with the proper structures in place, it is possible. Such changes, particularly those concerning human capital development, can take a long time, although not as long as North envisages. As Aho (2006) notes:

---

original). It invested over 469 million Euros in 2007 in over 2,000 research and development projects of which 185 million Euros went to universities, polytechnics and research institutes (TEKES 2007). It maintains offices throughout Finland as well as six outside the country.

Many factors have contributed to Finland's academic success, from highly trained teachers to a culture that encourages reading. One key – *and exportable* – ingredient often gets overlooked, however. Finland's remarkable performance today springs directly from education policies and reforms set in motion *four decades ago*. (1; emphasis added)

PART II
Case Studies

Chapter 6
Singapore

From Founding to Independence

Early Singapore

The British presence in Malaya dates from 1786 when Francis Light founded Georgetown on a sparsely populated Penang Island to serve East Asian trade routes. Expansion down the peninsula began in 1795 with the capture of long-established Malacca from the Dutch and continued in 1819 when Stamford Raffles claimed the island of Singapore, with a native population of approximately 1,000, concluding a treaty with a local Johor prince of questionable authority (Baker 1999). Penang, Malacca and Singapore were joined as the Straits Colonies in 1826. The Straits Colonies were held not by the British government, but by the East India Company (the EIC) which enjoyed a British monopoly on Asian trade. The EIC's interest in the colonies was strictly commercial, limited to their utility as duty-free trans-shipment points along the England-India-China route. Following the 1858 dissolution of the EIC the Straits Colonies were consolidated under the British Colonial Office in 1867 into a single Straits Settlements Colony.[1]

Commercially, Singapore was an instant success. By 1825, merely six years after its founding, Singapore's population had grown to almost 10,000, the vast majority of the new arrivals coming from China. Its volume of trade was already double that of Penang and Malacca combined (Baker 1999). While the British governed the Colonies, the Chinese increasingly filled positions from manual labour and clerical services to shopkeepers and merchants, some becoming very wealthy entrepreneurs, primarily from the packaging and distribution of goods trans-shipped through those ports. English and Chinese schools were established and the physical infrastructure and ancillary enterprises required to support trading operations, such as banking and insurance, were built and developed. A Chinese middle class emerged as well as an English-educated Chinese elite. By 1860, the Caucasian population, primarily British, of the Straits Colonies remained exceedingly small and transient; only 466 in Singapore out of close to 81,000 inhabitants, 316 in Penang and a handful in Malacca (Turnbull 1989).[2]

---

1   The Straits Settlements Colony also included the minor possessions of the Dindings Islands and a small coastal piece of land at the mouth of the Perak River between Penang and Malacca and the island of Labuan off the coast of the British colonies of Brunei and North Borneo (now the Malaysian state of Sabah).

2   Based on the first census of the Colonies conducted by the British in 1860.

Singapore's growth continued through the end of the nineteenth century and accelerated into the twentieth century. In 1921, its population was 75 per cent Chinese and growing daily, the remainder being primarily Indian and Malay. An estimated 360,000 Chinese immigrants arrived that year, an overwhelming majority of whom were male (Turnbull 1989). In 1911 the ratio of males to females in Singapore was 8:1 (Turnbull 1989). It had moderated somewhat ten years later and by the early 1930's was down to 2:1, still an abnormal situation (Baker 1999). World War II and the Japanese occupation of Singapore shocked the local economy and its population putting a sudden halt to its expansion. The British returned at war's end, but it was clear that Singapore's days as a colony were numbered.

The Radical Singapore of the 1950s

By the mid-1950s Singaporean politics had become fractious, but based on political and economic ideology and social class rather than ethnicity. Housing and public services failed to keep up with a quickly increasing population. Living conditions for many were 'abysmal' (Baker 1999; IBRD 1955). The trade union movement became exceptionally strong and the 1950s were marked by strikes, demonstrations and, occasionally, violence to people and property such as during the seminal Hock Lee bus strike. In 1955, it is estimated that 946,000 man days were lost to over 300 strikes whose aims were often as political as economic (Chen 1983; Baker 1999). Chinese language schools became highly politicized and anti-colonial feelings ran high. The political spectrum ranged from left to further left.

In 1954, the British introduced a new constitution for Singapore which provided for limited self-rule through the creation of a legislative council. The first Chief Minister was not Chinese, Indian or Malay, but David Marshall, a successful British-educated criminal lawyer from a Jewish family of Iraqi ancestry and the Labour Front leader. The elections also marked the first presence of the People's Action Party (PAP) established the previous year and led by an equally brilliant British-educated lawyer who throughout his school years was known as Harry Lee, but upon his return to Singapore reverted to his Chinese name, Lee Kuan Yew. Driven by ideology, as one of the party's founders, S. Rajaratnam (1964) argues, the PAP claimed to be a democratic socialist party (26). Winning three of the four constituencies it contested, the PAP considered, but rejected, an alliance with the Labour Front concluding, the 'Labour Front was going to be an election party and not a genuine socialist movement' (Rajaratnam 1964: 280). Elections for a larger, more powerful legislature were called for 1959 and this time the PAP ran a full slate of candidates. Viewed as more moderate than the parties further to the left, the PAP won 43 seats, having attacked the Labour Front as the 'corrupt pawns of capitalists' (Baker 1999: 284).

The new government faced an array of daunting issues particularly in employment, housing and education. Singapore's economy relied heavily on its status as an entrepôt for the trans-shipment of goods between Asia and Europe and as a source of regional distribution. Of Singapore's 1.1 million inhabitants, over half the workforce was employed in shipping and its related industries (IBRD 1955) and investor confidence was still fragile from the years of labour unrest. Its population was booming. Between 1947 and 1953 the natural rate of growth reached 3.5 per cent per year. 'Overcrowding in the central part of Singapore, bad before the war, [had] become appalling' (IBRD 1955: 180). The rapid increase in population strained the education system. Steady progress had been made in its provision of education, but the number of school children was poised to grow rapidly. In 1947 there were 81,000 primary school pupils and 5,900 in secondary schools. This had risen to 158,500 and 21,900, respectively, by 1954. It was projected that the volume of students entering the education system would require Singapore to construct 'an average 18 new schools a year and, to staff them for two sessions a day, recruit more than 600 teachers annually' (IBRD 1955: 167). Secondary education would have to be increased by an estimated 35,000 places by 1960.

In the run up to the 1959 legislative elections, the PAP set out a series of detailed policies to address Singapore's challenges which were collected and published as a comprehensive platform titled: *The Tasks Ahead: P.A.P.'s Five Year Action Plan, 1959–1964* (The Tasks Ahead). Elements of The Tasks Ahead bear a striking resemblance to the recommendations set forth in a report published subsequently by a United Nations study team headed by Albert Winsemius, a Dutch economist and successful businessman with shipping interests. The Winsemius Report, as it is commonly known, eventually formed the blueprint for Singapore's development efforts. Both The Tasks Ahead and the Winsemius Report, for example, recommended the creation of an Economic Development Board (EDB) to be provided with SG$100 million in funding to oversee industrialization. More than money, however, the PAP recognized that the development of a manufacturing sector would require technology and human capital, both of which were in short supply in Singapore. Technology could be acquired from FDI, but investors would only establish operations with more advanced technology if there was a sufficiently skilled labour force. Education and training levels would have to be improved.

The priority to be given to improving skills runs throughout The Tasks Ahead. It was promised that a PAP government would completely revamp the school curriculum to emphasize languages, math and science. Vocational schooling would be expanded, polytechnic institutions created and the science and technical departments at the University of Malaya and Nanyang University would be upgraded. Echoing the need for such facilities, Goh Keng Swee, who would become the Finance Minister, minced no words in describing the weaknesses that needed to be overcome, 'Not only is our technology backward, but the facilities for training technical and engineering workers are grossly inadequate' (People's Action Party 1959: 21). A similar message was delivered by Long Nyuk Lim who would become the Education Minister. Long promised that a PAP government would provide six years free schooling to all children and make secondary school available to all qualified students. In addition, a teaching and training institute would be established to foster the study of technology. He also gave a hint of how the PAP would go about its reforms to ensure they were effective. An advisory council comprised of representatives from the English, Chinese, Malay and Tamil communities as well as the government would be established to determine how to revise the curriculum and implement school reform. The vocational schools and training programs would be created after consultation with the EDB which, in turn, would consult with business leaders, scientists, engineers and trade unionists (People's Action Party 1959).

Industrialization, however, was still seen by the PAP within an import substitution model of economic development and within the context of a united Malaya and Singapore. Underlying the PAP platform was the belief that the best way to escape from colonial rule and to address Singapore's economic needs was through a merger, which became the PAP's first priority (People's Action Party 1959: 7). Union with Singapore was not a similar priority in Malaya and did not generate much public debate, given the historical and economic integration between the two there was widespread belief that federation would prove economically beneficial. In addition, the Singaporean constitution of 1954 was to expire in 1963 at which time it was expected to gain full independence. The Malayan leadership was fearful that an independent Singapore would become a 'second Cuba' (Turnbull 1989: 253), particularly after the PAP party splintered and 12 members of its legislative caucus crossed the floor to join the more radical Barisan Socialis (Socialist Alliance) opposition almost defeating the PAP government in 1962. These events led Malayan Prime Minister Tunku Abdul Rahman to suggest a federation between Singapore and Malaya. To counter fears that Malays would become a minority within the combined state, it was also proposed that the British colonies of Sarawak, Brunei and North Borneo simultaneously join the federation. A referendum approving the merger was held in Singapore in September 1962.[3] On September 16, 1963 Singapore joined Malaya together with Sarawak and Sabah, as North Borneo became known, to form the Federation of Malaysia, Brunei having decided to remain a British possession. The marriage did not go well. Singapore and Malaysia parted ways with Singapore becoming an independent republic on August 9, 1965.

In retrospect, the period from 1961–1965 may be viewed as economically stagnant. As Winsemius (1984) reflected in a much later speech, 1961–1963 were lost for economic development due to labour unrest that led to political instability, scaring investors away. Union with Malaya in 1963 proved to be no solution for

---

3 Singaporeans were offered three choices of the preferred method of merger. None of the choices allowed for its rejection. The Barisan Socialis campaigned against the merger and encouraged its supporters to leave their ballots blank, as voting was compulsory. Of the three options, the choice supported by the PAP, garnered 71 per cent of the votes while 24 per cent were left blank. Blank ballots were considered by the PAP as votes in favour of the government's option, allowing it to announce that its option had garnered 95 per cent of the vote.

Singapore's economic challenges. Singapore emerged independent in 1965 with little to show for the previous five years. Goh Keng Swee summarized Singapore's initial economic development efforts:

> So the first phase of our economic development ended with little achieved. In terms of industrial hardware, there emerged a small petroleum refinery, a steel rolling mill producing metal bars, a soap factory, a number of garment factories producing for export, mostly branches of Hong Kong firms trying to evade quota restrictions and some wood processing plants. (1986: 24–5)

An independent Singapore was ready to become almost entirely focused upon economic development.

Investment and FDI

Independence – Charting a New Course

Singaporean federation with Malaya underlay PAP economic policy from its inception in 1954. Termination of the union left its leadership bewildered. Lee Kuan Yew approached the path ahead with 'great trepidation' (2000: 25), while Goh Keng Swee described it as a 'terrifying experience ... Our economic problems remained unsolved, we had no natural resources and the population had been growing at a brisk pace' (1986: 24). In his autobiography, Lee quotes an editorial from an Australian newspaper as reflective of widespread sentiment: 'An independent Singapore was not regarded as viable three years ago. Nothing in the current situation suggests that it is more viable today' (2000: 19–20).

Singapore's population had grown to slightly under two million by 1965 while its real gross domestic product per capita stood at approximately US$900, its economy having contracted in 1964 (Heston et al. 2011). The number of people engaged in manufacturing approached 50,000, only a moderate percentage of the total workforce (Goh 1986), while the unemployment rate remained stubbornly above 10 per cent (Soon and Tan 1993). Labour unrest had declined to 388,000 man days lost to strikes in 1964 and dropped further to 46,000 in 1965 (P.S.J. Chen 1983), but political instability remained a concern to potential investors (Goh 1986). The entrepôt trade constituted the core of the Singapore economy and the British military presence provided employment for approximately 40,000 Singaporeans.[4] Thus, it was a heavy blow when a phased withdrawal of all military personnel was announced by London. The government needed to create jobs. It quickly concluded that the import substitution policies previously pursued failed

---

4   The Winsemius Report (United Nations Commissioner for Technical Assistance 1963) cites 35,000 as the number of Singaporeans employed by the British military in 1960 while Goh (1968) calculated there were over 42,000 in 1967.

to produce the desired results and, with most of its domestic market now gone upon the split from Malaysia, it was no longer a practical strategy (Goh 1986). Singapore's only option was to turn to an export oriented manufacturing strategy welcoming foreign capital and investment, as the Winsemius Report had originally suggested.

Although such a strategy was not the prevailing philosophy of the time, there were dissenting economists of the view that export orientation could provide a means for industrialization and economic growth. Two, in particular, may have influenced Singapore's leaders, particularly Goh Keng Swee who received his doctorate from L.S.E. in 1954; Peter Bauer and Hla Myint. Originally from Hungary, Bauer arrived at Cambridge in the 1930s and spent time in Malaya immediately after the war before returning to England and a teaching position at L.S.E. Myint, originally from Burma, who also taught at L.S.E. during the same period, maintained an abiding personal and academic interest in Southeast Asian affairs. Professionally, both were originally focused upon international trade before turning to issues of international development. They would have been among the relatively few high profile academics familiar with Southeast Asia at the time that the future leaders of Singapore were British university students (Goh 1983).[5]

Myint believed that 'the various arguments in favour of economic development through industrialization and import substitution do not stand up to critical scrutiny' (1973: 132). The smallness of most developing countries' domestic markets would limit industrialization. It was preferable to reduce tariff barriers, institute tax reform and provide subsidies, where required. The result: 'would have the effect of expanding international trade by enabling the country to realize more fully its *potential* comparative advantage in export production' (Myint 1973: 134, emphasis original). Consequently, Myint argued that export expansion offered a more promising path to economic development than import substitution for many less economically developed countries. Countries inclined to protect their declining industries, such as textiles, would do better to let them go and adopt 'the newer technologically more sophisticated industries where they have a comparative advantage' (Myint 1973: 136).

Bauer, a critic of foreign aid, fought passionately against comprehensive central planning. In his view, such planning was far more likely to deter material advancement than promote it. His dislike of central planning did not suggest that he believed government had only a small role to play in economic development (1969).[6] On the contrary, government played a crucial role in economic development. He envisaged a range of tasks 'sufficiently wide to exceed the human, administrative and financial resources of governments of all poor countries which I know' (Bauer 1971: 27).

Post-independence Singapore heeded Myint's and Bauer's advice and focused on setting core policy initiatives that provided flexibility 'to ensure quick and

---

5   Goh refers to their work in a speech he presented in London in 1983.
6   See also his criticism of Gunnar Myrdal's *Asian Drama* in Bauer (1971).

competitive response' (Huff 1995: 1433) to the international market. Goh pointed to three such policies that formed the basis of Singapore's industrial strategy. They suggest an active developmental state approach by the Singapore government and an early recognition of the importance of the factors that later literature would recognize as the key elements in mediating the relationship between technology and growth:

> Let me sum up the discussion so far on government policy and action in promoting industrial growth. These were related to three important areas:
>
> 1. Improving infrastructure – electricity, water, roads, ports, telecommunications, air transport, etc.;
>
> 2. Setting up the EDB to attract MNCs;
>
> 3. Expanding science, engineering and technical training facilities in schools, polytechnics, universities and special institutions. (Goh 1983: 42)

The Winsemius Report – Attracting Investment and Technology

Myint's and Bauer's sentiments found voice in the Winsemius Report. It set forth a course of action for Singapore to expand its manufacturing sector primarily through the attraction of FDI. Even if the right 'investment climate is created and given the necessary incentives' (United Nations Commissioner for Technical Assistance 1963: 13) the Winsemius Report believed that it was more likely that foreign participants would invest in Singapore's industrialization efforts than domestic businessmen. While there was wealth in Singapore, it tended to be highly concentrated among those active in the entrepôt trade. Its entrepreneurs were traders and merchants, not manufacturers. Local businessmen lacked international distribution channels. Consequently, Singapore would have to seek investment from foreign sources, predominantly MNCs, in order to obtain the necessary technology and to help develop the skills needed to be competitive. The government concurred. In his 2001 examination of the role MNCs played in the growth of Singapore's economy, Kwong concluded that: 'The story of industrialisation in Singapore is basically one of drawing foreign direct investment' (Kwong 2001: 5).

Singapore needed to compete internationally on quality and price, not low cost labour as its wages were higher than elsewhere in Asia (United Nations Commissioner for Technical Assistance 1963). Consequently, it would have to raise its level of productivity beyond that of its neighbours necessitating 'a comparatively high degree of mechanization' (United Nations Commissioner for Technical Assistance 1963: 14). A more highly productive workforce also implied one that was more skilled. This posed something of a problem for Singapore as, despite the high unemployment rate there was a shortage of foremen and skilled workers. More positively, Winsemius noted years later, labour in Singapore was very industrious and possessed good English skills (Winsemius 1984).

Investment Incentives

Attracting FDI required a different set of incentives and a different relationship with MNCs than were the case in Japan, South Korea and Taiwan where MNCs were kept out to the extent possible. Singapore had to gain their trust especially given its left leaning reputation and the PAP's self-proclaimed socialist orientation at a time of Cold War tensions. The Winsemius Report recommended guarantees against expropriation, entering into treaties to avoid double taxation, tax relief such as a five year tax holiday starting with the first profitable year, accelerated depreciation rates and a dividend instead of profit tax – incentives that were relatively novel at the time – as well as changes to immigration laws to facilitate investors bringing in management and technical staff to Singapore (United Nations Commissioner for Technical Assistance 1963). As a consequence, Singapore was amongst the first countries to enact many of the incentives referred to in Chapter 5 and to undertake measures to encourage investment by foreign manufacturers and exporters. The Pioneer Industries Ordinance granted a five-year exemption from taxes for companies that were recognized by the government to be among the first to introduce a new manufacturing industry to Singapore. Enacted contemporaneously, the Industrial Expansion Ordinance provided for a sliding scale of tax credits with the amount of capital invested for approved expansion projects by existing manufacturers. Subsequent incentives were broadened. Under the Economic Expansion Incentives Act profits from approved manufacturing activities were taxed at 4 per cent instead of the usual 40 per cent for 10–15 years.

The Pioneer Industry and Industrial Expansion programs were revised and a number of other tax-driven incentive programmes were introduced throughout the 1970s aimed at fostering a broader base in industrialization and encouraging FDI and manpower training. The Export Incentive Scheme provided tax relief mirroring the Economic Expansion Incentives for export oriented industries that were not eligible for pioneer status. An Investment Allowance was also instituted for approved manufacturing and related service projects whereby up to half of a company's profits could be exempt from taxes in cases where it was not eligible for pioneer status or export incentives. In an attempt to expand local engineering capability, the Warehousing and Servicing Incentives programme provided a five-year reduction of the tax rate from 40 per cent to 20 per cent for approved new or expanded services in repairing or otherwise servicing designated products. A similar tax reduction was granted under the International Trade Incentives programme for trading companies engaged in the export of Singapore manufactured goods or designated non-traditional commodity exports.

A number of financing programs also came into effect. The Small Industries Finance Scheme, jointly operated with local financial institutions, provided low interest loans aimed at fostering the technical upgrading of local small industries.

Equity and loan capital was provided under the Capital Assistance Scheme from an SG$100 million fund to assist companies, foreign or domestic, with 'specialized projects of unique economic and technological benefit to Singapore' (Chen 1983: 9). Under the Product Development Assistance Scheme, grants were provided to domestic manufacturers to develop new or improve existing products or processes.

The Winsemius Report argued that beyond incentives, Singapore should do everything it could to make it as easy as possible for foreign interests to establish manufacturing operations in Singapore. Even then, Singapore would need to be a 'super-salesman in overseas markets' (United Nations Commissioner for Technical Assistance 1963: 46). An export promotion council was recommended to seek out potential investors and to act as their one point of contact with the government, ensuring that their every need was met.

The Economic Development Board – Singapore's Institutional Template

John Kenneth Galbraith asserted that the first task of a less economically developed country 'is not to get capital or technicians, but to build competent organs of public administration' (Goh 1983: 229). Looking back in 1983 at almost 25 years of PAP rule, Goh cited Galbraith and agreed that the fundamental challenge faced by many poor countries 'is not the inadequacy of aid from, and trade with, the rich nations, but instead inappropriate social and political institutions' (Goh 1983: 229). Consequently, it is not surprising that one of the PAP's first economic acts was to create the EDB. Established in 1961, the EDB's initial object was 'to promote the growth of the manufacturing industry in Singapore' (Goh 1986: 25), but it quickly took on a more comprehensive role in the formulation and execution of Singapore's development strategy and it now views its purpose as 'the lead government agency that plans and executes economic strategies that enhance Singapore's position as a global hub for business, investment and talent' (Singapore, Economic Development Board 2010).

The Winsemius Report proposed that the EDB should both advise the government on industrialization policy and carry out part of the policy. Two broad principles were suggested in selecting industries upon which the Board's development efforts should focus: (a) industries that can take advantage of the 'relatively high aptitude and skill of workers in Singapore (thus offsetting the disadvantage of relatively high wages) and manufacture quality products' and; (b) industries that offer the best possibilities for immediate market expansion (United Nations Commissioner for Technical Assistance 1963: 128). Economic expansion was viewed as dependent upon Singapore's ability to expand its export industries 'which will have to compete in the world markets both in quality and price' (United Nations Commissioner for Technical Assistance 1963: 128). Other industries might provide more immediate employment, but over the long term opportunities were greater if Singapore's industrial sector could 'aim at high productivity and keep abreast with technological advance by employing modern machinery and production methods' (United Nations Commissioner for Technical

Assistance 1963: 128). It argued that foreign companies active in the targeted industries would 'introduce special skill in the labour force by starting assembling or production of simpler parts and quickly advance to more complicated products' (United Nations Commissioner for Technical Assistance 1963: 129).

The EDB's mandate specifically included the identification and attraction of MNCs to Singapore. In carrying out its duties, the EDB was empowered to administer fiscal and monetary incentives, such those under the Pioneer Industries Ordinance and, in appropriate cases, provide financing, such as for site development, through its investment arm. The Winsemius Report urged the EDB to be relentless in its pursuit of MNCs' investment. It would need travelling representatives armed with brochures and facts and figures relating to the cost and availability of land, utilities, transportation and labour. They were to cultivate relationships with banks, chambers of commerce, trade councils and manufacturers associations in Singapore and abroad. No detail was too minute not to be dealt with explicitly. Sample wording was provided for letters to prospective investors and the report advised that a first letter should be sent to the top person in the targeted organization. If that did not produce results then a second letter should go to the next person in the organization chart and so on. 'Do not give up with an initial refusal – keep trying, as perseverance will bring the desired results' (United Nations Commissioner for Technical Assistance 1963: Annex VII, 13). Letters should be typed on high quality paper and enclosed in an envelope 'of like quality' (United Nations Commissioner for Technical Assistance 1963: Annex VII, 13). Both letterhead and envelopes should reflect 'solidity, dignity, even affluence' (United Nations Commissioner for Technical Assistance 1963: Annex VII, 13).

The Winsemius Report was equally detailed regarding the structure of the EDB. Foremost amongst the recommendations was independence of the Board from political interference and influence. This would be accomplished through a governing board devoid of government ministers or officials without the security of permanent civil service status. It was explicitly stated that the presence of ministers, for example, could result in board members making recommendations to themselves as well as acting as an impediment to discussion. Representation from diverse business and labour elements as well as senior civil servants was crucial to ensure a diversity of ideas, but it was equally important that members be chosen for their personal qualities and not as representatives of a group so as not to become advocates for particular interests. Finally, appointments to the governing board 'should be regardless of political attachments' (United Nations Commissioner for Technical Assistance 1963: 118–19). The report stressed the need for the EDB to attract the best people possible as employees. To that end, it was recommended that the salaries of those working for the EDB be increased by 50 per cent to lessen the likelihood that they would be lured away by the private sector once they had acquired sufficient knowledge and skill through their intensive training.

No matter how well conceived the public policy or designed an institution, there is no guarantee the policy will be successfully carried out by the institution.

Success depends in large measure upon the quality of the people charged with implementation. Edgar Schein, a professor at the MIT Sloan School of Management and an expert on organizational culture, published an analysis of the functioning of the EDB in 1996. He argues that the EDB was crucial to the success of Singapore's economic development strategy and that it serves as an important institutional model to other less economically developed nations. One must:

> ... look beyond the actions of the leadership of the society and the particular economic conditions that prevailed at the time ... [and] focus on the organization that helped create an economic strategy and was responsible for its subsequent implementation. (Schein 1996: 2)

Echoing Galbraith, Schein states that economic growth may have: 'more to do with the processes of economic development than the actual content of a given strategy of growth' (Schein 1963: 2).

Schein's examination of some of the early activities of the EDB and, in particular, its pursuit of Hewlett-Packard (HP) as one of the first major investors proves illuminating. In the mid-1960s, HP decided to explore the possibility of establishing a manufacturing facility outside the United States. A short list of potential locations based on HP's own research included Singapore. Schein quotes Clyde Coombs, the HP manager assigned the task of investigating foreign manufacturing:

> I then telephoned Eric Goh, who headed the San Francisco office of the EDB. The minute I told him what we were thinking about, he was all over me; he was really a salesman who just wouldn't quit. If I needed any information he would get it immediately, and he just wouldn't give up until we had at least agreed to visit Singapore and see for ourselves. (Schein 1996: 2)

Upon arrival in Singapore, HP representatives met with the Chairman of the EDB. They were impressed with 'his clear sense of Singapore's strategy, and his clarity about the rules and what HP could expect from Singapore ... "They had clear rules and they kept their promises"' (Schein 1996: 20). The project officer assigned to the HP file acted as a one-stop service providing information on land, labour, fiscal incentives, training programs and financial aid. Again, Schein quotes Coombs:

> If you asked them about something, it would be on your desk the next day; if other government agencies were involved, they would do all of the negotiating and problem solving for you. (Schein 1996: 20)

The EDB even arranged for a 'gigantic cable extension cord' (Schein 1996: 21) to take power from one building to the not quite completed one next door that would house the sixth floor HP offices to provide electricity for the elevator and lights when William Hewett decided to visit on short notice. At the time of Schein's writing, the HP investment in Singapore had grown to over US $300 million 'and a staff of more than 6,000 managed primarily by Singaporeans' (1996: 21). Schein emphasizes that the relationship between HP and the EDB was not an isolated case, but indicative of a course of conduct by the EDB with companies prepared to make a long term commitment that would bring with their investments the technology and training Singapore sought. Such cases 'abound and, in most of those cases, a key variable appears to be the manner in which the EDB recruited, persuaded, and subsequently supported the companies who chose to invest there' (Schein 1996: 22). Blomstrom et al. (1999), for example, cite the example of Texas Instruments' experience in the 1960s whereby its Singapore facility was in operation within 50 days of its investment decision being taken.

As Johnson (1982) and Amsden (1989) noted about Japan and South Korea, respectively, the Singapore government recognized early that quality people were the key to an effective organization. Hon Sui Sen, described by Lee Kuan Yew as 'our most capable permanent secretary' (2000: 70) within the civil service became the first chairman of the EDB. Schein argues that Hon's appointment was indicative of the government's philosophy of human resource development; 'a reliance on excellent people and an assumption that they could learn whatever the job required even if they had not been specifically trained for it' (Schein 1996: 39–40). This attitude was reflected in the government's selection of the first Managing Director of the EDB, a choice that also foreshadowed the government's willingness to import foreign talent where the need arose.

Goh Keng Swee first met E.J. Mayer on a trip to Israel in 1958. Mayer was then Israel's director of industrial planning within its Ministry of Commerce and Industry. That meeting was followed by discussions during his trips to the region with Lee, who felt that Israel's position as a small country without resources surrounded by countries who did not want its products was similar to Singapore's. Lee was also impressed by Mayer's emphasis upon employing and nurturing the best people one could find and then training them for their specific tasks. Mayer was hired in late 1961 as Managing Director of the EDB. His initial job description, as quoted in the Singapore Straits Times newspaper is reproduced by Schein. It provides insight into manner in which the EDB fit within Singapore's developing institutional framework and is illustrative of the consultative nature required for the formulation of public policy and the creation of good institutions:

The director is expected:

a) to assist in the formulation of economic policy ... and when necessary to advise the Government on the direction of the policy,

b) to liaise with Government Ministries and statutory boards such as the proposed Port Authority, Public Utility Departments, Housing and Development Board and Singapore Telephone Board, in matter relating to policy and details of economic development, ...

f) to co-ordinate with other competent authorities of Government in the planning
of physical facilities for industries and port facilities ... (Schein 1996: 40–41)

The job description stressed the expectation that the Director would communicate
and align the EDB's actions with other government bodies as well as provide
input to the government's formulation of economic policy. This, combined with
the structure of the EDB itself which provided for input and advice from interested
parties outside the civil service, ensured, at least in theory, that a multiplicity of
views would be solicited and considered in the formulation and implementation of
government policy and in the actions of the government institutions charged with
carrying out that policy.

Economic and Institutional Expansion

Singapore's initial development efforts were extremely successful. By 1979, GDP
per capita had grown to US$5,815 (Heston et al. 2011). and the manufacturing sector
employed quadruple the number of people it had in 1960 representing 29 per cent
of all employment, almost double the 1960 level (Huff 1995). Direct manufactured
exports rose from 10.7 per cent of GDP to 47.1 per cent during the same period
(Huff 1995). The government also reigned in the unions through the Industrial
Relations (Amendment) Act 1968 which curtailed the right to strike and its close
relationship with the National Trade Union Congress which came to represent
almost all unionized workers in Singapore. By 1969, hourly wages for comparable
job classifications in electrical and electronics assembly industries fell to 'less than
one-eleventh of the US level, and below those in South Korea, Taiwan and Hong
Kong' (Huff 1995: 1424). Full employment was reached in 1975 (Goh 1986).

By the late 1970s, Singapore confronted new challenges. Full employment and
falling birth rates began to exert pressure upon wages. Manufacturing, too, was
evolving with 'more automation and robotics, where knowledge of the processes
and skills in maintenance would be the critical labour resource' (Schein 1996:
49). It became evident that Singapore's workforce would require greater skill
levels if it wished to retain and continue to attract MNC investment as the main
engine of growth. Singapore needed to provide 'not only a competent workforce
on the factory floor, but also a range of supervisory, technical, engineering and
management skills at higher levels' (Goh 1986: 30). Increasingly, Singapore
would have to rely on more capital intensive and higher technology industries.

Focusing on ICT

Singapore's focus evolved naturally in the 1980s as the use of increasingly
sophisticated technology in the manufacturing sector came to imply the ever greater
usage and production of ICT goods. In 1981, Goh Chok Tong, then the Minister
of Trade and Industry and future Prime Minister, stressed the need to develop
industries and services based on science, technology, skills and engineering in

the effort to transform itself into a knowledge-based economy (Schein 1996). While the precise meaning of 'knowledge-based economy' may be somewhat vague, it is centred upon developing manufacturing and service industries that harness technology, innovation and capabilities (Blomstrom et al. 1999). Even if the focus of Singaporean development policy had evolved, its means for achieving its revised ends were consistent. FDI would be the source of ICT just as it had been for earlier technologies.

Wong Poh Kam attributes Singapore's continued economic growth to constant technological upgrading almost exclusively through technology transfer from MNCs, 'not indigenous research and development' (2004: 1). Singapore was quick to recognize the 'global shift towards an information economy by attracting large MNCs in the global ICT industry ... and by promoting the rapid adoption and diffusion of ICT in all sectors of the economy' (Wong 2004: 1). He notes that by 2000, Singapore's promotion of both ICT production and consumption allowed it to be ranked within the top ten countries in the world on most measures of ICT diffusion (Wong 2004).

Singapore's economic success was derived from its ability to transform itself into a key manufacturer of electronics and ICT products. The industry remained in the hands of foreign-controlled MNCs. Approximately 75 per cent of Singapore's manufacturing output in the early 2000s came from MNCs and 60 per cent of the equity in manufacturing facilities was foreign owned (Wong 2004). Within the electronics sector, foreign firms represented over 80 per cent of the equity investment and over 90 per cent of the value added in the 1990s. In 1991, foreign firms accounted for all of the top thirty electronics manufacturing enterprises by sales in Singapore. By 2001, five Singaporean firms had entered the top 30 but their cumulative sales reached less than 8 per cent of the total (Wong 2004).

The government's approach to ICT manufacturing mirrored its earlier approach to other forms of manufacturing. Once a manufacturer had established a presence in Singapore, it would then be encouraged through the programs and incentives and a great deal of personal contact between management, the EDB and other relevant institutions to expand its role by using its Singapore operations as a regional headquarters and by upgrading its local operations through the assumption of increasingly complex and technology intensive activities (Wong 2004). The EDB role did not end with the MNC's establishment of a presence.

> EDB also coordinates the subsequent 'leveraging' activities with other agencies, including industry-specific manpower training programs, upgrading programs for local suppliers, and R & D collaboration with public research institutes. (Wong 2004: 10)

The government's strategy to improve skills came to depend largely upon in-house training by the MNCs. The EDB again played a critical role. It brokered arrangements with companies such as Rollei and Phillips to 'develop crash programs to upgrade its labour force' (Schein 1996: 48) as well as joint training institutes between Singapore and Germany, France and Japan under a programme called the Local Industry Upgrading Programme. The theory was that the MNCs and foreign training institutes would be in a better position than the government to ensure that the right set of skills was being taught. The EDB's focus also shifted to attracting MNCs that would be willing to create 'jointly sponsored training programs that would quickly enhance the skill levels of the Singaporeans' (Schein 1996: 48). Funds were also provided by the EDB to MNCs to institute their own training programs for Singaporean workers.

The dependence on MNCs to provide so much of the training, however, had drawbacks that would become more apparent in the 1990s. In his examination of the impact of FDI on human capital expansion in Southeast Asia, Ritchie concludes that the empirical evidence demonstrates that MNC training has led to increased knowledge and skills, but it is 'unclear whether these skills are appropriate to develop endogenous technological capability' (2002: 18). Blomstrom et al. (1999) note that despite the EDB's joint efforts with MNCs to establish training centres and schools to train workers not employed by MNCs, the importance of local firms as suppliers to MNCs or, more generally, as contributors to the economy, did not increase. In fact, the local manufacturer share of value added was lower in 1990 than in 1980. As Goh Keng Swee noted of Singapore's efforts in this field, 'our attempts to solve these problems were not completely successful' (1986: 31).

Infrastructure and ICT

Early Focus on Telecommunications Infrastructure

Since independence, the Singapore has directed resources 'into strategically essential investments, such as communications infrastructure' (Ure 2008: 239). It has played a highly activist role in the building of telecommunications infrastructure and fostering the adoption of ICT. Singapore's accomplishments success in this area, as with industrialization, are due to clearly enunciated policies, the establishment of an institutional structure with clear mandates, a high level of coordination between government, the relevant public sector institutions and private sector organizations, and the provision of the human and financial resources needed to implement its policies effectively. The Economic Development Institute of the World Bank issued a study in 1997 looking back at the development of East Asian infrastructure. Although it did not examine the telecommunications sector in depth, it viewed the Singaporean approach to telecommunications infrastructure development as analogous to that of the other forms of infrastructure development that it studied more closely. The authors attributed Singapore's success to the government's 'vision, leadership and commitment' for instilling the values of 'efficiency, meritocracy and intolerance of corruption' into the statutory boards charged with developing and managing infrastructure projects (T.Y. Lee 1997: 69, 71).

Singapore started from a relatively advantageous position. The World Bank, in its 1955 review of Malaya's economic prospects, considered Singapore's telephone, telegraph and overall communications infrastructure to be of a high quality for the times (IBRD 1955). Domestic telephone service was provided by the Singapore Telephone Board, established in 1953 as a government body to take over the telephone monopoly of the privately owned Oriental Telephone and Electric Co. Ltd. After Malayan independence in 1957, responsibility for international trunk lines, which had been handled from Kuala Lumpur, was assumed by the Telecommunications Department of the Singapore government. The operational monopolies were merged in 1974 to create the Telecommunications Authority of Singapore (TAS), a statutory body which also carried out the telecommunications regulatory function. Internal structures kept the operational and regulatory functions separate.

TAS was reorganized in 1982. It took on the operations of the Postal Department and Singapore Telecom (SingTel), a newly created unit of TAS, assumed operational responsibility for telecommunications provision. It was not until 1992 that the regulatory and operational functions carried on under the TAS umbrella were separated with TAS giving up its operational functions, but retaining regulatory oversight of a rapidly evolving competitive telecommunications industry. SingTel was corporatized and its shares held indirectly by the government through Temasek Holdings. At the time of corporatization, SingTel was granted a fifteen year monopoly over both domestic and international telephone communications. The monopoly over mobile telephone services ended in 1997 and the remaining land line monopolies were terminated in 2000, at which time the existing foreign ownership restrictions placed upon industry participants in the sector were also dropped. The main focus of TAS and its predecessors in the 1960s and early 1970s was 'to make massive investments in basic infrastructure to increase line capacity' (Koh and Lim 2002: 239) and to increase telephone penetration rates. From a relatively low 36 telephone lines per thousand of population in 1960, telephone usage increased to 78 lines per thousand in 1970 and 345 lines by 1982 (Chen and Kuo 1985).

Building for the Computer Age

By the beginning of the 1980s it was becoming increasingly clear to the Singaporean government that productivity would have to be improved in order for Singapore to continue to attract the FDI it desired to maintain its economic growth and progress up the technological ladder. Productivity gains could only be achieved, it reasoned, through the greater use of automation and information technology in both the private and the public sectors. Singaporean society itself would have to become more technologically sophisticated as a matter of national competitiveness (Gilbert 1989). As a first step, the government devoted resources to building telecommunications infrastructure and investing heavily in the computerization of the public sector, which the government believed would provide an example both to the private sector and the broader public to do likewise. As a result, 'telecommunications and information technology infrastructure became a formal element in development strategy' (Gilbert 1989: 25).

Prior to the 1980s, Singapore had never enunciated a formal science and technology policy (Kwong 2001). Since then it has regularly produced plans and strategies to bring Singapore to the frontier of ICT usage accompanied by on-going institutional reform and infrastructure upgrading (Koh and Lim 2002). The Committee on National Computerization (CNC) was created in 1980. Chaired by the Education Minister and comprised of ministers, civil servants, statutory board executives and representatives from the private sector the CNC was a high level policy-making body 'focused on developing the human resources and infrastructure necessary to build a core of information systems for the government' (Gilbert 1989: 25). In 1981 it recommended the creation of a permanent statutory board, to be known as the National Computer Board (NCB), to manage the computerization of the civil service, to establish an accreditation system for information technology specialists based on the British model and to develop incentives aimed at fostering the spread of information technology beyond the government. The same year, the NCB produced a National Computerization Plan (NCP), a significant component of which was the Civil Service Computerization Plan designed to upgrade information systems in nine ministries as a model to the rest of the civil service as well as the private sector.

Other initiatives under the NCP included the placement of computers in every secondary school and the offering of a computer science course within the 'A' Level course of study. Singapore also entered into agreements with more technologically advanced countries to provide training while encouraging joint public-private forms of cooperation. The Japan-Singapore Institute of Software Technology was created to train information technology professionals at the polytechnic level and the Centre for Computer Studies was established in partnership with the British Council. A joint venture between the National University of Singapore (NUS) and IBM created the Institute for Systems Science to produce systems analysts and educate chief executives and policy makers about the uses of information technology. The success of the CNC's efforts was demonstrated in the increase in the number of information technology professionals in Singapore from 850 in 1980 to over 5,000 in 1986, an expansion deemed 'remarkable not so much because new skills were produced, but because they were employed by the market' (Gilbert 1989: 27).

A goal of the National Computerization Plan was also to foster computer use in the growing number of Singaporean statutory boards such as the Housing & Development Board (HDB), Singapore's largest employer outside the civil service and the military (Gilbert 1989). The HDB computerization programme took close to five years to implement, at a time when most people had no familiarity with computers and had to be trained from scratch. Aside from their use as internal administrative tools, computer systems were also initially integrated into the HDB's operations such as to monitor elevator cars by linking each car to a central office from which maintenance personnel could be immediately dispatched in the case of car malfunction or trapped passengers.

> Within two years, new software was acquired to perform report generation, data inquiry, document composition, structural engineering, quantitative analysis, and graphics tasks, and to support interactive statistical analysis and construction management activities...Within four years, end-user development of applications was an integral component of HDB information systems. (Gilbert 1989: 28)

By the end of 1986 an early electronic mail system for the distribution of documents and messaging was in place in every department at HDB headquarters, all 37 area offices and all remote offices (Gilbert 1989).

Promoting ICT Usage

The emphasis shifted from the public sector to the private sector with the National IT Plan 1986–1990. A collaborative effort between the NCB, the EDB, SingTel, NUS and TAS, its goal was to develop the information technology sector and 'exploit it for national competitive advantage' (Koh and Lim 2002: 240). The plan signalled an even greater emphasis by the government on developing technology intensive industries and it signals the recognition by the government of the growing convergence between information and telecommunications technologies (Loh et al. 2000). Its objective was to position Singapore as both a major user and a producer of ICT related goods and services. Implementation was spearheaded by the corporate partners of the plan, NCB, EDB and SingTel, while TAS continued to build telecommunications infrastructure allowing Singapore to become the first fully digital country with an island-wide fibre optic ISDN network, critical for merged voice and data traffic.

Goh Chok Tong, who succeeded Lee Kuan Yew as Prime Minister in 1990, enunciated his ICT strategy for Singapore's future in 1991 with a pictorial, coffee table type publication entitled *Singapore: The Next Lap* which envisaged a highly educated, internationally competitive society at the forefront of technology with the ubiquitous use of ICT throughout Singapore. *The Next Lap* spurred the NCB to produce a study later that year called *IT 2000: A Vision of an Intelligent Island* (IT 2000) examining ways to increase ICT usage in eleven discrete economic sectors.

> The study tapped the practical and visionary expertise of more than 200 senior executives from both the public and private sectors to see how IT could be applied to improve business performance and the quality of life. (Loh et al. 2000: 243)

IT 2000 argued the need for Singapore's telecommunications infrastructure not merely to keep up with international standards but to move to the forefront, both for competitive economic reasons and to improve living standards. A reconstituted CNC became the National IT Committee with the task of overseeing and coordinating the implementation of IT 2000. The most important initiative fostered by IT 2000 was the launch of Singapore ONE (One Network for Everyone) which was designed to bring high-speed, high-capacity connectivity to homes and offices throughout the island to permit multimedia programming and create a secure environment for e-commerce (IDA 2003). The project involved the cooperation of local internet service providers, cable operators and government bodies including the TAS, EDB, NCB, SingTel, the National Science and Technology Board and Singapore Broadcasting Authority in a 'type of public-private collaboration [that] remains a characteristic of infrastructure development in Singapore' (Ure 2008: 247).

Accelerated convergence between communications and information technologies led the government to merge the TAS and NCB in 1999 to form the Infocomm Development Agency (IDA) which produced three new strategic plans in quick succession; Information and Communications Technology for the 21st Century (Infocomm 21) in 2000; Connected Singapore in 2003; and Intelligent Nation 2015 (iN2015) in 2005. Infocomm 21 aimed to develop the broadband multimedia industry as well as initiate the push to mobile wireless internet services and move up to 90 per cent of government services on-line (Ure 2008). Connected Singapore reiterated the view that ICT use would provide an engine of growth, but emphasized that such would only be the case if Singapore continued to build individuals' capabilities, continued technological training and provided an environment conducive to business (Ure 2008). Under the 'Got To Be Connected' umbrella, programs were launched to spread basic ICT literacy, improve access to computers at school and home for lower income families, provide greater technical support for new users and instil greater consumer confidence in e-commerce.[7] A number of manpower training programs were also created – Critical Infocomm Technology Resource Programme; Infocomm Training and Attachment Programme (iTA); E-business Savviness Programme; and the Infocomm Competency Programne – to enhance ICT skills among ICT professionals, business leaders and to train 'workers in the essential infocomm skills for today's competitive workplace' (IDA 2003: 22). The iTA programme, for example, provided funding for ICT programmers and developers to gain 'hands-on experience through local and overseas attachment opportunities with selected infocomm organizations in the area of hot and emerging technologies' (IDA 2003: 22).

The iN2015 master plan continued the major thrusts of previous plans. The main 147-page plan rests atop ten detailed subject specific reports ranging from specific industry sectors, manpower training, infrastructure and entertainment. It recognized ICT as potentially transformative of government and key economic sectors and set a globally competitive infocomm industry as a goal to be achieved through an ultra-high speed, pervasive and trusted infrastructure network and an infocomm-savvy workforce and globally competitive infocomm manpower (IDA 2005).

---

7   The IT Literacy programme, PC Reuse Scheme, e-Ambassadors programme and the Trust SG programme, respectively.

The Infocomm Development Authority

Primary responsibility for the implementation of Singapore's ICT policies falls upon the IDA. The IDA is not a 'textbook' regulator as described by the ITU Toolkit in that its mandate combines both the promotion of ICT and the regulation of telecommunications, as did its predecessor, TAS, thereby creating a potential conflict of interest (Painter and Wong 2006). Its impartiality was questioned in its early days. 'Allegations of inexperience, lack of corporate transparency, and partiality towards incumbent SingTel appear to plague it' (Koh and Lim 2002: 244).[8] While there is no evidence of favouritism being displayed by the IDA, Ure argues that the failure to attract more FDI into the telecommunications market in Singapore, for example, may have been affected by perceptions of potential bias as well as the actual 'dominance of government-linked corporations in the facilities-based market' (Ure 2008: 241). Ure notes, however, that competition gained momentum and criticism of the IDA abated with the introduction of a new 'Code of Conduct for Competition in the Provision of Telecom Services' in the mid-2000s. SingTel was required under the Code, for example, to produce a reference interconnection offer to any service provider prepared to agree to the mandated terms. The IDA followed the ITU Handbook procedure in making that decision.

> SingTel was required to publish its RIO in a short space of time, allowing a period for industry submissions, followed by comments by the IDA, redrafting and final approval. (Painter and Wong 2006: 185)

The lack of competition may have also initially inhibited ICT uptake, such as with broadband internet service. Singapore ONE originally envisaged that broadband service would reach 400,000 subscribers by 2001. By January 2001, however, there were only 85,000 subscribers (Ure 2008). Increased competition after 2002, a greater range of services and improved technology drove ADSL costs down and subscriptions up to 780,000 by 2007 (Ure 2008).

Overall, Singapore's efforts have borne fruit. Singapore's position as a regional air hub and the continued importance of its port, for example, 'owe much of their success to the vital supporting role played by the telecommunications industry' (Koh and Lim 2002: 240). As discussed in the Introduction, the ITU attempts to measure the level of ICT advancement in countries and the extent of the Digital

---

8 SingTel, a government linked corporation, as state-owned enterprises are referred to in Singapore, was not merely owned by the government but closely bound to it through personal relationships. Lee Hsien Yang led SingTel while his brother Lee Hsien Loong was prime minister. Both are sons of Lee Kuan Yew. The government's majority interest in SingTel is held by Temasek Holdings, as are a large number of other government linked corporations, including SingTel's largest competitor, Starhub. Until late 2008, Ho Ching, the wife of Prime Minister Lee Hsien Loong, was the Executive Director and CEO of Temasek Holdings.

Divide through its ICT Development Index. The 2010 index, which covers up to 2008, ranks Singapore as the fourteenth most advanced nation. It ranks even more highly in the ICT access sub-index (tenth) and the ICT use sub-index (fifth), but a relatively poor 77th in the ICT skills sub-index, which is a function of adult literacy, where Singapore ranks relatively well, as well as secondary and tertiary enrolment, where it does not (ITU 2009). A similar pattern is found in the WEF's *Global Competitiveness Report 2010–2011* which ranks Singapore as the world's third most competitive economy. It receives very high marks for the quality of its institutions (first) and infrastructure (fifth), but is 15th in secondary enrolment, 30th in tertiary enrolment and 17th in capacity for innovation. The WEF's 2010-2011 Networked Readiness Index ranks Singapore second, behind Sweden (WEF 2010b). These figures are all consistent with an economy that has been highly successful in attracting technology through FDI and spreading its use, but despite government leading the way in ICT usage and innovation, less successful at developing indigenous talent, creativity and innovation more broadly throughout the society.

Education and Human Capital

As discussed in Chapter 5, an education system should be built from the ground up (de Ferranti et al. 2003). Singapore has effectively done so by focusing first upon primary and then upon secondary, technical and vocational education as well as adult manpower training, to the point of providing a minimum of ten years of schooling to its citizens. Its two largest universities, NUS and Nanyang Technological University, rank 25th and 47th, respectively, in the 2012 QS World University Rankings. Enrolment at the tertiary level, however, remains relatively low for a country of its wealth. The development and implementation of education policy in Singapore stand in contrast to the government's efforts in its economic fields of endeavour. While Singapore has provided excellent schooling to its citizens, education reform has been marked by uncharacteristic confusion about how best to achieve as yet unreconciled pedagogical, social and economic goals. Literacy, math and science skills at the secondary level, de Ferranti (2003) argues, are the most important for economic growth and ICT adoption in newly industrializing societies. Singapore has excelled in teaching those skills and has grown in less than forty years from a poor country to one that is highly economically developed. Singapore continues to face, however, challenges in reaching the forefront of the 'knowledge economy', its stated goal, where innovation and creativity play dominant roles. The salient aspects of the education system, knowledge and skill acquisition, have contributed to Singapore's current wealth by supplying the needed pool of labour to MNCs, thereby allowing it to attract increasingly technologically sophisticated FDI, but the political and economic goals of its education system may work against it becoming an innovator in the new knowledge-based economy.

1959–1969

At the time it became effectively self-governing in 1959, education levels in Singapore were low and the education system was poorly equipped to handle the impending boom in school age children occasioned by its rapidly expanding birthrate. There were four school systems – English, Chinese, Malay and Tamil – with the British colonial government providing funding only for the English system in an amount equal to 5 per cent of the colony's annual budget (Yip et al. 1997). The other systems were funded by the local communities and there was no common curriculum. Of the approximately 272,000 children in primary school, 47 per cent of those entering Primary 1 in 1959 chose English schools, marginally fewer picked the Chinese system and the remaining few were divided between the Malay and the Tamil (Goh and Gopinathan 2006). Upon forming the government in 1959, the PAP government released a five-year plan under which the Ministry of Education took control of the education systems, established the principle of equal treatment for each system and imposed a common curriculum with an emphasis upon math, science and technical subjects. It also ambitiously promised to make free primary schooling available for all children (Yip et al. 1997).

Spending on education rose to an average of between 20–25 per cent of all budgetary expenditures from 1959–1965 during which time 83 new schools were built allowing over 350,000 primary students to attend school in 1965, thereby largely accomplishing the government's goal of free primary education for everyone as well as allowing freedom of choice for parents in the language of instruction for their children (Goh and Gopinathan 2006; Yip et al. 1997). A common structure of six years of primary education, four years of secondary schooling and two years of pre-university study, following the British system, was imposed upon the different linguistic streams. Common examinations were also instituted at the completion of each level and annual loans of free textbooks were made available to students who could not afford them (Yip et al. 1997). During those years, teacher training and recruitment became a high priority. The number of teachers rose from slightly under 10,600 in 1959 to approximately 17,000 by 1965 (Goh and Gopinathan 2006; Yip et al. 1997).

Attention was also devoted to secondary education, although primary education remained the top priority. The government strove to provide space in secondary school to anyone who qualified, as determined by the Primary School Leaving Examination, and who wished to attend. Secondary enrolment in the 1959–1965 period rose from 48,700 to close to 115,000 due to growing numbers of secondary school age children and the increasing availability of facilities. The Chan Chieu Kiat Report of 1961 examined the need for technical and vocational education to prepare students not continuing from primary school to the academic secondary level for the workplace. Vocational, technical, commercial and secondary schools were created as well as secondary level vocational institutes. In addition, Singapore Polytechnic and Ngee Ann Polytechnic were 'greatly expanded and restructured to accommodate new courses to meet the new needs of the changing economy' (Yip et al. 1997: 9). By 1965, approximately 12,000 students attended the new type of secondary schools (Seah and Seah 1983).

Despite proclaiming itself to be driven by democratic socialist principles in the 1950s, a guiding societal philosophy seems to be entirely absent from the educational reforms instituted by successive PAP governments, although they clearly sought to implement political and economic goals. As Seah and Seah note in their 1983 review of the history of education in Singapore, although 'Singapore is not ideologically committed to any political system of thought, political unity and integration is vital' (244).[9] In their view, the education system had three objectives. The first two were 'instilling the national interest and political commitment in the young' (Seah and Seah 1983: 244). These goals have continued to underlie the Singapore education system. In 2000, among the 'Desired Outcomes of Education' determined by the Ministry of Education, pupils at the end of primary school should 'Love Singapore'. By the end of secondary school students should 'know and believe in Singapore' and by the end of junior college they should 'understand what it takes to lead Singapore' (Singapore, Ministry of Education 2000: 197).

Economic growth provides a third objective that drives structural and curriculum reforms in education to an even greater extent than the political goals. Loh et al. argue that between 1959 and 1965, the most noteworthy aspect of reform:

> ... is the shift in the exploitation of education for political and ethnic primordial interests to the economics of education. In other words, there is a perceptible switch in emphasizing the link between education and economic development. (Low et al. 1991: 53)

Seah and Seah agree. They state: 'Of the many aims education has to fulfil ... that for economic growth and development is perhaps a supreme and overriding objective in Singapore' (Seah and Seah 1983: 244). This is not to suggest that the education system serves only political or economic ends. Seah and Seah note that 'knowledge ... as well as other ideals' (1983: 244) are among education's aims and Low et al. provide assurance that 'Moral education, together with national interests, ideas and values, continue to be taught in the schools' (Low et al. 1991: 53). Such educational purposes, however, appear to be held subservient to political and economic ends.

The expansion of secondary, particularly vocational, education attracted more attention in the late 1960s and 1970s (Yip et al. 1997). The shift in emphasis was accompanied with institutional reform aimed at strengthening the ties between the education system and industry. A National Industrial Council, whose membership included the Ministers of Education, Labour and Finance was created to oversee the coordination of training with manpower needs. The Technical Education

---

9   This is an interesting comment given the publication in 1976 of a speech by Goh Keng Swee entitled 'A Socialist Economy That Works' before becoming Minister of Education in 1979.

Department within the Ministry of Education was established in 1968 under which four industry-specific institutes were created[10] to be replaced in 1973 with the formation of the Industrial Training Board which assumed responsibility for industrial training. It, in turn, was merged in 1979 with the Adult Education Board to form the Vocational and Industrial Training Board (VITB). The Council on Professional and Technical Education (CPTE) was established the same year under a newly formed Ministry of Trade and Industry, which took over manpower planning from the National Industrial Council.

The CPTE was created 'to link up all the ministries, bureaus and agencies involved with either education or manpower planning' (Low et al. 1991: 61). It was initially composed of the relevant ministers, Vice-Chancellor of NUS, the Chairs of the EDB, Public Service Commission and National Wages Council as well as the Secretary-General of the National Trade Union Congress. The job of the CPTE was to predict education and manpower needs, recommend enrolment plans and forecast the financial and staffing requirements of Singapore's post-secondary institutions, including those operated by the VITB and EDB, 'to ensure that an adequate reservoir of trained professional, technical and skilled manpower is provided' (Low et al. 1991: 61).

1970–1979

Despite the rise in the overall level of education at the primary and secondary levels, both in the academic and the vocational and technical streams, there was growing unhappiness in the 1970s with the content of the education system. The initial emphasis of education policy was to build schools and provide universal primary and then secondary education to all Singaporean children. Structures and curricula in the different systems had been standardized, but little attention had been paid to the quality of the child's educational experience. Dropout rates were high. Of those who failed the Primary School Leaving Examination, upon which admission to secondary school depended, most left the school system entirely and very few went to vocational school. On average, 70 per cent of a cohort leaving primary school continued their education (Goh and Gopinathan 2006). Of those who did move on, merely half passed their 'O' Levels and 'of the remaining 35 per cent, only 14 per cent enroll for Pre-University education with only 9 per cent of these passing the "A" level examination' (Low et al. 1991: 98). Morale was low among teachers and principals, leading to high resignation rates (Goh and Gopinathan 2006). At the top, there had been seven ministers of education, including three within a fifteen month span, an extremely high number given the stability of the government. Unusually for a country where a great deal of emphasis is placed upon structures that permit for a diversity of opinion to be canvassed and consensus to be achieved prior to taking action, there was 'no attempt to hear the

---

10   The four new technical institutes focused upon training welders and machinists for the shipbuilding, oil refining, engineering and the chemical industries.

views of teachers or parents before new policies were implemented' (Goh and Gopinathan 2006: 19). To address these concerns, Goh Keng Swee was picked to lead a team to study the education system and recommend changes.

The Goh Report, as it is commonly known, led to the creation of the New Education System (NES) in 1979 which implemented reforms in the structure, curriculum, organization and management of schools and the Ministry of Education. Most importantly, 'the introduction of the NES resulted in a radical restructuring of the education system into a system of ability-based streaming' (Yip et al. 1997: 17). It was felt that a common curriculum for all students was unfair to the slower learners as it failed to take variations in learning abilities into account. A diversity of streams was proposed to provide alternatives to the existing system which had resulted in a choice of 'up or out'.

> A fundamental feature of the new education system is the categorization of pupils into the brilliant or ablest group, the average and above average group and the below average or poor group. (Seah and Seah 1983: 258)

Under the NES reforms, students would be tested and placed into one of three academic streams at the end of Primary Three, at roughly age eight. Further streaming would occur after Primary Six where pupils would be divided between those who would normally continue to follow a path that could lead to university and those whom would not. 'O' Level tests would be administered to the students in the university stream at the end of four years of secondary school to determine whether they would continue to a two or three year pre-university course, at the end of which 'A' Level examinations would be administered, or be channeled to the polytechnics and institutes run by the EDB and the VITB.

Although, in theory, lateral movement between the streams could occur as students caught up academically, the reality was that this did not occur often (Low et al. 1991). Those in the lowest category of learner for their last three years of primary school had very little chance of continuing to secondary school, their only options being vocational and technical training. The Goh report created a complex and technical structure that was criticized as reflecting the training of those Goh chose to work with him on the reforms. All in their thirties or younger, the team 'comprised mainly system engineers rather than professional educationists and specialists' (Seah and Seah 1983: 258). The reforms failed to address many of the existing educational shortcomings although several advances were achieved.

1980–1995

The NES did produce better test results among those in the academic stream while other students received more schooling in the technical and vocational streams. Success rates at the Primary School Leaving Exam and 'O' Levels improved, and the high attrition rates noted in the Goh Report declined sharply. By 1986, dropout rates had declined to the point that less than one per cent of students left school without at least ten years of education and by 1990, among the then 25–29 year old cohort, the number of people with only primary education had fallen to 38 per cent while the number with secondary or upper secondary, including technical or vocational schooling, had risen to 54 per cent and those with at least some university education had climbed to eight per cent (Goh and Gopinathan 2006; Gopinathan 1997).

Despite the reforms, Singapore still suffered from shortages of skilled labour, qualified technical and engineering staff and scientists as well as modern management well into the 1990s leading Gopinathan to remark that Singapore produced 'obedient labour used to working hard but not especially large numbers of high-skilled labour' (Gopinathan 1999: 297–8). For every 10,000 workers, 114 were engineers and only 29 engaged in research. Both Nanyang Technological Institute and NUS were expanded to accommodate more students, but still only '9 per cent of the annual cohort of students entered universities or polytechnics (as compared to 20 per cent in Taiwan and 40 per cent in Japan)' (Goh and Gopinathan 2006: 36).

Efforts to address the problems in the technical and vocational streams did not take place until the late 1980s, by which time very negative attitudes towards such education had developed. In addition to the 'stigmatization' felt by those left out of the academic path, Singaporean society viewed being streamed into the vocational education system as failure (Low et al. 1991). 'Vocational institutes became "dumping grounds" or "catch-nets" for those who failed to meet up with academic rigour' (Goh and Gopinathan 2006: 32). Extensive efforts were made to upgrade the quality and perception of technical and vocational education. The VITB was completely reorganized and renamed the Institute of Technical Education. New campuses were built with 'excellent educational and sports infrastructure and cutting-edge technological support' (Goh and Gopinathan 2006: 32). The non-university track secondary stream was re-vamped and greater opportunities to switch streams or progress to universities or pursue other tertiary options were introduced. Manpower training was further enhanced through the Modular Skills Training Programme and Worker Improvement through Secondary Education Programme introduced in 1986 and 1987, respectively, while individual skills needed for industry were met primarily through polytechnics and joint training centres operated by the EDB and private firms (Gopinathan 1999).

By the end of the 1980s Singapore had clearly closed the education gap required to produce a trained workforce able to respond to the demands of late twentieth century industrialization. The challenge for Singapore was no longer whether it could pull itself out of less economically developed country status or even whether it would grow to be a relatively wealthy nation, but whether it could join the ranks of the world's leading economies. The evolution towards a knowledge-based economy was becoming an increasing pre-occupation of the Singapore government as evidenced by the release of *Singapore: The Next Lap* in 1991 which maintained that henceforth: 'Education will receive the highest emphasis as it is resourcefulness, not resources, that will increasingly determine winners and losers in the future' (15).

Problems, however, persisted within the NES creating uncertainty about whether Singapore could produce the type of resourceful graduates it wanted to respond to the new economic challenges. The government's economic strategy had long been to rely on foreign technologies to build its industrial base. These technologies, however, changed more rapidly than anticipated. Consequently, Singapore resorted to importing skilled labour and more highly trained engineers, scientists and management in order to keep pace (Blomstrom et al. 1999). Singapore's education system produced workers with skills to respond to the needs of MNCs, but it was 'unclear whether these skills are appropriate to develop endogenous technological capability' (Ritchie 2002: 18). The problem, however, was possibly more fundamental in nature making the solution more complex. Goh and Gopinathan remarked that the 'strictly top-down, approach to planning, disseminating and enforcing educational changes' (2006: 28–9) had led to troubling outcomes.

> Firstly, it generated the 'yes-man' syndrome and the acceptance of change without question by those below. Secondly, it inculcated an over-reliance on the top leaders for direction. Thirdly, it nurtured a spoon-feeding culture. The end-result was an education service which lacked autonomy, initiative and a general sense of detachment from the policy-makers. Within schools, teachers and children alike are 'mechanically' fed by a bureaucratically designated and rigid curriculum. (2006: 30)

Singaporean students learned how to study for and write exams, but not necessarily how to think independently.

1996–Present

Gopinathan believed Singapore required fundamental change if it wished to train the people needed to compete at the forefront of an innovation driven international economy. The existing problems were structural and necessitated more than modest revisions to the curriculum or new facilities, as desirable as they were. Singapore's dilemma was that the order and discipline that permitted it to move from poverty to wealth were the same attributes that could stifle the talent needed to respond to the opportunities of the knowledge economy. Writing with Sharpe, Gopinathan argued:

> In Singapore what were strengths in the past are now routinely noted by policymakers to be handicaps for the future. The centralized, standardized, top-down system, the emphasis on school socialization and rote learning, the practice of tracking and, perhaps most of all, the quiescence of students ... all of which were used successfully by the developmental state in its joint

project of economic growth and nation building — have become impediments
in post-industrialism. There is a consensus among policy makers that a radical
transformation of education is required if schools are to play their part in
producing the creative, autonomous and flexible work force required to compete
in value-added markets. (Sharpe and Gopinathan 2002: 152)

The Ministry of Education eventually acknowledged the need to adopt an
'ability-driven approach to education' and to emphasize 'intellectual capital to
develop a knowledge-based economy' (2000: 186). In 1997 it adopted a new vision
statement, 'Thinking Schools, Learning Nation' (TSLN), reflecting a shift to an
educational philosophy that sought to be adaptable and cater to individual student
interests and aptitudes (Ministry of Education of Singapore 2000). New reforms
proposing far more flexibility were advanced. Initially, Gopinathan and Sharpe,
expressed great enthusiasm for the TSLN reforms, believing that Singaporean
education policy had 'been turned on its head' and that the 'range and depth of
educational reforms ... is remarkable' (Sharpe and Gopinathan 2002: 151). The
reforms pointed 'to a profound change in the direction of educational policy' made
even the more extraordinary because they demonstrated 'a willingness to make
fundamental changes just at a time when the school system has gained international
recognition for its high standards' (Sharpe and Gopinathan 2002: 151) such as in
the 1995 and 1999 international TIMMS evaluations where Singaporean students
placed at or near the top.[11]

Unlike the reforms under the Goh Report, Gopinathan noted that the quality
of the proposed 1997 reforms could be traced to the fact that for 'the first time
university academics and other education personnel, particularly principals,
were extensively involved' (Gopinathan 2007: 60). In contrast to the widespread
consultation normally associated with institutional development in Singapore,
previous educational reform efforts were marked by a lack of input from interested
parties. Singapore desperately wanted to produce more creative, independent
thinking professionals, particularly in engineering and the sciences where the low
number of graduates caused special concern. In their 2006 article, Gopinathan
and Goh approved of the government's recognition that in order for Singapore
to develop its technological capabilities it would have to nurture an indigenous
supply of scientists and engineers and not rely upon MNCs or the importation of
foreign talent (Goh and Gopinathan 2006).

By 2007, Gopinathan's enthusiasm for the TSLN reforms had become somewhat
muted. The reforms implied, but did not deliver, a tolerance for 'experimentation,
innovation and uncertainty where output is not always guaranteed or even

---

11   TIMMS, by which name the tests are commonly known, stands for Trends in
International Mathematics and Science Study. The international tests of math and science
are administered at the Fourth and Eighth Grade levels every four years. Singapore has
consistently finished extremely highly, often first or second, in both tests at both levels in
1995, 1999, 2003 and 2007.

expected' (Gopinathan 2007: 60). While the TSLN reforms did provide greater flexibility than previously, they did not generally address the structural issues or the 'considerable rigidities caused by tracking at the secondary level' (Gopinathan 2007: 62). Testing and streaming remain essential elements of the school system and so long as such assessment determines the opportunities available to students it will only encourage 'studying for the test' and an avoidance of risk. 'Policy is still dictated by the core assumptions that ability can be detected early and must be differentially developed' (Gopinathan 2007: 67). Streaming after Primary Three has been eliminated, but the Primary Six exam remains in place suggesting that the assumptions of what constitutes ability may be somewhat narrow. While the ability to synthesize material, analyse issues and apply knowledge to problem solving forms more of the curriculum since the reforms, the testing of such skills through high stakes examinations leads Gopinathan to criticize the reforms as merely bolting on new elements to the existing structure so that 'a technique-oriented view of creativity prevails' (Gopinathan 2007: 68).

The problem may be more profound than the structure of the education system. It may be that the education system reflects the structure of Singaporean society which itself militates against the formation of large numbers of creative, innovative people. Blomstrom in a study examining the policies developed in Sweden, Finland and Singapore aimed at spurring growth and innovation in a knowledge-based economy questions Singapore's ability to educate the type of person it claims to want in order to continue to be competitive.

> Other policies than educational changes are likely to be important in developing creativity in Singapore. For instance, Singapore is lagging behind many other East Asian countries in the pace of political liberalization. Whereas countries such as Korea, Taiwan, the Philippines, and Indonesia have achieved or been moving towards democracy in recent years, Singapore still has limits on the freedom of media, the cultural sphere, civil society, trade unions and political activities. The result has been a society where people are said to be cautious about expressing own ideas [sic] and views and where most people opt for the safe strategy to follow officially sanctioned paths. A society that oppresses alternative views is obviously not encouraging independent thinking and creativity. It is also uncertain if the government can expect people to think independently and to be creative in some areas such as in science or businesses, without allowing them to express independent views on for instance politics.
> (Blomstrom et al. 1999: 45)

Singapore wants a creative, innovative entrepreneurial class, but it is uncertain how such a class can develop in the business world without creativity and innovation being permitted free voice in whatever fields of endeavour they choose to express themselves. The Singapore of the 1950s was a cauldron of debate, passion, political and labour movements and ideas. If the PAP had not had to articulate its vision and defend it vigorously against opposing views it is an open question whether it would have developed the coherent and detailed set of policies enunciated in The Tasks Ahead or exhibited the same drive to transform Singapore into a modern, dynamic, prosperous society. One need only compare the PAP's 1959 election platform, The Tasks Ahead, with its brief, glossy 2006 Election Manifesto of platitudes, pictures and intellectual pabulum, or the marginally better 2011 Election manifesto to wonder how a government that eschews the public battle of ideas can hope to create the innovative republic it envisages.

In Summary

In the 45 years since its independence, the Singaporean approach to economic development has transformed a poor, small country without resources into one of the wealthiest countries in the world. Much of the credit can be attributed to enlightened leadership, wise policies, institution building and superb execution by those institutions. Generally, Singapore's institutions are the result of careful planning, on-going consultation with a wide range of interested stakeholders, independence from political interference and the employment of the best talent available, regardless of nationality. Singapore's economic gains have relied extremely heavily upon MNCs and FDI for industrialization, jobs, technology and skills development. The economy continues to be highly dependent on foreign firms. As Wong (2004) argues, there is no guarantee that a strategy that did more to encourage the growth of indigenous firms would have been more successful in terms of economic growth or that the overall size and competitiveness of Singapore's manufacturing sector would have been comparable. Wong acknowledges, however, Singapore's policies and approach to development can be credited with taking Singapore to the edge of the global technological frontier, but may unconsciously also have constrained it from joining the most technologically advanced and innovative societies. While research and development, innovation and creativity have always been important to technological and economic advancement, success in an ICT dominated knowledge economy may place greater emphasis upon such attributes and activities than in the past. Singapore was spectacularly successful in raising education levels and the quality of its education, as measured by standardized international testing of literacy, mathematics and science, but the structure of its economic system and the focus of its education system may have sacrificed individual expression and creativity in order to create a workforce that responded to the need required to attract, service and expand MNC investment, thereby providing Singapore with wealth and a standard of living comparable to many of the most economically developed countries, but destined to remain a step behind the technological innovators.

Chapter 7
Malaysia

Colonizing the Peninsula

The initial development of the Straits Colonies had little impact on Peninsular Malaya's Sultanates which continued to be ruled by hereditary royal families and small, elite circles of advisors, administrators and merchants. Royal monopolies controlled exports. Most Malays were poor, illiterate and tied to their kampong (village), where they were generally engaged in either subsistence farming or fishing. Prospects for economic improvement for the average Malay were few due to the tight control maintained over land ownership and commercial activity. Education levels remained low and: 'No commercial institutions or middle class evolved' (Turnbull 1989: 110). Consequently, the Chinese in the Straits Settlements and Malays on the peninsula lived very different, separate lives; their point of contact being the British administrators and the Sultans' courts. The British developed a keener interest in the peninsula late in the nineteenth century. The reason was tin.

The Malay Peninsula was found to hold some of the richest deposits of tin in the world. Chinese entrepreneurs from the Straits Colonies were approached to develop Malayan tin operations by the British and the Sultanates, which lacked sufficient capital and labour. Tin mining was dangerous, dirty and low paying work, providing little economic incentive for the Malay to leave their kampongs. Conditions in China, however, were different. The influx of Chinese labour on the peninsula to work and service the tin mines became a flood in parts of the Malayan peninsula. In 1850, for example, there were no Chinese or tin mining operations in the Larut Valley in Perak. By 1870 there were 40,000 Chinese and by 1911 the number of tin miners alone in the valley had risen to 196,000 of which 95 per cent were Chinese (Bruton 1992).

Tensions inevitably arose between the local Malay and the Chinese (Turnbull 1989). In order to protect their mutual commercial interests, the Sultans invited the willing British to provide security, leading to the appointment of resident 'advisors' accompanied by a small military presence in several Malay States. By the mid-1890s, the British were strongly established in four of the southern Malay States[1] and in 1895 those states officially came under colonial rule as the Federated Malay States with a centralized administration established in 1896 in

---

1   Selangor, Perak, Pahang and Negri Sembilan.

Kuala Lumpur. The other five Malay States[2] remained separate political entities known as the Unfederated Malay States 'administered with the aid and advice of British officials' (IBRD 1955: 4–5), but without formal British residents.

Rubber provided the impetus for further foreign involvement in peninsular affairs in the early twentieth century. First planted commercially in 1895, over 16,000 acres of rubber trees were under cultivation by 1902. Twenty years later over two million acres were in production, supplying approximately half the world's rubber (Baker 1999). As with tin mining, the average Malay did not participate economically. Only 5 per cent of the land used for rubber trees was owned by Malays and much of that was comprised of small agricultural plots producing low quality rubber. Fearful that the Malays might move away from growing food, the Federation 'banned the growth of rubber in some designated Malay-reserved land, further obstructing the entry of the Malays into this industry' (Baker 1999: 179). Tamils, brought by the British from India, provided most of the labour for the rubber plantations. Consequently, Malays were effectively shut out of tin mining and rubber cultivation, the two largest industries in Malaya.

The growth of the Chinese and Indian populations was troubling to the Malay, but the predominant view held equally by the immigrants, Malay and colonial authorities was that the new arrivals' time in Malaya would be temporary, viewing 'their stay in the country as a prelude to their retirement in their villages' (Ryan 1963: 108). Hence, few efforts were made to integrate the ethnic groups or to permit the Chinese or Indians input into the administration's decision-making process. As an extension of this policy, the British began to admit locals without regard to race into the Straits Settlements' civil service in the 1930s, but only Malays could seek such employment on the peninsula. Hugh Clifford, Governor of the Straits Colonies and High Commissioner for the Federated Malay States, enunciated the broadly understood social contract in 1927 when he rejected any movement towards majority rule. Majority rule would lead to:

> … the complete submersion of the indigenous populations ... and this would produce a situation which would amount to a betrayal of the trust which the Malays of these states ... have been taught to repose in His Majesty's Government. (As quoted in Turnbull 1989: 203)

Post-War to Independence

Continued poverty and turmoil in India and China after World War II made a return to their homelands an unappealing prospect for the immigrants to Malaya. Furthermore, given the decades that had passed since their first arrival, Malaya was for many the only home they knew. The permanent settlement of the short-

---

2   Kedah, Perlis, Trengganu and Kelantan in the north, which continued to pay tribute to Siam until 1909 when a treaty with Siam fixed the boundary, and Johor in the south.

term guests became a political issue. A new Labour government in Britain sought to chart a different course from its pre-war predecessors. It proposed the creation of a Malayan Union comprised of all the Malay States, Penang and Malacca. Singapore would become a separate colony. The Sultans would be stripped of much of their power and citizenship would be widely conferred upon Chinese and Indians. Administrative positions in the civil service would be opened to non-Malays.

The Malays offered fierce resistance to the plan seeing 'equality for immigrants as a foreign intrusion which threatened to destroy the character of the country' (Turnbull 1989: 232). The British had broken the understanding enunciated by High Commissioner Clifford in a 'gross betrayal of all the premises upon which British-Malay co-operation was based' (Turnbull 1989: 233). Already economically marginalized, the Malays feared that they would also lose political power. Whereas prior to the war there were no Malay political organizations that spanned the Malay States and little pan-Malayan identity that transcended attachment to one's state, the proposed Malayan Union quickly spurred a sense of unity among the Malay (Turnbull 1989).

Opposition to the Malayan Union reforms was led by the newly formed United Malay National Organization (UMNO) led by Dato' Onn bin Jaafar. The British backed down. Instead, the Federation of Malaya encompassing all the Malay States, Penang and Malacca came into existence in 1948. The Sultans' traditional powers were respected, the distribution of powers between the central government and states remained untouched and citizenship rights were curtailed with the result that of the three million citizens, as opposed to residents, of the reconstituted colony, 78 per cent were Malay, 12 per cent Chinese and 7 per cent Indian.

Elections for part of the legislative council were called for 1951. While Dato' Onn sought to open UMNO to all races, he could not convince the majority of UMNO members leading him to leave the party, to be replaced by Tunku Abdul Rahman. UMNO, however, recognized the electoral importance of the other ethnic groups and proved willing to form alliances. The Malayan Chinese Association (MCA) entered into an alliance in 1951, followed by the Malaysian Indian Congress (MIC) in 1954. The Barisan Nasional or the Alliance, as it became known, won the 1951 elections and, still composed of ethnically-based parties dominated by UMNO, has won every national election since. The Alliance leadership was 'essentially a conservative, English educated, upper-middle class, propertied group who did not want to see radical social or economic change' (Turnbull 1989: 250).

Independence came to Malaya on August 31, 1957. Its constitution mirrored the Federation Agreement, enshrined Islam as the state religion, Bahasa Malay as the national language and ensured that political power remained in the hands of the Malays.[3] Quotas were imposed on the number of non-Malay civil servants.

---

3   Baker (1999) suggests that approximately 70 per cent of constituencies are drawn to ensure a Malay majority.

Malays were also 'given preference in educational opportunities, including quotas for scholarships, and preference in entering institutions of higher learning' (Baker 1999: 258). In return, citizenship rules were relaxed allowing the immigrant communities to comprise roughly 42 per cent of the population at independence.

In anticipation of their eventual independence, the World Bank sent a survey mission to Malaya and Singapore in 1954 to address 'broad issues of development policy and general lines of priority investment' (IBRD 1955: vii). The report, released in 1955, greatly influenced Malaya's subsequent economic development efforts (Jomo 1986). It paints a picture of a relatively healthy economy by Asian standards, but with growing social needs (IBRD 1955). Rubber and tin formed the basis of the Malayan economy. Together these products accounted for 85 per cent of its domestic exports and approximately 20 per cent of its national income (IBRD 1955). Agriculture, including rubber which accounted for 65 per cent of cultivated land, dominated as the most important economic sector. Rice represented the second largest agricultural product with just under half of all Malays involved in small-scale cultivation (IBRD 1955). Nevertheless, Malaya still imported over half its rice needs with foodstuffs accounting for close to 40 per cent of its imports in 1953. Manufacturing, primarily of consumer items such as soap and beverages, was the second largest contributor to national income and was 'fairly advanced' (IBRD 1955: 16), within the Asian context, accounting for almost ten per cent of employment. Most industrial activity, however, was on a very small scale and associated with packaging agricultural products and trading activities.

Pressure would be exerted upon the economy by the rapid rate of population growth. Estimated at 5.7 million in 1953, Malaya was growing at the rate of over 3 per cent per year and with a moderation of the gender imbalance and a majority of females under the age of 19, it could reasonably be expected to rise further. Education was of increasing concern. In 1947, the last year for which statistics were available, 62 per cent of the population over 15 was illiterate. After the war, there were 300,000 children in school. The number had grown to 800,000 by 1954 and with an additional 60,000 school age children a year, it was expected to rise to 1.7 million by 1960. It was unlikely that the government would be able to provide places for all children, particularly as it could only accommodate between 55–60 per cent in 1954 at the primary level and only 1 in 14 at the secondary level in government run or assisted schools. Vocational training was extremely limited with about 700 students at the secondary level, 239 at the post-secondary level, 300 adults in full-time training classes and 1,000 in part-time evening classes (IBRD 1955). As bleak as such figures seem, 'enrolments compare favourably with those in many countries of Asia and other continents' (IBRD 1955: 143).

The World Bank report envisaged very few prospects for industrial expansion for Malaya placing its emphasis on agricultural development. While manufacturing had grown since the war, it was no more than commensurate with population growth which, given its increased rate in the 1950s, would become more difficult to maintain. The 'highly mechanized and capital-expensive industries' were not appropriate nor were industries attracted solely by cheap labour 'at the expense of equipment and training' as was the case elsewhere in Asia given the relatively high wages in the colonies (IBRD 1955: 121). It was difficult to envisage industries competing with those based outside the region particularly as their domestic markets were small. A better strategy would be to strive for gradual advances over a wide range of industries. Such an approach could be expected to contribute significantly to economic growth rather than the 'establishment of large mass-producing units along "Westernized" lines' (IBRD 1955: 31). Little thought was afforded to pursuing a course of action that might lead to a level of economic development approaching western levels, as it likely struck the authors as unrealistic.

The major issue in the Malayan legislative elections of 1955 concerned the rights of the ethnic groups, not economic development. On economic matters, it is questionable whether the Alliance had 'a specific, detailed vision of its own about the direction and content of the policies it would follow' (Bruton 1992: 175). Consequently, the Alliance was prepared to adopt the World Bank report as its economic development road map.

Investment and FDI

Independence to 1970 – Maintaining the Status Quo

The World Bank's 1955 comprehensive study of Malaya's economic prospects, which formed the basis of Malaya's economic strategy, urged the government to continue the exploitation of the existing natural resources-based rubber and tin industries, the expansion of palm oil exploitation and the encouragement of the entrepôt trade (IBRD 1955). Relatively little attention was paid to increased industrialization, the development of a manufacturing sector or to the social and economic status of the rural Malay who depended heavily upon subsistence farming. The only government action of note in the early days of independence to stimulate the manufacturing sector was the enactment of the Pioneer Industries Ordinance in 1958 with the goal of reducing the country's reliance on imported consumer goods (Andaya ad Andaya 2001). The Ordinance provided Pioneer status and tax holidays for companies establishing factories, but only in industrial sectors that had not previously been serviced domestically. Due to the structure of the tax measures provided, however, 'even at the time they were generally considered to have little or no effect on the absolute amount of investment' (Bruton 1992: 260). In many cases the tax holidays granted under the Ordinance proved illusory as they expired quickly, prior to the new businesses showing a profit. By 1968, only 22,000 people were employed at firms with Pioneer status.

A second World Bank Report (the Rueff Report), released in 1963 to coincide with Singapore, Sabah and Sarawak's union with Malaya to form Malaysia, foresaw bright prospects for manufacturing in the combined state (IBRD 1963). Guided by import substitution theories of growth, the enlarged national market presented a 'golden opportunity' (IBRD 1963: 9) to expand the sector. It noted that both Thailand and the Philippines, with roughly half Malaysia's per capita income, supported substantially larger manufacturing sectors (IBRD 1963). The Rueff Report recommended that Malaysia raise its comparatively low tariffs, but only to the extent that it did not threaten the entrepôt trade. As a counter-balance, it proposed the creation of free trade zones and bonded warehouses, suggestions which when first acted upon towards the end of the decade would have a profound impact upon Malaysia's economic growth. The creation of a Federal Industrial Development Authority (FIDA) to coordinate federal support for industrial site development and lending was urged. The specific recommendations in the Rueff Report relating to FIDA mirror those in the Winsemius Report describing the initial functions of Singapore's EDB.

Singapore's departure from Malaysia in 1965 did not produce the same re-evaluation of its economic growth strategy in Malaysia as it did in Singapore. Shortly after the split, the Government of Malaysia (1965) released its first five year plan, entitled the *First Malaysia Plan*, a comprehensive statement of the country's plans for economic development. The Economic Planning Unit (EPU) of the Prime Minister's Department has continued to publish such plans every five years. The EPU undoubtedly receives input from outside sources, but as such input is provided informally, it is impossible to know how widely the EPU consults. There is no entrenched consultative process with outside organizations or formal means for outsiders to make their views heard. Unlike the statutory boards and ad hoc committees in Singapore which operate independently to implement the government's broad policy guidelines and are comprised of a variety of stakeholders, there are no analogous bodies in Malaysia. Economic policy and its implementation rest firmly with the government.

The First Plan focused upon the economy's agricultural sector while maintaining an import substitution strategy approach to manufacturing, but offered very little in the way of new policies or programmes to encourage industrial investment or economic diversification. The largely ineffective Pioneer Industries Ordinance was replaced in 1968 with the Investment Incentives Act in an effort to encourage job creation. This statute broadened the class of companies eligible for tax relief and tailored the granting of tax holidays to the nature of goods produced, the geographical location of the manufacturing facility and the extent to which local products were used as inputs for new business operations, regardless of whether they were 'pioneers' in their field of endeavour.

By the late 1960s, before the impact of the Investment Incentives Act could be felt, Malaysia's import substitution policies showed modest success. Manufacturing grew to account for 15–16 per cent of Malaysian GDP compared to 9–10 per cent ten years earlier and the range of consumer goods produced expanded to the extent that the value of such domestically produced goods exceeded imports compared to the beginning of the decade when their value had been less than half that of goods brought into the country (Bruton 1992). Employment in the manufacturing sector, however, 'was the major disappointment' (Bruton 1992: 263) of Malaysia's industrialization efforts. The manufacturing sector accounted for only six per cent of the labour force in 1963 (Turnbull 1989) and 8.7 per cent by 1970 (Rasiah 2002). Manufacturing came to resemble 'an enclave' with a relatively small, well-paid workforce, but only 'modest links with the rest of the economy' (Bruton 1992: 263). It was also an enclave with very little Malay representation.

Malaysia's economy showed strong growth through the 1960s averaging close to 6.5 per cent annually (Bruton 1992), as per capita GDP grew at a slower pace, from US$293 in 1960 to approximately US$425 by 1969, due to its high birth rate (Heston et al. 2009). Growth, however, was unevenly distributed and the plight of rural Malaysia, apart from the rubber and palm plantations, began to draw the attention of the government. Almost half of all government development expenditures during the 1960s were aimed at the Malay farmer.[4] The strategy behind such spending was not to alter the traditional Malay way of life or to diversify the rural economy so much as to make the rural Malay more prosperous.

> The most important thing to note about this strategy is that it is built on the notion that the Malays would remain paddy farmers, fishermen, and smallholder rubber farmers. There was to be no large-scale shift from rural to urban areas and activities ... The idea was to raise the income in these rural activities, not to shift the Malays to other, more profitable activities, and not to try to create new activities in the rural areas. (Bruton 1992: 233)

The results of Malaysia's initial efforts to improve the lives of rural Malays, however, were limited. In 1970, monthly income in almost half the households in peninsular Malaysia fell under the poverty line, of which 75 per cent were Malay (Andaya and Andaya 2001). Income in Chinese and Indian households, in contrast, rose during the same period (Bruton 1992). More than a decade after independence Malays continued to be disproportionately rural and poor as well as badly educated (Andaya and Andaya 2001; Turnbull 1989). The government's economic policies led to the perception among many Malays that they were being excluded from the industrial and commercial sectors of the economy and relegated to the agricultural sector (Andaya and Andaya 2001). By the end of the decade, income inequality and economic activity disparities had increased between the Malays and other Malaysians (Bruton 1992).

Independence had effectively vested political power in the Malay elite leaving the Chinese, for their part, feeling increasingly excluded from government and alienated from the ruling UMNO coalition. In the economic sphere, despite their relative affluence within Malaysia, there was anger due to the perception that under the Investment Incentives Act the government had provided preferences that in practice would primarily benefit foreign firms in order to prevent Chinese enterprises from playing an even greater role in the economy (Bruton 1992).

---

4   See Bruton (1992) who notes that rural did not include rubber and palm oil estates and referred to communities of 1,000 inhabitants or fewer.

Education reforms in 1967 which eliminated government funding of English language instruction at all levels as well as Chinese and Tamil education at the secondary level, while extending it at the primary level, left large elements of the Chinese and Indian minority unhappy as well as many Malays who felt that Bahasa Malay should be the only language of instruction at all government supported schools. In the May 1969 federal elections, opposition Chinese and Indian parties made strong gains at the expense of those forming part of the governing coalition. Celebratory demonstrations degenerated into race riots that left at least 200 dead (Turnbull 1989). A state of emergency was declared by the government and both the constitution and Parliament were suspended.

1970–1990: The New Economic Policy – Setting New Goals

Parliamentary rule was restored in February 1971 and the government quickly moved to introduce a New Economic Policy (NEP), the details of which were enunciated in the *Second Malaysia Plan* whose first sentence unequivocally states: 'National unity is the over-riding objective of the country' (Government of Malaysia 1971: 1). The government recognized that the main threat to the country's stability lay in the economic and political disparities between racial groups and the ethnic tensions they caused. The NEP would seek to redress the Malay's poverty and economic isolation as well as maintain their political dominance, while attempting to reassure the Chinese and Indian communities that their relative economic prosperity and 'legitimate interests'[5] would not be threatened.

The NEP rests on the pursuit of two goals. The first is the elimination of poverty by 'raising income levels and increasing employment opportunities for all Malaysians irrespective of race' (Government of Malaysia 1971: 1). In practice, the attainment of this goal would place a heavy emphasis upon the condition of rural Malays who constituted a disproportionate majority of those living below the poverty line. The second goal seeks to eradicate 'the identification of race with economic function' (Government of Malaysia 1971: 1) meaning, for example, that no longer would Malays be cast as farmers nor would the commercial world belong to the Chinese. The NEP undertook to create 'a Malay commercial and industrial community in all categories and at all levels of operation' (Government of Malaysia 1971: 1) so that they and other indigenous people (known collectively as the Bumiputera) could partake fully in Malaysian society. The government made no secret of its intention to intervene actively in the economy in pursuit of its stated goals. It would undertake such commercial ventures, devise such

---

5   Article 153(1) of the Malaysian constitution provides that it shall be the King's responsibility 'to safeguard the special position of the Malays and natives of any of the States of Sabah and Sarawak and the legitimate interests of other communities'. The terms 'special interests' and 'legitimate interests' have become oft-repeated catch phrases to describe the basis of government policy.

programmes, spend such government revenues and impose such quotas and other preferences in favour of the Bumiputera as it deemed advisable.

Against the background of socially motivated intervention in the economy, the NEP addressed broader questions of economic development. Most importantly, the NEP marked the abandonment of import substitution economic policies in favour of export orientation and a renewed emphasis on industrialization, particularly manufacturing, in order to provide the employment opportunities to lift Malaysians out of poverty. Under the NEP new institutions were created and existing ones were reorganized to foster industrialization. FIDA was renamed the Malaysian Industrial Development Authority (MIDA) in 1978 with a mandate that corresponded more closely to Singapore's EDB. MIDA's objectives were broadened to include the promotion of industrial investment, from both domestic and foreign sources, industrial site development, undertaking industrial feasibility studies and the making of policy recommendations to the Ministry of Trade and Industry. Other institutions included the Malaysian Industrial Development Finance Ltd (MIDF) which assisted private enterprises through the provision of medium to long term loans as well as equity investments and the Malaysian Industrial Estates Ltd, a subsidiary of MIDF, which acted as a developer of industrial estates.

Unlike Singapore, where institutions such as the EDB proved a dynamic force in Singapore's economic development from their inception, Malaysian bodies suffered initial growing pains. MIDF, for example, was criticized for lending to already solid ventures, in competition with commercial banks, instead of potentially riskier new ventures, as it was overly focused upon its financial returns. This led to a situation where not only the 'largest companies were preferred, but also that foreign companies often crowded out domestic ventures' (Spinanger 1986: 45). Whereas the EDB was praised by foreign investors as a highly effective 'one-stop shop' that worked seamlessly with other Singaporean government bodies, coordination among the Malaysian institutions and with the relevant government ministries 'was initially lacking and complaints about bureaucratic ineptitude were frequently raised' (Spinanger 1986: 47). Part of the reason may be that Malaysia attempted to copy the EDB as opposed to building MIDA, using the EDB as a precedent. The Malaysian government did not engage in the same detailed economic self-analysis as Singapore nor did it consult as widely. MIDA was also structured differently from the EDB. It was placed within the Ministry of International Trade and Investment and overseen by a board of directors with relatively little diversity.

By the end of the 1980s, the NEP's record was 'mixed' (Bruton 1992: 294). The government's immediate goal to eradicate poverty regardless of ethnicity was largely successful. Significant progress was made by 1990 that continued into the 2000s. The UNDP estimates that 49.3 per cent of all Malaysians, and close to two-thirds of Bumiputera, households lived below the poverty line in 1970. The overall poverty rate declined to 37.4 per cent by 1980, 16.5 per cent by 1990 and 5.1 per cent by 2002 while rural poverty fell from 58.6 per cent to 11.4 per cent of households over the same period (UNDP 2005). Although there are questions about the measures used by the UNDP,[6] and the UNDP (2005) acknowledges that its methodology is under review, there is little doubt that poverty levels have fallen sharply since the introduction of the NEP.

The NEP's second goal to erase the connection between ethnicity and economic activity by increasing Bumiputera participation in the economy would lead to more serious problems caused, in part, by the manner in which this objective was implemented. Bruton identifies the failure of the NEP to distinguish between inter-racial and intra-racial inequalities as the root of the NEP's implementation challenges (Bruton 1992). The wealth of Malays collectively grew through the 1970s and 1980s compared to the other ethnic groups, but income distribution amongst Malays became increasingly unequal.[7] A Malay commercial elite emerged that:

> ... profited enormously from the government program and exercised considerable influence on government policy. Rent seeking became common and complaints of favouritism and overt corruption were frequently heard. (Bruton 1992: 298)

The process is described by Hilley as the 'transfer of wealth and resources to selectively designated political-corporate elites' (2001: 59). Bruton notes that the 'granting of patronage and monopolistic practices meant that many Malay businesses were insulated from the pressures of competition' (1992: 294). The requirement that Malays own 30 per cent of the shares of most commercial enterprises was often circumvented through the use of Malay nominees as 'front-men', or 'Ali Baba corporations', to non-Malay businesses which 'promoted a rentier Malay class and did nothing to further their business skills and experience' (Bruton 1992: 294).

Apart from the social redistributive aspects of the NEP, the focus on export-oriented industrialization as a means of economic growth showed considerable, if narrow, success. The one extraordinary achievement in this area was the development of an electronics manufacturing and assembly sector in Penang and the Klang Valley which runs west from Kuala Lumpur to Port Klang. Penang stands as a model of economic and institutional development while the Klang Valley, despite its initial accomplishments, exhibits many of the challenges of poor policy execution and the conflicting goals of the NEP. The manufacturing sector's share of GDP grew over the course of the 1970s at an average annual growth rate of 10.9 to 19.1 per cent (Fong 1986), employing 15.8 per cent of the labour force in 1980, up from 9.1 per cent near the end of the 1960s. Electronics accounted for a mere 0.7 per cent of all manufactured exports in 1968 but grew to over 28 per cent in 1980, 53 per cent in 1990 and 71 per cent by 1997 (Rasiah 2002a). The

---

6   See, for example, Jayakumar (2004) who questions whether the poverty line is drawn too low by the UNDP.

7   Hilley (2001) claims that intra-racial disparities grew by 36.2 per cent among Malays from 1957–1970.

dominance of electronics manufacturing, however, serves to highlight the fact that manufacturing exports in most other sectors have been disappointing.[8]

Targeting FDI and Manufacturing – The Malaysian Electronics Industry

Initial Success – Penang and the Klang Valley   Lall suggests that electronics manufacturing, as opposed to a different manufacturing sector, was attracted to Malaysia 'more by good luck than by deliberate targeting' (2001: 339). It is true that the boom in electronics manufacturing did correspond to a time of rising wages in Singapore, Taiwan, South Korea and Japan as well as with Malaysia's efforts to broaden its education system at the primary and secondary levels thereby providing workers with the necessary skill to work for MNCs (Lall 2001). It was not luck, however, that caused MNCs to choose to locate in Malaysia especially when other countries such as Thailand and the Philippines had larger manufacturing sectors. It is more likely that the expansion of fiscal and financial incentives under the Investment Incentives Act and the roles played by MIDA and the Penang Development Corporation (PDC) proved far more important in recognizing and seizing upon investment opportunity.[9] In a survey of 121 foreign electronics firms that entered Malaysia between 1973 and 1991 'nearly all ... listed export incentives, low local wages and tax and investment incentives as being important motivating factors' (Driffield and Noor 1999: 7).

Electronics manufacturing in Malaysia dates from 1966 when Matsushita opened the first television assembly plant in the Klang Valley (Fong 1986). From there, Malaysian production initially focused upon the assembly of integrated circuits as well as consumer appliances and industrial equipment from imported components (Fong 1986). Fong describes three stages to the production of integrated circuits – mask-making; wafer fabrication; and assembling and testing – which each requiring different levels of machinery and labour intensity.

> Mask-making requires highly skilled labour and sophisticated computer-controlled equipment, and therefore can only be performed in countries endowed with such resources. Wafer fabrication is also highly equipment-intensive, and is generally undertaken in countries which have easy access to the specialized equipment needed for the process. Assembly and testing of ICs is the most

---

8   Apart from electronics, the largest manufactured exports in 1979 were metal products and food stuffs, at approximately 31 and 12 per cent, respectively. These sectors demonstrated some growth in absolute terms in the 1970s, but their contributions to exports declined in relative terms during the decade from 66 per cent in the case of metals and 18 per cent in the case of food stuffs from 1968. Aside from electronics, only the textiles sector contributed significantly more to manufactured exports at the end of the 1970s than at the beginning, growing from a little more than 1 per cent to over 7 per cent. See Rasiah (2002a).

9   Rasiah (2003b) refers to the 'exemplary roles' played by MIDA and PDC in attracting FDI in electronics manufacturing.

labour-intensive (unskilled), and is the activity most commonly undertaken in labour-surplus developing countries. (Fong 1986: 48)

Increasing levels of human capital and technology are thus needed for countries to progress from assembly and testing of integrated circuits to more sophisticated forms of electronics production (Lall 2001). Having attracted integrated circuit assembly and testing operations, Malaysia's challenge was to increase its human capital to allow it to move into higher level production functions in the sector.

It was a challenge Malaysia was able to meet initially, but has had difficulty maintaining as the complexity of manufacturing processes has grown. In his 2001 study of Malaysia, Lall noted that Malaysia had developed '[s]ignificant capabilities ... in process engineering and improvement, capital goods adaptation and manufacture, changes to product design and even some product development for mature products' (2001: 342). Furthermore, he noted that several MNCs supplying complex components for the goods produced by the first wave of MNCs to locate in Malaysia had established local operations which 'further deepened technological capabilities in Malaysia, with some spillover benefits to local firms and subcontractors' (Lall 2001: 342). Without growing its technological base further, however, Malaysia risked 'losing its place in the international production hierarchy' (Lall 2001: 344).

During the 1970s the average monthly wage in the electronics assembly firms had risen from MYR 175 at the beginning of the decade to MYR 343 (Fong 1986). Malaysia's response, in part, was to bring in cheaper, low-skilled foreign labour in order to maintain its competitive position as it suffered from growing deficits in skill and innovation stifling its ability to move into higher value-added activities. Rasiah estimates that foreign labour came to constitute 15–25 per cent of the workforce in the electronics industry and that 'sustained growth will require moving into more complex activities that can sustain high wages' (2003b: 312). Singapore was able to do so by enhancing its human capital, but 'this is where Malaysia is lagging' (Rasiah 2003b: 306–7). He argues that two issues must be addressed in order to build the necessary capacity if Malaysia wishes to 'attract FDI and benefit from the resulting agglomeration and learning economies' (Rasiah 2003b: 329). The first is the development of entrepreneurs and the second is skill formation which involves 'institutional development on a national scale' (Rasiah 2003b: 329). His approach emphasizes the critical role played by institutions in economic growth while illustrating some of Malaysia's institution building shortcomings both in the manner of their creation and in the execution of their mandates. Rasiah contrasts those efforts to those in Penang which proved to be far more successful.

In 2002, Rasiah published the findings of his comprehensive examination of the MNC-driven electronics clusters in Penang and in the Klang Valley 'where differences in systemic coordination have produced contrasting consequences' (2002b: 90). Rasiah's describes 'systemic coordination' as a melding of two approaches to human capital development (2002b). The first involves the provision of human capital through formal education at the primary, secondary and tertiary levels and 'is coordinated at the institutional level – by the Government, and private and intermediary organizations' while the 'second refers to refers to tacit and experiential knowledge acquired from learning by performing' (Rasiah 2002b: 91). It requires networks of 'inter-connected firms, institutions and other organizations' (Rasiah 2002b: 93) whose strength depends upon systemic coordination, or an established means of coordination created deliberately or through repeated patterns of conduct or a combination thereof. Rasiah concludes that:

> Ineffective federal governance of tertiary institutions of human capital constrained the first channel of human capital development throughout Malaysia. Strong systemic coordination locally helped Penang produce greater skilled, technical and entrepreneurial synergies for differentiation and division of labour. (Rasiah 2002b: 91)

The level of systemic coordination was weak within the Klang Valley. Penang was able to develop local institutions that compensated in some measure for the federal government's poor development of tertiary institutions to provide the necessary skilled human capital to allow the electronics industry to continue to grow and move away from dependence on lower wage labour whereas such was not the case in the Klang Valley.

Rasiah found that the Klang Valley quickly dissipated the initial advantages that it enjoyed over Penang such as the investment by Matsushita in 1966 and the presence of Kuala Lumpur and the head office of MIDA within the district. The Selangor government failed to compensate for the deficiencies of the federal government in manpower training. Despite the presence of more than eight public and private universities in 2000 it still faced 'severe demand-supply deficits involving engineers and technicians' (Rasiah 2002b: 113). He places much of the blame for poor systemic coordination on a lack both of institutions to facilitate communication and the poor quality of the local institutions charged with industrial development. Rasiah notes that the Selangor State Economic Development Council (SEDC) 'hardly gathered and disseminated information, matched firms and mediated technology and skills development, or R & D activities' (2002b: 113). In contrast to Singapore's EDB or the PDC, Rasiah quotes an SEDC official as stating: 'We take potential inventors [sic] around to show what Selangor has to offer, allocate land and facilitate the starting of the factories. Our tasks end the moment firms start their factories' (2002b: 114).

Penang's Continued Success – The Nathan Report and Institutional Development Penang has no control over tertiary education in the state, but it has improved its human capital through local institutions that have attracted FDI to the electronics manufacturing field and has taken advantage of that investment through concerted planning and focused implementation of its policies. As a result, according to Rasiah:

> Penang has developed systemic coordination and network cohesion to support
> flexibility and inter-firm technological interface. TNCs in Penang enjoy strong
> linkages with local firms and better coordination with support institutions.
> (2002b: 102)

Penang in the mid-1960s was in economic decline. Its importance as a
port had been eroded by the shift of trade to Port Klang. It was 'besieged by
depression, spiralling inflation, labour unrest and political instability' (Rasiah
1996: 189). Unemployment hovered around 15 per cent and 'Penang was in such
a chronic depression that some circles referred to the state as a "dying fishing
village"' (Singh 1975: 270). Within this context, an American firm of consulting
economists, Robert R. Nathan Associates, was engaged by the Penang Master Plan
Committee to devise a strategy to revive the Penang economy. Delivered in March
1970, the report (the Nathan Report) was enthusiastically adopted by the newly
elected government which made the report 'an integral part of its development
plan' (Rasiah 1996: 189). In particular, it seized upon the opportunity to create
Malaysia's first free trade zone at Bayan Lepas in 1972, shortly after the enactment
of the federal Free Trade Act, 1971 (Ismail 1999).

The Nathan Report recognized that in terms of natural resources, Penang was
the 'least favourably endowed of the States of Malaysia' (Nathan et al. 1970:
1). Its economic growth lagged Peninsular Malaysia in almost all respects in
the 1960s other than in trade, transportation and communications owing to its
historical importance as an entrepôt. Manufacturing provided approximately ten
per cent of employment in Penang. Penang's share of Malaysian manufacturing
determined by gross sales hovered around the same figure (Nathan et al. 1970).
Its greatest asset, the Nathan Report (1970) argued, lay in its workforce, which
was young and close to universally literate providing the base for a programme to
accelerate economic growth. A key goal of the proposed economic development
plan would be to change negative attitudes towards factory employment and to
create opportunities in industries with broader markets (Nathan et al. 1970). In
particular, Penang needed to attract industries using labour intensive technologies
such as those using Malaysian raw materials such as rubber and wood (Nathan et
al. 1970). Electronics was not mentioned in the Nathan Report.

The report does devote considerable attention, however, to the quality and
importance of Penang's infrastructure, particularly its institutional infrastructure
as a potential driver of economic growth. It discusses Penang's industrial
infrastructure, such as transportation, communications and electricity, and its
social infrastructure, such as housing, schools, shopping and recreational facilities,
but in language startlingly similar to that used by North and Putnam twenty
years later, it devotes its greatest attention to Penang's institutional infrastructure
'through which the complex relationships that characterize a modern society
are coordinated' (Nathan et al. 1970: 10). Together, the industrial, social and
institutional infrastructure comprise 'the accumulated stock of social capital –
tangible and intangible – which serves as a factor in the production of goods and

services' (Nathan et al. 1970: 10). In addition to the legal system, the Nathan Report views institutional infrastructure as including 'a number of private and Governmental bodies concerned with commercial matters and economic policies and programmes' (1970: 21).

The Nathan Report acknowledges that the nature of Malaysian federalism is such that most economic planning and development powers are vested in the federal government leaving the state government's role greatly circumscribed. Hence, it argues, the need for local 'institutional infrastructure for coordination of development policies and implementation of programmes is critical' (Nathan et al. 1970: 24). The existing institutional infrastructure, however, was inadequate as it provided 'little or no opportunity for private sector participation in the planning and implementation of development programmes' despite the private sector being the primary source of 'the capital, managerial talent and direction required for economic development in Penang' (Nathan et al. 1970: 25). Consequently, the Nathan Report recommended the creation of three semi-autonomous development organizations concerned with land development, tourism and industrial promotion, responsible only to the State Government. The creation of an additional body, a Development Planning Council, comprised of State Officials and the heads of the three semiautonomous development organizations was also recommended. It was anticipated that the government would 'delegate the responsibility for preparing comprehensive, overall development plans' (Nathan et al. 1970: 95) to the new organization. The Council would also be the legal authority for the development of physical sites, similar to the initial responsibility of Singapore's EDB for the development of industrial estates.

The PDC, like its counterpart, the EDB, came into existence prior to the final report recommending its creation was submitted. Established in 1969, Rasiah argues that the PDC played a 'pivotal' (Rasiah 2003b: 104) role in Penang's economic development and that it and MIDA played 'exemplary roles' (Rasiah 2003a: 315) in attracting FDI to export-oriented manufacturing industries in Penang. While its role is similar to the EDB, it operates within a much smaller scope for action as the State of Penang's powers are greatly restricted in its ability to formulate economic policy, enact laws and implement them. Its success has been in building relationships between the state government and investors and between investors. Unlike in the Klang Valley, the PDC views its mandate as continuing subsequent to an investor's facility beginning operation. This has led to the growth of vertical and horizontal linkages between MNCs and local entrepreneurs. Where 'strong integrated business networks emerged, as in Penang, MNC activity led to considerable local sourcing' (Rasiah 2003a: 314).

Within the realm of its limited powers, the PDC has endeavoured to improve the quality of the human capital available in Penang. While it could not alter the availability or quality of tertiary education, it has focused upon the provision of manpower training programmes through close coordination with manufacturers to complement the in-house programmes provided by MNCs and to ensure that its programmes met local needs. In 1989, it spun out its training division as the Penang Skills Development Centre (PSDC). The PSDC's success can be attributed, in part, to the abilities of its CEO, Boonler Somchit, who has led the organization since its inception, and to its structure which seeks input from a wide range of interested parties. Its Management Council consists of 15 representatives of local businesses, mostly MNCs in electronics manufacturing[10] together with ex-officio members from State Government, PDC, the Small & Medium Industries Development Corporation and the Universiti Sains Malaysia. Yusuf and Nabeshima (2009b) state:

> One outstanding success story associated with the development of the electronics industry is the Penang Skills Development Centre (PSDC), which has become a world-class training center. (108)

Rasiah notes attempts were made to copy the PSDC's success in the Klang Valley through the establishment of the Selangor Human Resources Development Center in 1992, but it has failed to stimulate off-site training among MNCs in the Klang Valley due to its inability to build relationships between government and the business and academic communities (Rasiah 2003b).

Vision 2020 – Pursuing a Knowledge-Based Economy

By the 1990s, the forces of global economic integration and the spread of ICT caused Malaysia to re-evaluate its economic strategy. While Malaysia was able to increase significantly its wealth over the course of the NEP from per capita GDP of US $468 in 1970 to $4,100 in 1990 (Heston et al. 2011), Malaysians were concerned that their climb up the economic ladder faced increasing challenges as ICT's economic importance grew. At the inaugural meeting of the Malaysian Business Council on February 28, 1991, then Prime Minister Mahathir presented his view of Malaysia's future development path. Vision 2020, as it became commonly known, established the goal of creating 'a Malaysia that is a fully developed country by the year 2020' (Mahathir 1991: 1). The conceptual themes underlying Vision 2020 found further expression in the official ten year Second Outline Perspective Plan that proclaimed a New Development Plan (the NDP), marking the formal end of the NEP.

In order to achieve its ambitious economic goals, Vision 2020 acknowledged that Malaysian GDP would need to grow at an average rate of seven per cent annually for thirty consecutive years (Mahathir 1991).[11] Such growth would be achieved through greater industrialization and technological proficiency whereby the economy would be 'increasingly technology-intensive, moving in the direction

---

10   As at 15 April 2012, Management Council members included top management from Agilent Technologies, Intel, Motorola, Bosch, Seagate and Osram (http://www.psdc.org.my/html/default.aspx?ID=9&PID=42).

11   See also Sheriff (1993).

of higher and higher levels of technology' (Mahathir 1991: 71). It was not until 1996, when the creation of the Multimedia Super Corridor, recently renamed MSC Malaysia, (the MSC) was announced, that a more substantive change in economic policy was contemplated. The MSC would lead the transformation of the economy to one that was knowledge-based, incorporating ICT throughout Malaysian society. Two years after its unveiling, Mahathir described the MSC as follows:

> The MSC is a giant test-bed for experimenting with not only multimedia technology, but also, and more importantly, the evolution of a new way of life in the unfolding age of information and knowledge. The MSC is, therefore, 'Malaysia's gift to the world', a creation that welcomes the involvement of the global community in sharing the useful lessons of multimedia development. (Mahathir 1998: 7)

Putting aside the hyperbole, the MSC was presented by the government as a transformational undertaking that would drive Malaysia's economic growth to the level of the world's most prosperous nations. Given that manufacturing's contribution to GDP was expected to 'peak at around 38 per cent by the year 2005' (Mahathir 1998: 8) another source of growth would have to be found. Having 'put our finger on the pulse of the forces that will shape the socio-economic tapestry of the future' Mahathir proclaimed that ICT would become 'the engine of growth in all economic sectors' (1998: 9).

The MSC's genesis can be found in a confidential mid-1990's McKinsey & Co. study commissioned by the Malaysian government to provide a comprehensive plan to turn Malaysia into a Southeast Asian centre of ICT research, development and production. The result, the MSC, was an ambitious attempt by the Malaysian government to create a greenfield ICT industry, literally turning a fifteen by fifty kilometre strip of mostly palm oil plantations into an ICT-intensive oasis, incorporating a new administrative capital, Putrajaya, and a small city, Cyberjaya, to serve as the ICT industry's epicentre. The corridor is anchored by a new international airport at one end and the Petronas twin towers in the heart of Kuala Lumpur at the other end.

In the late 1990s the Malaysian Parliament began to adopt a variety of laws, notably those relating to electronic signatures and intellectual property rights that were then at the forefront of the ICT field. Four MSC 'flagship applications' were announced, such as paperless government and telemedicine, to provide Malaysia with state-of-the-art services and purchasers for the products that would be developed. A venture capital arm was established and companies that qualified for 'MSC status' due to the nature of their activities wishing to locate in the corridor would be eligible for tax breaks and concessions on a variety of matters such as import duties and visas for 'knowledge workers'.

> MSC Malaysia's vision is to transform the nation into a knowledge based economy driven by a knowledge society. With this commitment, MSC Malaysia

is determined to spearhead this transformation through ICT via industry and
capacity building and socio economic development. (Multimedia Super Corridor
Malaysia)

By the mid-2000s it became clear that neither the NDP nor the MSC would
transform Malaysia into a knowledge-based economy and that ICT would not
become an engine of economic growth. McKinsey & Co., which wrote the
confidential blueprint for the MSC, was quoted in 2001 as citing key gaps, such
as a lack of world class telecommunications infrastructure in attracting large and
innovative operations to the MSC facilitating wealth and knowledge transfers to
the broader economy (Low 2001; Chen 2001).

   The MSC has failed to generate much economic activity by itself or act as a
catalyst for ICT adoption or economic transformation elsewhere in the economy.
Its boast of MYR5 billion in annual ICT exports and 63,000 knowledge workers
in 2008 (Multimedia Super Corridor Malaysia), even if taken at face value, as
it is not clear how the figures were derived, represent only 0.75 per cent of all
Malaysian exports (Treasury Department Economic Report 2008/2009) and 0.50
per cent of the labour force (Malaysia External Trade Development Corporation).
More important is the apparent lack of integration of the MSC, in particular, or
ICT more generally, into other sectors of the Malaysian economy judging by
Malaysia's relatively poor standing in most measures of ICT adoption. As the
Ninth Malaysia Plan acknowledged: '... with regard to content development and
the extent of cutting edge products and services, these have yet to reach expected
levels' (Government of Malaysia 2006: 146). The MSC's current focus now seems
restricted to software development which remains a very small niche industry
within the Malaysian economy (Government of Malaysia 2010).

Education and Human Capital

Building Primary and Secondary Schooling

As with economic development, which was guided by the twin objectives of
eliminating poverty and the identification of ethnicity with economic function,
education policy has attempted to balance two goals: the promotion of the social
and economic status of Malays throughout Malaysian society and Bhasa Malay as
the national language; and the creation of a system that provides the best education
possible to all students regardless of ethnicity (Azmi 2000). Despite huge efforts
and significant resources being devoted to education by successive Malaysian
governments, the lack of human capital is the most often cited impediment to
continued economic expansion. The achievement of the social aims of the NEP
and the educational reform it engendered have resulted in many Malaysians,
particularly Malays, receiving an education denied to their parents, but one that

does not provide them with the skills Malaysia needs to maintain its upward economic trajectory.

Formal education in Malaysia is a matter of exclusive federal jurisdiction. The States may provide manpower training, but primary, secondary and tertiary schooling are the responsibility of the central government. At independence there was no national, standardized, publically funded system of education. Schooling at the primary and secondary levels was available in English, Malay, Tamil and a variety of Chinese dialects, but only the English language stream, modelled on the English grammar school system, provided a pathway to higher education, the professions and economic and political leadership (Azmi 2000). Attendance was not compulsory. The main campus of the University of Malaya, an English language institution, was located in Singapore.

The new Malayan government's initial education reforms were guided by a 1955 report prepared by Abdul Razak, the country's first education minister and eventual prime minister. Designed to promote national unity and to provide a 'Malaysian outlook and an intensely Malaysian curriculum' (Azmi 2000: 115), the reforms led to the enactment of the Education Act in 1961 under which free primary education, with a common curriculum, in each of the four main languages would be available to all children beginning with the 1962 school year. Bhasa Malay and English were compulsory subjects in all schools. The government also pledged to provide funding for Bhasa Malay and, until 1967 as required under the constitution, English secondary schools. Thereafter, publically funded English secondary education would be phased out.

Malaysian efforts to promote basic education proved very successful, following the model advocated in Chapter 5 of building the system systematically from the ground up (de Ferranti 2003). By 1968, primary school enrolment had increased by 60 per cent. By 1980 over 90 per cent of Malaysians of the relevant age group had completed primary school and by 2005, that figure had climbed to 98 per cent (UNESCO Institute for Statistics 2005). The literacy rate rose to 60 per cent in 1975 from 53 per cent at the beginning of the 1960s, growing steadily into the 2000s when close to universal literacy was attained (Gan 1995). The push to educate Malaysians then reached beyond primary school into the secondary level. By the late 1960s, the 'total enrolment rate in secondary schools [had] increased by a factor of more than 5' (Gan 1995: 169). The greatest increase was in the Bhasa Malay secondary schools where enrolment leaped by a factor of 45, which serves to underscore how few Malays attended secondary school during colonial rule (Bruton 1992). After the initial surge, secondary school enrolment climbed steadily from 34 per cent of the cohort in 1970 to 69 per cent in 2005 (Beyond 20/20 WDS: Key Statistical Tables on Education), a large increase, but one which still leaves room for significant improvement (Gan 1995). In particular, the aggregate graduation rate indicates that the drop-off between lower secondary school graduates and upper secondary school is fairly steep. Nearly 93 per cent of the cohort graduated from lower secondary school, but only 70 per cent completed an upper secondary course of study and only 15 per cent obtained secondary school diplomas in courses of study that would allow them to pursue tertiary level studies that could lead to a degree, the second lowest among the nations studied according to UNESCO's 2005 review of world education indicators in nineteen middle income countries. Malays, however, have caught up to the other ethnic groups in Malaysia in terms of the number of years of schooling they attain.[12]

Challenges in Meeting the Educational Needs of a Knowledge Economy

The announcement of Vision 2020 followed by the creation of the MSC required a critical re-evaluation of education in Malaysia in order to meet the goal of turning Malaysia into a knowledge-based economy. Its manufacturing sector, especially its electronics industry, had continued to expand its contribution to GDP throughout the 1980s, providing jobs for Malaysians. The quality of those jobs, however, began to stagnate as rising wages and changing technology threatened the sector's continued prosperity. Vision 2020 anticipated the levelling off and decline of the sector's contribution and pointed at ICT usage and production as the means to offset such losses. More Malaysians would thus require more education, particularly in engineering and the sciences at the tertiary level, in order to accomplish the desired transformation of the Malaysian economy.

Under the *Seventh Malaysia Plan*, beginning in 1996, the budgetary allocation for education grew to 15.4 per cent of all public development expenditures of which approximately 81 per cent of the education budget was to be used to increase capacity at the primary, secondary and tertiary levels and 78 per cent of the training budget was allocated towards establishing new training institutes and upgrading and expanding existing ones. Over 140 new primary schools were built and in excess of 3,000 more classrooms were added at the secondary level to overcome crowding. Computer accessibility at both the primary and secondary level increased and secondary vocational schools were converted into technical schools with a revised curriculum that stressed skill acquisition over specific job training (Malaysian Communications and Multimedia Commission 2002).

The Education Act and the Universities and University College Act were amended, new statutes including the Private Higher Education Institutions Act and the National Accreditation Board Act were passed and bodies such as the National Council on Higher Education and the National Higher Education Fund were created (Azmi 2000). Privately owned universities would receive accreditation and foreign universities were given permission to open branch campuses. Telekom Malaysia, Tenaga Nasional (the National Electricity Company) and Petronas

---

12   In 1970, Malays constituted merely 51 per cent of the Lower Secondary graduates and 49 per cent of the Upper Secondary graduates. Only 43 per cent of those with some post-secondary education and 40 per cent of tertiary degree holders were Malay. By 1980, Malays had risen to 60 per cent of Lower Secondary graduates and 66 per cent of Upper Secondary graduates, figures that more closely reflected the ethnic composition of Malaysia and which have remained relatively stable since. See Gan (1995).

all own universities and the University of Nottingham, England and Monash University, Australia have created campuses in Malaysia.

As a consequence, within a very short time, tertiary enrolment boomed, growing from approximately 76,000 enrolled in university degree courses in 1995 to 171,000 in 2000 with the number of science and technology students growing from 40.7 per cent of those enrolled in 1995 to 52 per cent in 2000 (Malaysian Communications and Multimedia Commission 2002). A similar trend occurred amongst those studying for certificates and diplomas at the tertiary level as enrolment increased from 13,500 to 28,100. By 2005, the *Ninth Malaysia Plan* reported that the number of first degree candidates had risen to over 212,000 in public universities plus an additional 110,000 in private universities and by 2010, the *Tenth Malaysia Plan* reported that the number had risen to 272,012 in public universities and 206,209 in private universities (Government of Malaysia 2010).

Malaysia's Institute of Strategic and International Studies (ISIS) released a study in 2002 titled *Knowledge-Based Economy Master Plan* (the 'Master Plan'), the importance of which was underscored by the introduction written by Prime Minister Mahathir. Particularly worrying to ISIS was the quality of the education delivered by the Malaysian school system. It highlighted several areas where the development of the human capital needed for a knowledge-economy in Malaysia was lagging. In particular, ISIS found that 'Malaysia has still some scope for improvement' (2002: 33) with regard to enrolment rates, investment in education, access and participation at the tertiary level and teacher education and conditions where Malaysian efforts almost universally lagged those of the more economically developed countries. ISIS stressed that although Malaysia had achieved significant quantitative success at educating its people compared to previously it 'must now focus on achieving qualitative improvements at the primary, secondary, and tertiary levels' (2002: 31).

ISIS felt the qualitative problems resulted from poorly trained teachers, little incentive for young people to pursue teaching careers due to low salaries, uncertain career paths and heavy workloads as well as with the curriculum itself in terms of content and implementation. Quality issues were apparent at both the secondary and tertiary levels. For a country determined to participate in the knowledge economy, access to ICT at the secondary level posed a special concern. ISIS cited shortcomings in co-ordination among agencies responsible for supporting ICT education programmes and research and development, an issue also noted by Lall (2001), poor training of teachers in the optimal use of computers as a teaching tool, inadequate computer time for students and an over-investment in hardware at the expense of software development for courses and 'peopleware (training)' (ISIS 2002: 46). These shortcoming had led to a harmful brain drain of science and engineering graduates.

At least 50,000 professional and technical personnel have migrated to Singapore, Australia, New Zealand, US, Canada and Europe over the last 15 years. Currently between 500 to 1,000 Malaysians work for high-tech US firms in the Silicon Valley area alone. An estimated 51 per cent of foreign IT workers in Singapore are Malaysian nationals. The over 100,000 Malaysian students overseas are another source of potential out-migration. (ISIS 2002: 45)

Rasiah has repeatedly argued in the same vein as ISIS. He has noted that 'sustained growth will require moving into more complex activities that can sustain high wages, design, development and innovation' (Rasiah 2003b: 306). Doing so will require 'strenuous efforts to raise human capital—this is where Malaysia is lagging' (Rasiah 2003b: 307). Firms complain that the lack of skilled labour is their most significant constraint (Wee 2003). While the number of tertiary graduates with science, technology and engineering specialties has undoubtedly grown in number through the 1990s and 2000s, Rasiah concurs with ISIS that the aggregate numbers of university and technical college graduates trails behind many of Malaysia's Asian competitors and is far below those countries Malaysia wishes to catch up with economically by 2020 (Lall 2001; Rasiah 2002b, 2003b).

Conflicting Goals

The roots of the human capital deficiency can be traced to the transformation of the Malaysian economy beginning with its industrialization in the late 1960s and the introduction of the NEP in the early 1970s. Success of the government's social restructuring plans came initially to depend heavily on the success of manufacturing. The government increased spending on education in order to facilitate rural Malays moving into the 'labour-intensive and low-technology industries' (Gan 1995: 171) that had been attracted to Malaysia. These new industries required a disciplined, reliable, literate workforce with a basic education that could be easily trained to carry out relatively simple, repetitive tasks.

Bruton was early to recognize the dilemma faced by Malaysian educators as they strove to improve the well-being of the rural Malay (Bruton 1992). They had to contend with the fact that 'schools in rural Malaysia in particular were historically rote-learning institutions' (Bruton 1992: 250). Schooling became to be viewed by many as merely a means to a defined outcome, namely a job. Improved educational opportunities were greeted warmly by the rural Malays, but the expectation was that schooling would lead to a specific end that would prove more profitable for their children than remaining in subsistence agriculture. The onus was viewed as being upon the government to ensure that an appropriate job was available to those who achieved a certain level of schooling. This led to a further emphasis upon rote learning, memorization and repetition. The student would attend school to receive ready-made answers to a set of specific questions and could then be certified as qualified and entitled to a specific job with salary and social position (Bruton 1992). In Bruton's view, most Malays in university were enrolled in fields that led them to anticipate government jobs upon graduation. The government obliged as 'the number in government service jumped from 397,000 in 1970 to 710,000 in 1980' (Bruton 1992: 249–50). Bruton further argued that the rapid expansion of tertiary institutions beginning in the 1980s resulted in immediate signs of dilution of their quality:

> ... education as a claim to 'be something' rather than as a preparation to 'do something' continued in evidence. It is also undoubtedly correct to say that the quality of education fell at all levels as enrolments increased, although expenditures rose sharply. Many observers seem to think that, at least at the university level, quality suffered as entrance requirements were lowered and more students were admitted from rural areas, where elementary schools were usually of lower quality. So the best (and wealthiest) students went abroad. All of this meant that the educated product probably deteriorated over the decade, and firms seeking to hire Bumiputera were often disappointed in their capacity. (Bruton 1992: 249–50)

In 2005, Francis Loh expressed serious concern about the deterioration of Malaysian universities in response to the fall of the University of Malaya's ranking in the QS-Times world university survey from 89th to 169th. In his view, the rapid expansion of Malaysian universities came at the price of academic standards in two ways. First, Malaysia could not recruit a sufficient number of qualified academics to teach at its universities and, second, the academic culture which values research and teaching was replaced with a 'hybrid of corporate and bureaucratic culture' (Loh 2005: 1) that was over-focused upon raising money for the university and had reduced the role of professors in determining their direction. This, Loh argued, led to a loss of senior faculty to the private sector, foreign universities and international organizations. He noted that the attrition rate among senior faculty where he taught, the Universiti Sains Malaysia, had grown from 7 per cent in 1990 to 27 per cent per year in 2000. Other factors cited included government interference in the administration of universities and inadequately prepared students who had achieved high marks through grade inflation, but were unable to embark upon independent research.

If university rankings have merit, then Loh would be further distressed by more recent results. The University of Malaya ranked 207th according to the 2010 QS ranking of global universities, recovering in 2012 to 156th, and only three other Malaysian universities rank in the top 400 (QS World University Rankings 2012). Malaysian universities fare even worse in the Shanghai Jiao Tong University Academic Ranking of World Universities. Its 2012 survey did not rank any Malaysian universities among the top 500 globally or top 100 within Asia (ARWU 2012).

Loh had picked up on the challenges cited by Lee in her 1999 review of public primary and secondary education in Malaysia. She viewed as problematic the 'highly centralized and bureaucratic system where most of the important policy decision-making occurred outside the schools' (N.N. Lee 1999: 89). Historically, she argued, the Ministry of Education took a very top-down approach to school reform without undertaking a consultative process with local administrators, teachers or parents. Attempts at decentralization and the provision of greater autonomy to local authorities and teachers, 'seemed to be shackled by the traditional practice of waiting for directives from the top rather than making independent decisions' (N.N. Lee 1999: 92). Local administrators and teachers wished to 'avoid the risk of being accused of doing something wrong' and thus became 'unresourceful and over-dependent on the ministry's directives and handouts' (N.N. Lee 1999: 92). The attitude was reflected in the classroom as she, like Bruton, noted that the 'over-emphasis on public examination results have resulted in certain teaching-learning strategies such as rote-learning and spoon-feeding' (N.N. Lee 1999: 92).

Brown, in his 2007 review of the history of ethnic tension surrounding the Malaysian education system, blames political and social-engineering goals for the deterioration of the Malaysian education system. He argues they have come to play a significant role in primary and secondary school where students 'are encouraged to participate in the Malaysian nation uncritically through the virtual worship of development symbols and unquestioning deference to political leadership' (Brown 2007: 319). At the university level, Brown maintains, the system is used 'as a tool for the promotion of ethnic Malay interests' and has discriminated against non-Malays (2007: 318). Lee (1999) concurs that the desire to improve Malay access to university, particularly those from rural Malaysia, resulted in quotas, special assistance and financial aid to Malays that was unavailable to others. Brown (2007) notes that between 1980 and 1984, Bumiputera students were awarded over 95 per cent of government grants to study overseas. In 2001, he argues further, 560 top scorers on the examination used to determine admission to university were denied places. All were ethnic Chinese who have likely pursued their education elsewhere (Brown 2007). Malaysian policies may thus be pushing some of their best students out the country, as ISIS indirectly suggested in the Master Plan discussion of the number of science and engineering professionals working abroad, at the very time they are needed the most at home.

Infrastructure and ICT

Malaysia was slow to establish an independent regulator and, once established, its independence was not statutorily secured. The governing legislation permits the Minister responsible for telecommunications to hover like a 'Sword of Damocles' above the regulator, ready to override its authority at any time. Prior to the appointment of an independent regulator, political considerations played a significant role in the granting of licences with decisions being made by Cabinet, not by the regulator. Since the creation of the regulator further market liberalization has proceeded slowly. The quality of Malaysia's ICT infrastructure outside major urban areas and ICT penetration rates lag behind those of its neighbours. While there does not appear to be any empirical work that demonstrates directly that the structure of telecommunications regulation in Malaysia has led to the deficiencies in ICT usage, given the experience elsewhere it is likely that it is at least a contributing factor. Historically, telecommunications regulation in Malaysia has demonstrated few of the desirable attributes of an independent regulator in structure or functioning as described in the ITU Toolkit discussed in Chapter 5.

Early Telecommunications Service

Prior to independence, telecommunications services throughout the Malayan Peninsula were a monopoly of the Department of Telecommunications. The government monopoly continued after independence and following various ministerial reorganizations was ultimately held by Jabatan Telekomunikasi Malaysia (JTM), an agency under the Ministry of Energy, Telecommunications and Posts. JTM also acted as the telecommunications regulator, a common situation where the government enjoyed a telecommunications monopoly. Decisions regarding the granting of licences were made by the Ministry itself.

The Malaysian government began to reform the telecommunications sector in the early 1980s. It first allowed the private sector to sell terminal equipment in 1983 thereby ending JTM's monopoly. Competition was permitted in value-added network services in 1984, radio paging in 1985 and mobile cellular services in 1988 (C. Lee 2004). The Telecommunications Services Act, 1985 modified the legislation governing telecommunications for the first time since 1950 bringing changes to the structure of the industry effective January 1, 1987. JTM was split in two, with Syarikat Telekom Malaysia (STM) taking over the service operations and 98 per cent of the staff from JTM, which remained the telecommunications regulator and an agency of the Ministry (Painter and Wong 2006). STM was corporatized upon its spin-off and 20 per cent of its equity was sold to the public in 1990, at which time it gained a stock exchange listing and was renamed Telekom Malaysia Berhad (TMB).

Sectoral Reform

Consistent with the goals of increasing Malay participation in the economy under the NEP, the privatization of JTM and opening of the telecommunications sector represented an opportunity to increase Malay ownership of the sector. 'Thus, reforms that were carried out in Malaysia had both efficiency and equity considerations. It is difficult to ascertain the extent of conflict between these two objectives' (C. Lee 2004: 120). Licences were granted for paging, cellular telephones, satellite communications, value-added services and fixed-line networks upon the termination of TMB's monopoly in the 1990s. The manner in which such licenses were awarded, however, was criticized as 'opaque ... so much so that the ... Director General of [JTM] ... was not always informed until after the event' (Ure 2008: 286). Salazar (2007) maintains that the awarding of licences was decided on political grounds by the Cabinet, while Ure, in his 2008 review of the telecommunications sector in Malaysia, states:

> Requests for licences frequently bypassed the JTM, going directly to the Prime
> Minister's Office and notable political allies and personal associates of UNMO's
> [sic] leadership were successful. (286)[13]

As Ure recounts, and Salazar describes in great detail, the opening up of the
telecommunications industry 'fell prey to widespread "crony capitalism"' (Ure
2008: 285) whereby licence recipients for mobile cellular service, satellite
communications including television broadcasting and basic network services,
were closely linked to the country's most senior politicians, almost none of whom
had any experience in the sector (Ure 2008: 285; Salazar 2007: 161–2). Painter
and Wong in their 2006 review of regulatory reform in Thailand and Malaysia
portray the privatization process as 'an instrument of political patronage for
UMNO' (31). TMB's first direct competition in 1993, for example, came from
Time Communications, a unit of the industrial conglomerate, the Renong Group,
which is controlled by UMNO (Ure 2008). The fixed-line market continues to be
dominated by these two companies with TMB controlling approximately 95 per
cent of the market and Time the remainder.

> In sum, the first phase of the liberalization of the telecoms industry in Malaysia
> was about dividing up the spoils and positioning the winner—all of them
> well-connected with the UMNO political elite—to reap the benefits. License
> decisions were made by cabinet, and were inextricable from a series of intricate,
> politically-inspired deals over ownership and control. Only later did the basic
> elements of a pro-competitive set of regulations begin to develop. (Painter and
> Wong 2006: 31–2)

In 1994, the government released a National Telecommunications Policy (the
NTP) ostensibly revealing a path for ICT development that would contribute to
the achievement of Vision 2020. The NTP's primary goal, as with every other
aspect of government policy, was 'national unity and integration by encouraging
interaction between the races and regions through telecommunication facilities and
services' (Government of Malaysia 1994a: 2–3). Under the NTP, the Government
of Malaysia (1994a) would encourage competition in the telecommunications
sector between both participants and technologies in all segments of the industry.
There would be particular support of the 'aspirations of Bumiputera entrepreneurs
to participate actively in the telecommunications sector' (Government of Malaysia
1994a: 7). The NTP is long on statements of principle and short on specifics
making it difficult to discern how the enunciated policy would differ from the
government's previous practice. Salazar (2007) notes that by 1995, the year after
the announcement of the NTP, licences had been granted for seven basic network
providers, seven cellular systems and five international gateway facilities, a very

---

13   For a detailed description of the awardees of licences and their relationship to the
government see Salazar (2007).

large number given the size of the Malaysian market. The licensees were connected to the government and all but one of the licences had been issued prior to the announcement of the NTP, suggesting that the NTP served as an *ex post facto* rationalization of a scheme to provide economic benefit to cronies rather than a liberalization of the telecommunications market for the benefit of Malaysians.[14]

The Communications and Multimedia Commission – Independent Regulation, Legislative Overhang

Telecommunications legislation was again completely overhauled in November 1998 with the passage of the Communications and Multimedia Act (the CMA) and an Act creating a new regulator, the Malaysian Communications and Multimedia Commission (the CMC) which would begin to function in April 1999 as part of the flurry of legislation stimulated by the creation of the MSC. Despite the apparent independence and broad powers granted to the CMC, the CMA vests the Minister responsible for the Act with an almost unfettered ability to intervene in any matter within the CMC's jurisdiction through any one of Ministerial Directions, Determinations, Declarations and Regulations, as appropriate.[15] Appeals from regulatory decisions were allowed for the first time through the creation of an Appeal Tribunal which the Minister may establish 'on an *ad hoc* basis, as the Minister considers necessary or expedient' (CMA, s. 17(1)). Subject to the right of the Minister to exercise his discretion to intervene in any matter, however, the CMA grants to the CMC the necessary authority and independence to regulate the telecommunications market.

Since its creation, the CMC has used its powers to consult with interested parties and the public on regulatory matters. 'Typically, discussion papers are published on the internet and the industry is invited to submit their views within a

---

14 'The NTP seemed to be an afterthought. One senior former Telekom official described it as an "act of trying to correct faults of what has been done, rather than a policy statement of the way forward."' (Salazar 2007: 161)

15 See Communications and Multimedia Act, Part 1, Chapters 1, 2, 3 and 4, respectively. The Ministerial Direction provisions permit the Minister to 'issue directions to the Commission on the exercise of [its] powers and the performance of [its] functions and duties under this Act' of a general or specific nature. A Ministerial Determination allows the Minister to 'determine any matter specified in this Act as being subject to Ministerial determination, without consultation with any licensees or persons.' Pursuant to a Ministerial Declaration, the Minister may alter the terms of an individual licence or a class of individual licences in such manner as he deems fit although, unlike a Determination, the CMA does provide for notice to be given to those affected by a proposed Declaration and for them to respond as well as for the CMC to make recommendations to the Minister. The Minister may also make Regulations on a wide variety of matters such as those pertaining to the CMC's procedures, procedures for the use of network facilities, the compounding of penalties and 'any matter for which this Act makes express provision' as well as 'such other matters as are necessary for giving full effect to the provisions of this Act'.

given period (at least 45 days)' (C. Lee 2004: 129). The CMC has also established consultative bodies, known as industry forums, to provide input on issues such as content and consumer rights and protection. By the mid-2000s the Consumer Forum had grown to 48 members including telecommunications providers, non-governmental organizations and public interest groups that oversee the handling of consumer complaints (Painter and Wong 2006). It has tried to stimulate competition and increased service provision and offerings where possible by, for example, granting 12 licences allowing new entrants to provide wireless local loops to office buildings, shopping malls, apartments and college campuses (Ure 2008). Being an entity apart from the Ministry has provided the CMC with greater flexibility in its hiring practices and, within its budget, remuneration allowing it to attract qualified employees from outside the civil service.

So long as the CMC is left to its own devices, it appears to operate in a fairly transparent fashion and enjoys a large degree of independence consistent with the recommendations of the ITU Toolkit. It is not clear, however, how the knowledge of the overhanging Ministerial power stifles the manner in which the CMC undertakes its responsibilities. Ure summarized the CMC's on-going challenges as follows:

> The major difficulty facing the MCMC is that after 20 years of 'managed market reform' only the cellular market is fully competitive while the state remains financially involved in the fixed-line market, which inevitably politicizes policy decisions. For example, the MCMC's proposal to unbundle state majority-owned Telekom Malaysia's network to encourage broadband services competition was apparently over-ruled by the government at the last moment in December 2006. (Ure 2008: 288)

Like Singapore's IDA, part of the CMC's mandate includes the primary responsibility to promote universal access and equity throughout Malaysia to 'ensure an equitable provision of affordable services [sic] over ubiquitous national infrastructure' (Malaysian Communications and Multimedia Commission 2002: 19). Its efforts to promote cellular coverage, the sector with the greatest competition, have proven successful with close to all populated areas now being covered and a relatively high penetration rate. The CMC has been much less successful elsewhere although it is questionable whether the government has provided it with the tools necessary to fulfil its mandate. The promotion of universal broadband service, for example, has proven problematic despite its importance. In Ure's view the problem is simple: 'For as long as Telekom retains an effective monopoly in the fixed-line business, Malaysia will continue to fall behind other countries in the provision of broadband' (2008: 294).

The Middle Income Trap

Malaysia has risen from being a poor country in the early 1960s to one that is solidly middle income. Extreme poverty has been reduced to very low levels, literacy rates are high and the economy has been transformed from one where tin mining, rubber production and subsistence farming predominated to one with a vibrant electronics manufacturing industry and a growing services sector. Malaysians can be proud of their country's accomplishments and, despite the inevitable comparisons to Singapore, Malaysian growth stands as a model for many countries that have not been able to sustain economic growth over the same period. Yet, there is a growing concern that Malaysia's standard of living has reached a plateau from which it if unable to progress further.

Prime Minister Najib (2009) made the middle income trap a recurring topic of his speeches subsequent to becoming Prime Minister in April 2009 and it provides an underlying theme to the *Tenth Malaysia Plan* released in June 2010. The *Tenth Malaysia Plan* describes the country's economic position as being a one that is 'neither a low cost imitator nor a high value add innovator.' Noting that the economy has reached 'the point of diminishing returns' it compares Malaysia's progress unfavourably to that of South Korea's whose per capita income was lower than Malaysia in 1970, but almost triple by 2009. Growth momentum, which was high from the early 1970s until the mid-1990s, has slowed noticeably. Vietnam is cited by the Plan as a country that could be ready to leapfrog Malaysia technologically (Government of Malaysia 2010).

Malaysia's predicament suggests an inability to harness ICT effectively and fully bridge the Digital Divide. The MSC, which was to anchor the creation of a dynamic ICT production hub as well as act as a catalyst of ICT usage throughout the Malaysian economy, has failed on both counts despite, by one estimate, having 'swallowed US$3.7 billion in state funds' by 2000 alone (K.Y. Lee 2000). As discussed, the MSC itself has generated only very modest employment and exports. Malaysia's rankings in the ITU and WEF indices demonstrate that ICT's penetration nationally lags far behind the aspirations expressed in Vision 2020.

The Malaysian rankings reflect trends that ISIS highlighted in its 2002 Master Plan that compared ICT penetration in Malaysia with its regional neighbours as well as recognized world leaders in ICT usage such as Germany and the United States in view of the country's stated goals. It found that Malaysia fared better than Thailand and the Philippines in ICT penetration, but otherwise lagged behind the other countries surveyed, ranking ninth of eleven overall.[16] Compared to Singapore, Malaysia trailed in every category ISIS that measured. Unfortunately, the warning failed to generate a set of policy alternatives to reliance upon the MSC.

---

16 The surveyed countries were United States, New Zealand, Singapore, United Kingdom, Japan, Germany, Taiwan, Korea, Malaysia, Thailand and the Philippines, in order of their ranking (ISIS 2002).

The *Ninth Malaysia Plan* reiterated that government policy remained to turn Malaysia into a knowledge-based economy:

> With ICT as a key determinant in the development process to move the economy up the value chain, efforts will be intensified to mainstream ubiquitous access to ICT services and facilities and, equally important, to promote the wider adoption and usage in all aspects of everyday life. (Government of Malaysia 2006: 133)

The focus of ICT development would be upon a number of specific goals including, 'enhancing Malaysia's position as a global ICT and multimedia hub' as well as expanding networks to ensure more equitable access and 'intensifying efforts at bridging the digital divide' (Government of Malaysia 2006: 133). The government, however, did not devote the necessary funds towards accomplishing its goals.[17] The resultant modest spread of ICT penetration in Malaysia may be disappointing, but it is not surprising.

Malaysian growth seems increasingly reliant on petroleum production and the largest contributor to the Malaysian economy appears to be Petronas, the national oil company. The financial relationship between the government and Petronas is kept opaque, but the CEO, Hassan Marican, announced that Petronas had paid approximately MYR73 billion (US$24 billion) to the government in royalties, dividends, taxes and export duties during its fiscal year ended March 2009, accounting for 44 per cent of the Malaysian government's total revenue. Over five years, it contributed MYR268 billion (US$89 billion) or slightly under MYR30 million (US$10 million) for every Malaysian (Lopez 2009). While the declining contribution of manufacturing to GDP from close to 40 per cent in the late 1990s to approximately 30 per cent in the late 2000s (Malaysia Treasury Department Economic Report 2008/2009) has been offset, to some extent, with growth in the services sector, primarily the communications, finance, real estate and hospitality and tourism industries, the unstated fear is that Malaysia is becoming a petro-dependent economy.

The *Tenth Malaysia Plan* has promised a new approach with the government assuming a less interventionist role and more of one of an enabler pursuant to what it has termed the 'New Economic Model'. If the government is to be successful

---

17   The government undertook to allocate MYR 12.9 billion over the five years of the Plan to ICT-related programmes. The largest portion of the funds, MYR 5.7 billion, would be allocated to the continued computerization of government agencies, with another MYR 3.3 billion towards schools. Approximately MYR 1.5 billion would be spent on unspecified 'ICT Funding' and MYR 1.1 billion towards the MSC and its flagship applications with close to 80 per cent being allocated to e-government and the Government Multipurpose Card which functions primarily as an identity card for Malaysian citizens. A mere MYR 474 million would be devoted to ICT research and development, MYR 180 million to ICT/ Training and services and MYR 150 million to 'communications infrastructure service provision programme'. (Government of Malaysia 2006)

in moving Malaysia back on the road to high income status, it will have to foster more effectively the usage of ICT throughout the country. It is not clear that the government recognizes this imperative. In a small section on ICT, reference is made to the need to fact that greater usage of ICT will boost productivity, but far greater emphasis is placed on ICT production and becoming a 'niche producer of selected ICT products and services' (Government of Malaysia 2010: 129).

In an effort to foster greater ICT usage, the government should focus on the factors that have been shown to mediate the relationship between ICT and economic growth. Far more needs to be done by the government to spur private sector investment, in general, and in ICT, in particular. Investment has become too dependent on government with the private sector's share of investment declining from approximately 25 per cent of GDP in the 1990s to about 10 per cent of GDP in the 2000s (Government of Malaysia 2010). In the same manner that the government enacted numerous incentives to attract FDI in the 1970s, incentives to invest in ICT should now be considered. Malaysian telecommunications infrastructure development has been hobbled by an historically poor regulatory structure and politically motivated interference in opening the various market segments to competition and in the granting of licences. The CMC has attempted to generate discussion among, and receive input from, interested organizations and parties through its industry forums, but its scope for action is severely curtailed by the CMA which reserves to the Minister an unfettered right to intervene in any matter.

Human capital development, however, may prove to be Malaysia's greatest challenge due to the time it takes to reform the education system and educate a new generation of students. Simply put, Malaysia's education system does not produce a sufficient quantity or quality of graduates to meet its goals. The situation is exacerbated by the university entry and scholarship preferences that cause too many top students to forsake their country to pursue higher education and subsequent employment opportunities. At a broader institutional level, the elaborate matrix of interconnections between individuals, organizations and government bodies that are present in Penang are generally absent federally or in other States. Malaysia's reform efforts have tended to be top down exercises from the Prime Minister's office and the EPU with few attempts to engage in widespread consultation on an on-going basis with all interested parties. If Malaysia wishes to build the institutions needed to allow it to progress to high income status, it will need to focus much more on the process by which effective institutions are built.

Chapter 8
Separate Paths

Continuing Similarities

Given Singapore's current status as a wealthy nation and Malaysia's relative prosperity when compared to much of Africa, South America and Asia, it is easy to forget that they were both poor countries fifty years ago as they emerged from colonial rule although neither lay at the very bottom of the economic development ladder. Living conditions in Singapore in the mid-1950s were described by the World Bank as appalling and the majority of Malaysians lived below the poverty line. By 2000, Singapore was among the world's richest nations ($34,090) and Malaysia ($8,102) was solidly middle income. Throughout the decade, Singapore continued its steep climb ($51,230), surpassing the United States, but Malaysia's per capita wealth, which climbed commensurately by 50 per cent to $12,778 fell further behind in absolute terms, thereby giving credence to the suggestion that Malaysia had fallen into what its Prime Minister calls the middle income trap.[1]

While there are historical, geographic and demographic differences between the countries, their shared history and similar ethnic composition, albeit in different proportions, make them particularly relevant subjects of comparative study. British colonization inextricably intertwined their histories. Penang and Malacca, once part of the same Straits Settlements Colony as was Singapore, are now part of Malaysia. So closely were their economies connected that in the late 1950s the Singaporean government considered union with Malaysia as crucial to its economic viability. Their divergent paths since the dissolution of their brief union in 1965 are all the more striking as it might have been logical in 1965 to assume that Malaysia would become the wealthier nation, given its larger population and greater natural resources.

Since 1965, Singapore has clearly achieved a much higher level of economic prosperity than Malaysia. Although Singapore's economic progress may be attributable, in part, to its decision to shift from an import substitution economic orientation to one that is export-driven before Malaysia that alone does not sufficiently explain the growing gap in per capita wealth between the two countries. There do not appear to be fundamental differences in their respective development philosophies as enunciated in Singapore in the Winsemius Report and its subsequent actions and in Malaysia through the regular five-year plans since the introduction of the NEP in 1972. They view the respective roles of the public and private sectors similarly. Malaysia pursues additional social goals concerning

---

1   All figures US dollars, Heston et al. 2011.

the participation Malays play in the country's economic life, but its approach to economic development otherwise corresponds closely to that of Singapore.

Both countries sought to spur their growth by attracting MNCs to their manufacturing sectors. Singapore is highly dependent on FDI, not just in manufacturing, but throughout its economy. Malaysia's natural resources allow its economy to be more diversified, but its manufacturing sector tends to be MNC dominated. In both countries, MNC investment was regarded as a means not only to provide employment, although that was an important goal, but as a source of technology upon which to build further growth. Nothing has changed. Singapore and Malaysia continue to recognize the need for improved productivity through the use of increasingly sophisticated technology in order to remain internationally competitive. As the computer age dawned and global economic integration hastened in the 1980s and 1990s, they were quick to understand that the nature of technology had shifted and that they needed to foster the adoption of ICT throughout their societies. They also acknowledged the complementary need to improve constantly their respective levels of human capital in order to attract FDI with increasingly sophisticated ICT and to use and to benefit from it.

Singapore stands as a model of achievement and economic transformation. Malaysia has also accomplished a great deal, but has not realized its full economic potential. While a number of factors may account for their different rates of economic growth, a significant contributor to their differing outcomes is the manner in which they carried out their economic policies, not their substance, and their ability, or failure, to build the institutions associated with those policies. The underlying reasons may be related, in part, to the quality of their respective leadership and levels of rent seeking or the lack thereof. Such differences, however, only serve to underscore the need to build good institutions. Singapore's government wanted the country to become prosperous and it was able to implement its policies spectacularly well. Malaysian leaders wanted the same thing, but they did not execute in the same manner.

Different Choices, Different Outcomes

Less economically developed countries should not necessarily attempt to replicate the specific actions taken by the Singapore government. The lesson to be drawn from the Singaporean approach to economic development is the manner in which its decisions were made and implemented resulting in institutions that were effective in achieving the purposes for which they were created. If Singapore made wise choices part of the reason is because it created processes that increased the likelihood of doing so. As emphasized in Chapter 5, continuing wide scale consultation is a key to successful policy formulation and implementation. The PAP consulted widely in preparing The Tasks Ahead and in commissioning the Winsemius Report at the beginning of Singapore's economic journey. Once having formed the government, it worked closely with outside expertise to analyse the

Singaporean economy's strengths and shortcomings. Goh Keng Swee, generally perceived as the architect of Singapore's economy and its first Minister of Finance, travelled widely to study how other countries approached economic development.

Goh and the PAP concluded there were three main functions for their new government: attracting MNCs, improving infrastructure (including telecommunications) and increasing Singapore's human capital. They did not attempt to pick winning companies or technologies although they stressed the need for industry to be as technologically advanced as possible. The government focused its efforts on creating the conditions that would allow the private sector to succeed. The greatest obstacles to economic development, in their minds, were outdated social, political and economic institutions which had to be replaced by those that responded to current needs. Consequently, the government's first major economic step was to create the EDB as the institution with primary responsibility for setting the country's economic agenda. Of equal importance to the role the EDB played directly in Singapore's growth, is the manner in which it is structured and operated and how it became the template for new institutions in Singapore. The EDB is shielded from government interference, overseen by a diverse board of directors and staffed by highly skilled individuals in a manner very similar to that of MITI in Japan described by Johnson (1982) and discussed in the examination of the developmental state literature in the Introduction. That model endures. Architect Moshe Safdie recently reflected on his experience working in Singapore:

> I'm completely taken and impressed by the planning authority of Singapore and its Urban Redevelopment Authority (URA). It's the most cutting-edge agency in the world. They have very effective guidelines for development and they review design as it evolves. They have an international review panel that meets annually … They seem to be able to attract impressive talent to their city ranks. (Rochon 2011: A16)

Malaysia's concern with economic development was initially very different from that of Singapore where the government's overriding priority has always been economic growth. UMNO's focus in its first election campaign was primarily upon social goals aimed at improving the material wellbeing and political engagement of the Malay community, not national economic growth. Its platform addressed Malay poverty and its economic policies targeted means of ameliorating the quality of rural Malay life, not changing its nature. The institutions it created sought to improve and maintain traditional rural life through better healthcare, infrastructure and crop yields. Industrialization received little attention. The 1955 World Bank report examining Malaya's economy emphasized the importance of tin and rubber production and the greater manufacturing of consumer products within the context of high tariff barriers and import substitution policies. That report guided the government's thinking without formal challenge or review, in contrast to the public debates that took place in Singapore at the same time.

The NEP, introduced in 1972, marked the formal abandonment of import substitution in Malaysia in favour of export orientation and the country's first concerted efforts at industrialization. Those efforts, however, were often overshadowed by the two social objectives of the NEP: the elimination of poverty; and the elimination of ethnic identification with economic function. Those social goals led to the creation of targets and quotas for Bumiputera, predominantly Malay, participation in the economy in areas such as employment and share ownership. On the industrialization side, the Malaysian government can claim success in helping to build a thriving electronics sector in Penang. Regarding its social goals, it was able to lower poverty significantly, but despite its activist role in the economy, it has not fostered widespread Malay participation in the economy to the extent it claims to desire. Following a path of affirmative action for the majority would, alone, produce economic distortions, but such may have been a price the country was willing to pay to achieve its social goals. The manner in which the government has attempted to achieve increased Malay economic participation, however, has produced a greater negative impact than necessary upon national economic development. Cronyism in the awarding of contracts and licenses, rent-seeking and an inadequate supply of skilled human capital due, in large part, to preferential hiring practices and declines in the quality of publicly funded education have hurt Malaysian economic development. Inequality within the Malay community has grown, sparking resentment and threatening UMNO's hold on power. As a result of the government's actions, Malaysia has only partially succeeded in building the strong institutions needed to carry out its economic agenda.

A number of institutions were created in response to the social-engineering goals of the NEP to increase Malay participation in the economy, but little was done institutionally to encourage the foreign investment Malaysia wished to attract to manufacturing. MIDA, which pre-dates the NEP, but was re-structured in its wake, enjoys a mandate that closely parallels that of the EDB. Structurally, however, the board of directors does not enjoy the same independence from the government as the EDB's nor does it serve as a forum for a diversity of opinions. It was only in 2011 that the initial steps were taken to move MIDA out from the direct control of the Ministry of International Trade and Investment. Most current board members are government civil servants at either the federal level or from strong UMNO states such as Johore, Sarawak and Sabah where overwhelming support for UMNO in the 2008 federal election allowed the government to maintain power. Not only are there few business people on the board, but none of the Malaysian members are employed by MNCs nor are there any foreign nationals.

While Rasiah (2002b) notes that MIDA has done an exemplary job working with local government and business in Penang to attract investment, it has achieved less success elsewhere as the contribution of the electronics sector to GDP greatly exceeds that of other manufacturing sectors. Outside of the electronics sector and textiles, to a much lesser extent, manufacturing has mostly involved the processing of natural resources – wood furniture, rubber and date palm products, frozen seafood and petroleum and petrochemicals – and has received relatively little FDI in comparison to the electronics sector. The contribution of manufacturing to GDP has shrunk commensurately with the decline since the mid-1990s of the electronics sector's contribution.

The development of the Malaysian electronics sector can be described as a tale of two States. Electronics manufacturing in Penang grew massively beginning in the early 1970s while that in Selangor, despite a head start in investment, has remained relatively stagnant, overly dependent on imported low wage labour to keep its costs competitive. The difference between the outcomes in the two States can be attributed in large measure to the quality of local institutions and what Rasiah has termed 'systemic coordination'. Penang's economic development efforts most closely parallel Singapore's. In a dire economic situation in the mid-1960s, the Penang government turned to foreign consulting economists to devise an economic strategy. Similar to the Winsemius Report, the Nathan Report closely analysed Penang's economy and proposed an approach to decision-making and the establishment of an economic development body, the PDC, to build upon Penang's strengths, rather than focusing upon specific economic sectors.

The Penang government followed the Report's methodology and, recognizing Penang's relatively well-educated workforce and historical dependence upon international commerce, seized upon the federal government's then recent legislation to allow free trade zones and a market opportunity in the electronics sector caused by rising wages elsewhere in the region to attract investment to Penang. The PDC and local government representatives began a course of conduct of consulting closely with the newly arrived MNCs to determine their needs. The necessity of continuously upgrading Penang's workers' skills led most notably to the eventual creation of the PSDC which worked closely with MNCs to create the programs needed to respond to those companies' human capital needs. Consequently, Penang was able to attract more, and more sophisticated, FDI and to begin to build linkages between local entrepreneurs and the MNCs to allow for the creation of local, related enterprises to a greater extent than elsewhere in Malaysia.

Selangor, in contrast, initially did little to build on its manufacturing base compared to Penang. Whereas Penang built institutions to provide manpower training to overcome federal shortcomings in education, Selangor failed to do so. The Selangor counterpart to the PDC, the SEDC, proved ineffective in its abilities to attract firms or introduce them to potential partners. Unlike the EDB or PDC, which view their mandate as extending beyond an MNC's initial investment, the SEDC viewed its role as terminating upon the opening of a manufacturing facility. In contrast to the situation in Penang, where a high tech cluster has formed, fewer local linkages have been formed in Selangor.

Fostering ICT Usage and Growth

The effects of Singapore's and Malaysia's differing approaches to promoting ICT usage and economic growth become more apparent when examining their institution building efforts specifically related to the other factors that mediate that relationship: telecommunications infrastructure; investment in ICT goods and services; and human capital. Singapore is amongst the world's leaders in ICT usage while ICT penetration in Malaysia is lower than would be suggested by its level of income.

Spreading ICT usage has comprised an important pillar in Singapore's economic growth thinking. For a country that forsakes the use of formal economic plans, it has produced a remarkable number of ICT strategies beginning in the 1980s with the National Computerization Plan and the National IT Plan and accelerating over the next 15 years.[2] Institutions such as the IDA and National Science and Technology Board have been created to implement the country's goals in this field. The common thread to the various ICT plans has been to foster its usage in business and to encourage all Singaporeans to become adept ICT users at home and at work.

Malaysia's efforts to stimulate ICT adoption and promote its spread relied primarily upon the MSC. The MSC was heavily promoted during the late 1990s and early 2000s. Its International Advisory Board included a who's who of top executives from global ICT companies, such as Bill Gates. 'Roadshows' to publicize the MSC were held in major cities around the world and its four initial flagship applications were to transform Malaysian life. The Malaysia Plans produced every five years also placed heavy emphasis on the catalytic role the MSC would play in spreading ICT usage throughout Malaysia. The MSC's failure to live up to its promise and its fading from prominence in Malaysia's public discourse have left a void. While the spread of ICT and the creation of a knowledge economy remain government aspirations, no comprehensive plans or strategies have replaced reliance on the MSC.

Singapore's small island state status undoubtedly makes its infrastructure task somewhat easier than Malaysia's. It need only decide what infrastructure to build, not where. Singapore has had both the financial resources and the political will to build state-of-the-art facilities that span the island. Malaysia, with more limited resources and a much larger country must make choices. It has been relatively successful at building a high speed network in and around Kuala Lumpur and other major cities, but other parts of the country lag in their access to a full range of up to date services.

Neither country has created a 'textbook' regulator as described in the discussion of the ITU Toolkit in Chapter 5 that stands independent of all other functions. The

---

2   Singapore's subsequent plans include *Singapore: The Next Lap* (1991), IT-2000 (1992), SingaporeONE (1998), Infocomm 21 (2000), Connected Singapore (2003) and iN2015 (2005).

CMC and the IDA combine promotional and regulatory functions although the necessary safeguards to separate the two have been instituted and are working well. Initial criticism of the IDA's operations seems to have dissipated while the CMC's reputation, when it is permitted to carry out its responsibilities, is good. The potential problem in Malaysia is the CMC's enabling legislation that allows the Minister to intervene in almost any matter at any time, thereby opening the door to the potential politicization of the decision making process which has historically been a problem, as described by Salazar (2007) and Ure (2008).

Ideological goals underlie education policy to a greater extent both in Malaysia and Singapore than in most prosperous countries giving credence to Prichett's (2007) argument that governments use school systems to inculcate a specific set of beliefs and to socialize citizens, not to maximize social welfare. Nevertheless, the pursuit of such goals has not proved to be incompatible their remarkable success since 1960 in providing their citizens with primary education and virtually eliminating illiteracy, a feat made even more impressive given that it was accomplished in the 1960s and 1970s at a time of rapid growth in the number of school age children. Both countries followed the path of building their public education systems from the ground up; first striving to provide universal primary schooling and then attempting to extend secondary schooling to an increasing number of students in the manner subsequently recommended by the World Bank (de Ferranti et al. 2003).

The importance of secondary education to the ability to harness ICT's potential, examined in Chapter 5, has been recognized in both Malaysia and Singapore. In principle, they should not lack the human capital needed to participate in the knowledge economy. Singapore and Malaysia, particularly Penang, have also done an excellent job of creating vocational training programs and institutions, such as the PSDC which works closely with industry to give students and employees the opportunity to improve their skills so as to allow industrial upgrading to take place. They have faced difficulties, however, at the secondary and tertiary levels. The number of secondary school graduates is good by world standards in both countries although lower in Malaysia than in Singapore. Graduation rates from post-secondary institutions lag especially in Singapore compared to other wealthy countries. Their challenges are different. Singapore has uncharacteristically continued to grapple with competing motivations in education policy. Much of the school system is geared to producing a pool of workers who possess the increasingly high skill set needed by MNCs, not just in manufacturing, but in other areas of high FDI concentration, such as the financial services, and the professional legal and accounting advisory services needed to service them. Streamed at the end of primary school and potentially twice again towards the end of secondary school, Singaporean students excel on international tests and do, in fact, provide a very large talent pool for the MNCs to draw upon. The Singaporean system, however, has been criticized for not producing a substantial pool of people who can create and innovate. Risk taking and entrepreneurism is lower than would normally be expected for a country with its wealth. As a result, few local companies are engaged in the space occupied by MNCs and linkages between local companies and MNCs are relatively weak. Singapore has advanced to the frontier of the knowledge economy, but taking the final step has proven difficult for it to achieve.

Malaysia's greatest problem relates to the quality of its education system. While many more people have access to, and are taking advantage of, a wider selection of options at the tertiary level than was available twenty years ago, thanks to changes in the rules relating to private and foreign institutions, too few graduates are of the calibre needed by the private sector. As Rasiah (2002b) and ISIS (2002) have argued, industry's greatest challenge is a lack of human capital. The issues in education have ranged from an emphasis on rote learning and learning for the test to low standards to pass to questions and preferences for places at university, scholarships and hiring practices. As a consequence, Malaysia suffers from having too many graduates who are unable to perform the jobs expected of them in the private sector while many others leave the country. The ICT companies in Penang, for example, employ thousands of locally trained engineers, but they are now looking to the Philippines, Indonesia, Myanmar and South Asian countries to fill their future needs.

Singapore: Not All Roses

Singapore's development can be seen as promoting economic growth and industrialization through attracting increasingly sophisticated FDI. Its government has acted in many ways that are reminiscent of the developmental state model although it does not fit perfectly into that analytical framework and there have been few 'explicit attempts among scholars specializing in Singapore to fit the city-state into an historical institutionalist framework' (Rodan et al. 2006: 138–9). Huff (1995) is one of the few academic writers to attempt to describe the Singapore government's role in developmental state terms. He suggests that Singapore 'had to find its own economic and political development model' (1434) and, as such, may have more to offer to less economically developed states seeking a model for industrialization than those that better fit the developmental states framework (1435).

In the early 1960s, when Singapore was still perceived as potentially a second Cuba, the PAP government created stability and certainty. It sought to understand and provide the ideal environment for MNCs to carry out their activities and for their employees in which to live. It broke the left wing opposition and co-opted the union movement while cutting wages. The government ensured that the labour pool needed by industry was well educated and that the mechanisms were put in place to train workers continually to meet the needs of MNCs. The EDB, as Schein (1996) described, acted as a one stop shop for investors, dealing with other branches of government to solve all their problems. Infrastructure was built; not just for telecommunications, but in all areas such as roads, airports, rapid transit, electricity and sewage treatment. Parks, museums, concert halls, bars, restaurants and shopping malls abound. Housing, at the upper end is plentiful, modern and spacious, if expensive. Imported domestic labour is cheap by international standards. The media is predominantly state controlled, public demonstrations are subject to permit and political dissent is muted. For foreign investors, their management and ex-patriot professionals willing to abide by the rules of conduct, Singapore can resemble Disneyworld run by the Swiss.

The downside of Singapore's extraordinary FDI-fuelled growth and reliance on foreign capital and expertise is the risk that events beyond the government's control will disrupt the MNCs' supply chains or their operations in some other manner, causing the economy to shrink relatively dramatically, as it did in the aftermath of the 1997 Asian financial crisis and the 2008 European-American recession. Technology changes quickly. Capital is highly mobile. Strong local linkages tying foreign investment to Singapore have not developed. There is always the possibility that, despite the government's best efforts, it will move elsewhere. The paucity of local industry makes it questionable whether Singaporeans could effectively step into a vacuum caused by a reduction in the foreign presence.

For many Singaporean workers, shopkeepers and taxi drivers, the Singapore enjoyed by MNCs and expats does not resemble their experience. Most cannot dream of leaving their comfortable, but far from luxurious HDB flats. The necessities of life have increased in price faster than their incomes. Social inequality has become a political issue (Rodan et al. 2006: 156–8). The 2011 general elections which produced a noticeable drop in the PAP's popular vote, although only a modest reduction in the number of constituencies it won, seems to have put fear into the hearts of the government. While not new, social inequality is being discussed more openly since the election as witnessed by the Institute of Policy Studies Singapore Perspectives 2012 conference, the main background paper to which addresses the issue (Institute of Policy Studies 2012). In response, the government promised in its February 2012 Budget to put more money into services and double the amount spent on health care for five years (Singapore 2012). It will thus be a challenge for Singapore to maintain its FDI-driven growth model that focused so greatly on national wealth while addressing social welfare issues. Like most governments of prosperous countries, Singapore may discover that balancing other interests with growth poses a range of new challenges.

Malaysia: Not All Thorns

Despite having fallen behind Singapore economically, Malaysia's accomplishments should not be overlooked. Many less economically developed countries would be pleased to be grappling with how to escape from middle income status. Malaysia, with its ethnic and social cleavages, is not an easy place to govern, yet with one major exception social peace has endured since independence. Most people's lives are materially better than their parents or grandparents. All Malaysians have access to at least nine years of free education. There is much to be proud about.

Malaysia's economic growth since independence has been impressive, but the period of dynamic expansion seems to have stopped and the upward trajectory stalled. Its approach to economic growth defies easy categorization. The government's intervention in economic matters since the introduction of the NEP in the early 1970s would leave few in agreement with the World Bank (1993) view that its growth can be attributed to neoclassical or neoliberal economic policies. Guided at least as much by political motivations regarding the specific economic and social role and wellbeing of the Bumiputera as by broader economic ones, Malaysia cannot be classified as a developmental state, to the extent that a defining characteristic of the developmental state is an almost single minded focus on economic development. It actions share more characteristics of the governed stated model described by Wade (2004), but do not fit comfortably into that theory either.

Khoo (2006) in an analysis of the political economy of Malaysian growth strategy argues:

> ... the main themes of Malaysian political economy cannot be understood by seeing economic transformation as an apolitical expression of rational choices, technocratic options, and market processes. Instead, policy choices, technocratic interventions, and market processes must be analysed in political terms ... (172)

Rasiah (2010) makes similar arguments. Classifying the development state literature as falling within a broader state-capital approach, he contends that government support for industrialization was not directed at domestic, overwhelmingly Chinese, sources of capital (9). Malaysia's industrialization efforts were aimed at attracting FDI. A further distinction with usual developmental state is found in its policies directed at human capital development. Quantity has been substituted for quality with the result that the level of human capital in Malaysia continues to be an impediment to growth. While raising the level of human capital was a major component of economic development efforts in Japan, South Korea and Taiwan, such was not the case in more broadly in Southeast Asia, apart from Singapore (Rasiah 2010: 9)

Malaysia's continued prosperity will depend on its ability to reconcile its conflicting social, political and economic goals. The current prognosis is troubling as Malaysia appears to becoming increasingly dependent upon oil revenues generated by the national oil company, Petronas, for its growing budgetary needs. Its inability to foster ICT usage and to create the strong institutions that have been shown to mediate its relationship with growth have restricted Malaysia's efforts to become a more knowledge-based economy. The brain drain of young people, predominantly from the Chinese and Indian communities, may be too late to stop in the short term. They are likely to look to Singapore and further afield to pursue their university education and career interests. Relatively few return. UMNO's social engineering policies have greatly reduced poverty among Malays, but while Malay wealth has grown collectively, it has become more unevenly distributed and intra-Malay tensions have grown. The issue may come to a head with the general elections that must be held before July 2013. Unless there is an unexpected surprise, the UMNO led government is likely to lose popular support although it is far from certain that it will lose power. Changes will be demanded if not of the social contract, then of the manner in which it has been pursued. The next government will have to pay far more attention to building the institutions that allow for economic growth and, at least as importantly, the consultative process by which those institutions are built.

In summary, it is not suggested that the differences in Malaysian and Singaporean economic development since 1965 can be attributed solely to their respective institutional development. Nevertheless, the examination of their paths demonstrates the importance to economic development of building good institutions. Singapore has been able to build the institutions needed to help formulate and implement public policy better than Malaysia. It is no coincidence that Penang, within the limits of its powers, which generally has built better institutions than the central government or other Malaysian States, has led Malaysian industrialization. Its substantial achievements in building a vibrant electronics cluster stand in marked contrast to the rest of the country. Singapore's and Penang's efforts at building institutions are characterized by a focus upon process in their design, widespread consultation and independence from government interference in their daily activities. Other Malaysian institutions tend not to exhibit such characteristics.

Chapter 9
Conclusion – A Final Word

Lessons Learned

What can governments and others concerned with economic growth take away from this book? The main point is that all governments can improve the well-being of their citizens by building the institutions that create a more effective enabling environment for economic endeavour. The existing literature cannot provide insight into which institutions are important for growth because the commonly used conception of institutions is flawed for that purpose. The most influential body of literature that examines the role of institutions in economic development and the one that enunciates the meaning of institutions most often used in the empirical research that attempts to measure their impact, the NIE, helps significantly in understanding why some countries are rich while others are poor, but it fails to explain why or how countries, notably in East Asia, have been able to transform their economies in a much shorter time than the theory contemplates. Two main reasons are suggested. First, the NIE fails to recognize the complexity of informal institutions by treating them as a homogeneous mass that changes only at a glacial pace. Second, the NIE's definition of institutions is unworkable for the prospective understanding of economic growth.

The most commonly used definition, enunciated by Douglass North (1990), as being the totality of humanly devised constraints, suits his purpose well. North was concerned with why some countries are rich and others are poor. He attributes wealth and poverty to the quality of a country's institutions. The manner in which the totality of a country's unwritten (informal) and written (formal) institutions interact determines the nature of that country's economic status. Informal institutions determine formal institutions and government's actions are circumscribed by them. He is likely correct. Where this book diverges from North is in his belief that informal institutions change at a speed that only historians can record. Informal institutions and societies are portrayed as being relatively homogeneous. In reality, there is a great deal of diversity in both. Some informal institutions, or core beliefs, may change only exceedingly slowly while others, which enjoy a greater impact on economic activity, can change much more quickly. Clearly, modern history shows that governments can affect their countries' economic trajectories. Far greater insight into the roles of culture, social capital, identity formation and other factors that affect informal institutions is needed to understand how the ones that stifle growth can be overcome relatively quickly.

Both endogenous growth theory, which considers technology usage to be a variable that differs in each country, and developmental state models, which see governments as actively guiding their economies, give institutions a central role. Those literatures use the term 'institutions' in a different sense from North as does the literature that attempts to test empirically the importance of institutions although it does not always acknowledge that fact. The proxies they use to test the importance of institutions, despite their imperfections, attempt to evaluate government institutions, or bodies, not the totality of constraints that govern human interaction. The most common proxy, Kaufmann's indicators, measure perceptions of governance. It may be justified to conclude that if a country's governance is good, the quality of its institutions is good, but those indicators do not measure institutional quality directly. The scope of institutions, as used by North, is too vast to allow for the accurate analysis of their place in how economic growth can be achieved.

For those charged with the daily practical necessity of fostering economic development this book argues that institutions need to be viewed as the means by which policies and laws are formulated, enacted, implemented and enforced. The institutions that lead to economic growth are the ones that governments build in order to accomplish their development strategies. Good institutions create the enabling environment in which economic activity can lead to prosperity. Poor institutions lead to inefficient economic performance and when too many of a country's institutions fail to work efficiently, sustained economic growth cannot be achieved. Implementation and institution-building are not abstract concepts; they require meticulous attention to detail.

The development strategies governments choose are important, but of greater importance may be their ability to implement their chosen strategies. The institutions that formulate policy and legislate start the process. Institutions that enforce laws ensure compliance when necessary. Most institutions, however, are created to implement laws. The point about the importance of institutions creating an enabling environment for growth is not always well made in the development literature, but in many respects it boils down to the ability of governments to execute their plans.

If it is correct that informal institutions and the manner in which they change need to be better understood and that institutional quality plays a critical role in determining economic outcomes, then it would seem that economists need to be joined in their examination of the development process by those with different expertise and that the usual analytical tools used by economists should be supplemented with different means of analysis. Social scientists such as sociologists and cognitive scientists may be better placed to understand culture, norm formation, the manner in which informal institutions change and how they determine government's scope for action. Similarly, political scientists and lawyers may better understand how institutions can be built so that they are effective in implementing governments' policies and laws. Case studies are one means of examining phenomena that are not easily quantifiable.

Good institutions are not created with a secret recipe. Regardless of the institution, the ingredients are basically the same: openness; transparency; input from all interested stakeholders; constant communication, consultation and feedback; independence from government and capture by special interest groups; fairness; and integrity. Throughout the book, one can see the recurrent themes of institution-building irrespective of whether the subject is the reformation of the Finnish education system, the functioning of the EDB in Singapore or the PSDB in Penang, small-scale project determination and implementation in Macedonia, the ITU Handbook or the microfoundations of organizational institutionalism. This may seem pedestrian when so much of the academic literature seeks to reveal a previously hidden key to unlock growth, but there are no holy grails in economic development any more than there are miracles.

Countries on the wrong side of the Digital Divide need to find a way to begin to bridge the gap. There is no quick fix to this challenge and doing so is a protracted process, but the incorporation of ICT usage into all aspects of a country's society must be the ultimate goal. ICT, however, must be viewed as more than hardware and software. It is equally about human capital development. ICT equipment and applications are tools for human thought and endeavour. They are extensions of the brain. By themselves they do nothing. Give tractors to farmers in rich and poor countries and they will plough their fields equally well. Put a computer in front of people from those same countries with educations that are at their respective national averages and the results will be very different. Sustained development depends on bridging the Digital Divide. There is no leapfrogging. There are no shortcuts. There is no choice.

Ultimately, a vast range of institutions are important for economic development, but for governments looking to bridge the Digital Divide, one place to start would be with the institutions associated with the other factors that mediate the relationship between ICT usage and growth. An independent telecommunications regulator has been shown to be crucial to the building of infrastructure and to the provision of telecommunications goods and services. A multiplicity of institutions is important to ICT investment, but where the development strategy involves the attraction of FDI, an effective investment promotion agency can be an important ingredient. Human capital is the most challenging, time consuming and expensive of the institutional reforms, but countries cannot afford to keep their populations uneducated. An education system must be built from the ground up providing both primary and secondary education to as much of the population as possible. Reading, writing and arithmetic are not sufficient to use ICT effectively. The cognitive and reasoning skills taught in high school are essential.

The case studies provide compelling evidence of the importance of building effective institutions. When Singapore's efforts and, to a lesser extent, Penang's are compared to those more generally in Malaysia, the importance of institutions to policy implementation becomes more apparent. Singapore has built the institutions needed for modern telecommunications infrastructure, investment in ICT goods and services and a highly educated and skilled workforce. It has, of course, also created a wide range of institutions needed for an enabling environment conducive to growth. Malaysia has achieved success, as well, but not to the same degree as

Singapore. Some of the reason lies in its government's legitimate pursuit of social goals as well as economic ones whereas Singapore has been almost exclusively devoted to economic development. A second significant reason is that it has not engaged in the needed institution-building process. Too often, its institutions have been subjected to government interference, opaque practices, a failure to seek the participation of interested parties and a lack of consultation.

Singapore and Malaysia have been able to transform their economies and achieve prosperity in less than fifty years. The success they have enjoyed is due to skilful planning, hard work and meticulous implementation of their development policies. A crucial point to emphasize for the governments of less economically developed countries is that it is within their powers to improve the economic condition of their citizens, but it is an exacting process. There are few shortcuts in obtaining the investment or building the infrastructure needed to bridge the Digital Divide and none in developing human capital. It took decades for Singapore and Malaysia to build their economies.

Spanning the Digital Divide need not be accomplished in a single bound, but less economically developed countries have no choice other than to narrow it progressively if they wish to enjoy sustained economic growth. The consequences of not doing so are likely to be economic stagnation or regression. Labour intensive industries are becoming fewer and while they may provide a first step up the development curve, reliance on cheap labour ultimately brings limited returns. Creating strong institutions allows governments to make wiser policy choices, enact better laws and implement and enforce them more effectively. The process of building the institutions needed to bridge the Digital Divide may be demanding, but all governments possess the tools required to begin the process and to improve the lives of their citizens.

Bibliography

Abdullah, H., R.C. Rose and N. Kumar. 2007. Human resource development strategies: the Malaysian scenario. *Journal of Social Science*, 3(4), 213.

Abdullah, W.A.W. 1994. Transnational corporations and human resource development. *Personnel Review*, 23(5), 50.

Academy of Finland. [Online: Academy of Finland]. Available at: http://www.aka. fi/en-gb/A/ [accessed: 8 May 2010].

Acemoglu, D. 1998. Why do new technologies complement skills? Directed technical change and wage inequality. *The Quarterly Journal of Economics*, 113(4), 1055.

———. 2011. *Why Nations Fail.* Presentation. Available at: http://econ-www.mit. edu/ files/6699 [accessed: 15 August 2011].

Acemoglu, D. and S. Johnson. 2005. Unbundling institutions. *Journal of Political Economy*, 113(5), 949.

———. 2008. The role of institutions in growth and development. *The Commission on Growth and Development Working Paper No. 10.* Washington, D.C.: World Bank.

Acemoglu, D., S. Johnson and J.A. Robinson. 2001. The colonial origins of comparative development: an empirical investigation. *American Economic Review*, 91(5), 1369.

———. 2002. Reversal of fortune: geography and institutions in the making of the modern world income distribution. *The Quarterly Journal of* Economics [Online], 1231–94. Available at:http://www.people.fas.harvard.edu/~jrobins/ researchpapers/publishedpapers/jr_ROFQJEversion.pdf [accessed: 4 May 2010].

———. 2004. Institutions as the fundamental cause of long-run growth, in *Handbook of Economic Growth*, edited by P. Aghion and S. Durlauf. Amsterdam: North-Holland, 1–92.

Acemoglu, D. and J.A. Robinson. 2006. *Economic Origins of Dictatorship and Democracy.* New York: Cambridge University Press.

———. 2012. *Why Nations Fail.* New York: Crown Business.

Adamali, A., J.O. Coffey and Z. Safdar. 2006. Trends in national e-strategies: a review of 40 countries, in *Information and Communications for Development: Global Trends and Policies*, edited by World Bank. Washington, D.C.: World Bank, 87–124.

Aghion, P. and P. Howitt. 1998. *Endogenous Growth Theory.* Cambridge, MA: MIT Press.

Agosin, M.R. and R. Mayer. 2000. *Foreign Investment in Developing Countries: Does it Crowd in Investment?* United Nations Conference on Trade and Development [Online]. Available at: http://www.unctad.org/en/docs/dp_146.en.pdf [accessed: 4 May 2010].

Ahmad, N., P. Schreyer and A. Wolfl. 2004. ICT investment in OECD countries and its economic impacts, in *The Economic Impact of ICT*, edited by OECD. Paris: OECD, 61–84.

Aho, E., K. Pitkanen and P. Sahlberg (eds). 2006. *Policy Development and Reform Principles of Basic and Secondary Education in Finland Since 1968.* Washington, D.C.: World Bank.

Aker, J.C. 2008. Does digital divide or provide? The impact of cell phones on grain markets in Niger, *BREAD Working Paper #177*. Durham, NC: Bureau for Research and Economic Analysis of Development.

Al-Jaghoub, S. and C. Westrup. 2003. Jordan and ICT-led development: towards a competition state? *Information Technology and People*, 16(1), 93.

Alatas, S.H. 1972. The second Malaysia plan 1971–1975: a critique, *Occasional Paper No. 15*. Singapore: Institute of Southeast Asian Studies.

Ali, A. 1996. Industrial technology capacity, in *Malaysia's Economic Development: Policy & Reform*, edited by K.S. Jomo and S.K. Ng. Petaling Jaya, Malaysia: Pelanduk Publications.

Amsden, A. 1989, *Asia's Next Giant: South Koreas and Late Industrialization*. New York: Oxford University Press.

——. 1994 Why isn't the whole world experimenting with the East Asian model to develop? Review of *The East Asian Miracle, World Development*, 22(4), 627.

——. 2001. *The Rise of 'The Rest': Challenges to the West from Late-Industrializing Economies*. New York: Oxford University Press.

Andaya, B.W. and L.Y. Andaya. 2001. *A History of Malaysia* (2nd edition). Houndmills: Palgrave.

Andonova, V. 2006. Mobile phones, the internet and the institutional environment. *Telecommunications Policy*, 30, 29.

Andonova, V. and L. Diaz-Serrano. 2007. Political institutions and the development of telecommunications, in *IZA Discussion Paper No. 2569*. Bonn, Germany: Institute for the Study of Labor.

Andres, L., J.L. Guasch and S. Straub. 2007. Do regulation and institutional design matter for infrastructure performance? *Policy Research Working Paper 4378*. Washington, D.C.: The World Bank.

Anwar, S. 2006. Manufacturing sector growth: a case study of Singapore. *Global Economic Review*, 35(4), 381.

——. 2008. Foreign investment, human capital and manufacturing sector growth in Singapore. *Journal of Policy Modeling*, 30, 447.

Ariff, I. and C.C. Goh. 1998. *Multimedia Super Corridor*. Kuala Lumpur: Leeds Publications.

Aron, J. 2000. Growth and institutions: a review of the evidence. *The World Bank Research Observer*, 15(1), 99.

Arrow, K.J. 1962. The economic implications of learning by doing. *The Review of Economic Studies*, 29(3), 155.

Aschauer, D.A. 1989. Is public expenditure productive? *Journal of Monetary Economics*, 23(2), 177.

Asian University Rankings 2009 [Online: TopUniversities]. Available at: http://www.topuniversities.com/university-rankings/asian-university-rankings [accessed: 9 May 2010].

ARWU 2012 [Online: Academic Ranking of World Universities]. Available at: http://www.shanghairanking.com/ [accessed 15 October 2012].

Audretsch, D.B. 2000. Knowledge, globalization, and regions: an economist's perspective, in *Regions, Globalization and the Knowledge-Economy*, edited by J.H. Dunning. York: Oxford University Press, 63–81.

Avgerou, C. 1998. How can IT enable economic growth in developing countries? *Information Technology for Development*, 8(1), 15.

Awang, H. 2004. Human capital and technology development in Malaysia. *International Education Journal*, 5(2), 239.

Azmi, B.Z. 2000. Educational development and reformation in the Malaysian education system: challenges in the new millennium. *Journal of Southeast Asian Education*, 1(1), 113.

Baily, M.N. and R.Z. Lawrence. 2001. Do we have a new e-economy? *The American Economic Review*, 91(2), 308.

Baker, J. 1999. *Crossroads: A Popular History of Malaysia and Singapore*. Singapore: Times Editions.

Balasubramanyam, V.N. 2001. Foreign direct investment in developing countries; determinants and impact, Paris: OECD.

Baliamoune, M.N. 2002. The new economy and developing countries: assessing the role of ICT diffusion. *Discussion Paper No. 2002/77*. Helsinki: UNU-WIDER.

Bardhan, P. 2005. Institutions matter, but which ones? *Economics of Transition*, 13(3), 499.

Barr, M.D. and C.A. Trocki. 2008. *Paths Not Taken: Political Pluralism in Post-War Singapore*. Singapore: NUS Press.

Bassanini, A. and S. Scarpetta. 2002. Growth, technological change, and ICT diffusion: recent evidence from OECD countries. *Oxford Review of Economic Policy*, 18(3), 324.

Bauer, P.T. 1969. Dissent on development. *Scottish Journal of Political Economy*, 16(3), 75.

——. 1971. *Dissent on Development: Studies and Debates in Development Economics*. London: Weidenfeld and Nicolson.

Bayoumi, T. and M. Haacker. 2002. It's not what you make, it's how you use IT: measuring the welfare benefits of the IT revolution across countries. *IMF Working Paper WP/02/117*. Washington: International Monetary Fund.

Bedlington, S.S. 1978. *Malaysia and Singapore: The Building of New States*. Ithaca, NY: Cornell University Press.

Bergara, M.E., W.J. Henisz, and P.T. Spiller. 1998. Political institutions and electric utility investment: a cross-nation analysis. *California Management Review*, 40(2), 18.

Berman, E. and S. Machin. 2000. Skill-biased technology transfer around the world. *Oxford Review of Economic Policy*, 16(3), 12.

Berman, E., R. Somanathan, and H.W. Tan. 2005. Is skill-biased technological change here yet? Evidence from Indian manufacturing in the 1990s. *World Bank Policy Research Working Paper 3761*. Washington, D.C.: World Bank.

Beyond 20/20 WDS: Key Statistical Tables on Education [Online: United Nations Educational, Scientific and Cultural Organization Institute for Statistics]. Available at: http://stats.uis.unesco.org/unesco/ReportFolders/ReportFolders. aspx?IF_ActivePath=P,50&IF_Language=eng [accessed: 7 May 2010].

Bhagwati, J.N. 1978. Anatomy and consequences of exchange control regimes. *Studies in International Economic Relations*, 1, 10.

Bhaskaran, M. 2003. *Re-Inventing the Asian Model: The Case of Singapore*. Singapore: Times Media.

Bhaskaran, M., Ho S.C., D. Low, Tan, K.S., S. Vadaketh and Yeoh L. K. 2012. *Inequality and the Need for a New Social Contract*. Singapore: Institute for Policy Studies.

Biswas, R. 2002. Determinants of foreign direct investment. *Review of Development Economics*, 6(3), 492.

Blanchard, O. 2004. The economic future of Europe. *Massachusetts Institute of Technology, Department of Economics, Working Paper 04-04*. Cambridge, MA: MIT Press.

Blomstrom, M., S. Globerman, and A. Kokko. 1999. The determinants of host country spillovers from foreign direct investment: review and synthesis of the literature. *SSE/EFI Working Paper Series in Economics and Finance, No. 239*. Stockholm: The European Institute of Japanese Studies.

Blomstrom, M. and A. Kokko. 2002. FDI and human capital: a research agenda. *OECD Development Centre, Working Paper 195*. Paris: OECD.

Blomstrom, M. and F. Sjoholm. 2002. Growth and innovation strategies for a knowledge economy: experiences from Finland, Sweden and Singapore. *Stockholm School of Economics, Working Paper 156*. Stockholm: Stockholm School of Economics.

Blondal, S., S. Field, and N. Girouard. 2002. Investment in human capital through upper-secondary and tertiary education. *OECD Economic Studies 34 2002/I*. Paris: OECD.

Bloom, M. 1992. *Technological Change in the Korean Electronics Industry*. Paris: OECD Development Centre.

Borensztein, E., J. DeGregorio, and J.-W. Lee. 1998. How does foreign direct investment affect economic growth? *Journal of International Economics*, 45, 115.

Branstetter, L., R. Fisman, C.F. Foley, and K. Saggi. 2007. Intellectual property rights, imitation and foreign direct investment. *NBER Working Papers 13033*. Cambridge, MA: National Bureau of Economic Research.

Bresnahan, T. and M. Trajtenberg. 1995. General purpose technologies: engines of growth. *Journal of Econometrics*, 65, 83.

Bresnahan, T.F., E. Brynjolfsson, and L.M. Hitt. 2002. Information technology, workplace organization, and the demand for skilled labor. Firm-level evidence. *Quarterly Journal of Economics*, 117(1), 339.

Breznitz, D. 2007. *Innovation and the State: Political Choice and Strategies in Israel, Taiwan and Ireland*. New Haven: Yale University Press.

Brinkley, I. and N. Lee. 2007. *The Knowledge Economy in Europe*. London: The Work Foundation.

Brown, A., M. Hossain, and D.-T. Nguyen (eds). 2004. *Telecommunications Reform in the Asia-Pacific Region*. Cheltenham: Edward Elgar.

Brown, A.C., J. Stern, and B. Tenenbaum. 2006. *Handbook for Evaluating Infrastructure Regulatory Systems*. Washington, D.C.: World Bank.

Brown, G.K. 2007. Making ethnic citizens: the politics and practice of education in Malaysia. *International Journal of Educational Development*, 27, 318.

Brownlie, I. 1981. The Reality and Efficacity of International Law. *British Yearbook of International Law* 52, 1.

Brunnée, J. and S. Toope. 2002. Persuasion and Enforcement: Explaining Compliance with International Law. *Finnish Yearbook of International Law*. XIII, 1.

Bruton, H.J. 1992. *The Political Economy of Poverty, Equity, and Growth: Sri Lanka and Malaysia*. New York: Oxford University Press.

Brynjolfsson, E. and B. Kahin (eds). 2000. *Understanding the Digital Economy*. Cambridge, MA: The MIT Press.

Buchanan, I. 1972. *Singapore in Southeast Asia: An Economic and Political Appraisal*. London: G. Bell and Sons.

Bunnell, T.G. 1998. *On Route 2020: Malaysia, Modernity and the Multimedia Super Corridor*. Nottingham, UK: University of Nottingham (PhD Thesis).

Bureau of Economic Analysis [Online: US Department of Commerce]. Available at: http://bea.gov/index.htm [accessed: 8 May 2010].

Calderon, C. and L. Serven. 2004. The effects of infrastructure development on growth and income distribution. *Econometric Society 2004 Latin American Meetings* [Online], 173. Available at: http://ideas.repec.org/p/ecm/latm04/173.html [accessed: 5 May 2010].

Calliano, R. and C. Carpano. 2000. National systems of technological innovation, FDI and economic growth: the case of Ireland. *Multinational Business Review*, 16.

Campbell, J.L. 1998. Book review – *Embedded Autonomy* by Peter Evans. *Theory and Society*, 27(1), 103.

Cardarelli, R. 2001. Is Australia a 'new economy? in *Australia: Selected Issues. Staff Country Report 55*. Washington, D.C.: International Monetary Fund, 5–26.

Carkovic, M. and R. Levine. 2002. *Does Foreign Direct Investment Accelerate Economic Growth?* World Bank Conference on Financial Globalization: A Blessing or a Curse, Washington, D.C., May 30–31, 2002.

Caselli, F. and W.J. Coleman II. 2001. Cross-country technology diffusion: the case of computers. *The American Economic Review*, 91(2), 328.

Cass, F. 2007. Attracting FDI to transition countries: the use of incentives and promotion agencies. *Transnational Corporations*, 16(2), 77.

Caves, R. 1996. *Multinational Enterprise and Economic Analysis* (2nd edition). Cambridge, MA: Cambridge University Press.

Chan, H.C. and O. ul Haq. 1987. *S. Rajaratnam: The Prophetic and the Political*. Singapore: Graham Brash.

Chan, T.H. and K. Horii. 1986. *Impact of the New Economic Policy on Malaysian Economy*. Tokyo: Institute of Developing Economies.

Chee, S. and S.M. Khoo. 1975. *Malaysian Economic Development and Policies*. Kuala Lumpur: Malaysian Economic Association.

Chen, E. 1996. Transnational corporations and technology transfer to developing countries, in *Transnational Corporations and World Development* edited by UNCTAD. New York: UNCTAD, 181–214.

Chen, H.Y. and E.C.Y. Kuo. 1985. Telecommunications and economic development in Singapore. *Telecommunications Policy*, 240.

Chen M.Y. 2000. Malaysia's multimedia super corridor struggles to live up to its own hype. *Asian Wall Street Journal*, 22 September, 32.

——. 2001. Glitches zap Malaysian tech corridor. *Asian Wall Street Journal*, 26 March, 1.

Chen, P.S.J. 1983. Singapore's development strategies: a model for rapid growth, in *Singapore Development Policy and Trends*, edited by P.S.J. Chen. Singapore: Oxford University Press, 3–25.

Chia, S.Y. 1986. Direct foreign investment and the industrialization process in Singapore, in *Singapore: Resources and Growth*, edited by C.Y. Lim and P.J. Lloyd. New York: Oxford University Press, 79–118.

Chidamber, S.R. 2002. An analysis of Vietnam's ICT and software services sector. *Kogod School of Business, Faculty Research Working Paper Series 03-005*. Washington, D.C.: Kogod School of Business.

Chong, T. (ed.). 2010. *Management of Success: Singapore Revisited*. Singapore: ISEAS Publishing.

Choong C.K., Y. Zulkornain, and S.C. Soo. 2005. Foreign direct investment and economic growth in Malaysia: the role of domestic financial sector. *The Singapore Economic Review*, 50(2), 245.

Chu, K.Y. 2004. A model of a rule of law and a rule of man. *Research Paper No. 2004/65*. Helsinki: UNU-WIDER.

Chua, A. 2003. *World on Fire*. New York: Anchor Books.

Clark, D.H. 1971. Manpower planning in Singapore. *The Malayan Economic Review*, 16(2), 194.

Clarke, M. 2003. E-development? Development and the new economy. *Policy Brief No. 7*. Helsinki: UNU-WIDER.

Co, C.Y. and J.A. List. 2004. Is foreign direct investment attracted to knowledge creators? *Applied Economics*, 36, 1143.

Coase, R. 1998. The new institutional economics. *The American Economic Review*, 88(2), 72.

Cohen, D. and M. Soto. 2001. Growth and human capital: good data, good results. *OECD Technical Paper 179*. Paris: OECD.

Cohen, J. and W. Easterly (eds). 2009. *What Works in Development? Thinking Big and Thinking Small*. Washington, D.C.: Brookings Institution Press.

Colecchia, A. 2001. The impact of information and communications technologies on output growth: issues and preliminary findings. *STI Working Paper No. 11*. Paris: OECD.

Colecchia, A. and P. Schreyer. 2002. The contribution of information and communication technologies to economic growth in nine OECD countries. *OECD Economic Studies No. 34*. Paris: OECD.

Collis, M. 1988. *Raffles*. London: Century Hutchinson.

Colyvas., J.A. and W.W. Powell. 2006. Roads to institutionalization: the remaking of boundaries between public and private science. *Research in Organizational Behavior*, 27, 305.

Committee of the Future [Online: Parliament of Finland]. Available at: http://web.eduskunta.fi/Resource.phx/parliament/committees/future.htx [accessed: 7 May 2010].

Cowen, T. 2011. *The Great Stagnation*. New York: Dutton.

Coyle, D. 2005. Overview. *The Vodafone Policy Paper Series* 3.

Crafts, N. 1997. Endogenous growth: lessons for and from economic history, in *Advances in Economics and Econometrics: Theory and Applications, Seventh World Congress, Volume II*, edited by D.M. Kreps and K.F. Wallis. Cambridge, England: Cambridge University Press, 38–78.

——. 2001. *The Solow Productivity Paradox in Historical Perspective*. London: London School of Economics. Available at: http://www.j-bradford-delong.net/articlcs_of_thc_month/ pdf/Ncwsolow.pdf [acccsscd: 6 May 2010].

Cuadra, E. and J. Moreno. 2005. *Expanding Opportunities and Building Competencies for Young People: A New Agenda for Secondary Education*. Washington, D.C.: World Bank.

Cubbin. J. and J. Stern. 2006. The impact of regulatory governance and privatization on electricity generation capacity in developing economies. *The World Bank Economic* Review, 20(1), 115.

Dahlman, C.J., J. Routti, and P. Yla-Anttila (eds). 2006. *Finland as a Knowledge Economy: Elements of Success and Lessons Learned*. Washington, D.C.: World Bank Institute.

Dasgupta, S., S. Lall, and D. Wheeler. 2001. Policy reform, economic growth and the digital divide: an econometric analysis. *Policy Research Working Paper 2567*. Washington, D.C.: World Bank.

Daveri, F. 2002. The new economy in Europe, 1992–2001. *Discussion Paper No. 2002/70*. Helsinki: UNU-WIDER.

David, P.A. 1990: The dynamo and the computer: an historical perspective on the modern productivity paradox. *The American Economic Review*, 80(2), 355.

——. 2000. Understanding digital technology's evolution and the path of measured productivity growth: present and future in the mirror of the past, in *Understanding the Digital Economy*, edited by E. Brynjolfsson and B. Kahin. Cambridge, MA: The MIT Press, 49–95.

David, P.A. and G. Wright. 1999. *General Purpose Technologies and Surges in Productivity: Historical Reflections on the Future of the ICT Revolution*. International Symposium on Economic Challenges of the 21st Century in Historical Perspective, Oxford, England, July 2–4, 1999.

Davis, K. and M.J. Trebilcock. 1999. *What Role do Legal Institutions Play in Development?* Draft prepared for the International Monetary Fund's Conference on Second Generation Reforms, Washington, D.C., November 8–9, 1999.

Davis, N. 2003. *Inward Foreign Direct Investment, Productivity Spillovers and Public Policy*. Wellington, New Zealand: Ministry of Economic Development.

de Ferranti, D., G.E. Perry, I. Gill, J.L. Guasch, W.F. Maloney, C. Sanchez-Paramo, and N. Schady. 2003. *Closing the Gap in Education and Technology*. Washington, D.C.: World Bank.

de Mello Jr, L.R. 1997. Foreign direct investment in developing countries and growth: a selective survey. *The Journal of Development Studies*, 34(1), 1.

Deardorff, A.V. 1990. Should patent protection be extended to all developing countries? *World Economy*, 13(4), 497.

Delors, J. 1996. *Learning: The Treasure Within*. Paris: UNESCO.

Deyo, F. 1987. *The Political Economy of the New Asian Industrialism*. Ithaca: Cornell University Press.

Dewan, S., D. Ganley, and K.L. Kraemer. 2004. *Across the Digital Divide: A Cross-Country Analysis of the Determinants of IT Penetration*. University of California, Irvine: Personal Computing Industry Center, Graduate School of Management.

Diamond, J. 1999. *Guns, Germs, and Steel*. New York: W.W. Norton & Co.

Digital Opportunities Task Force (DOT Force). 2001. *Digital Opportunities for All: Meeting the Challenge*. Genoa: G-8. Available at: http://www.g8italia.it/_en/docs/STUWX141.htm [accessed: 7 May 2010].

Dimelis, S. 2005. Spillovers from foreign direct investment and firm growth: technological, financial and market structures. *International Journal of the Economics of Business*, 12(1), 85.

Djankov, S. and B. Hoekman. 1999. Foreign investment and productivity growth in Czech enterprises. *World Bank Economic Review*, 14, 49.

Dobson, W. 2009. *Gravity Shift*. Toronto: University of Toronto Press.

Dollar, D. and A. Kraay. 2004. Trade, Growth and Poverty. *The Economic Journal*, 114, 22.

Doraisamy, T.R. 1969. *150 Years of Education in Singapore*. Singapore: TTC Publications Board.

Driffield, N. and A.H.M. Noor. 1999. Foreign direct investment and local input linkages in Malaysia. *Transnational Corporations*, 8(3), 1.

Dunning, J.H. 1996. Re-evaluating the benefits of foreign direct investment, in *Transnational Corporations and Investment: Companies Without Borders in the 1990s* edited by UNCTAD. London: International Thomson Business Press.

——. 1997. The advent of alliance capitalism, in *The New Globalism and Developing Countries*, edited by J.H. Dunning and K.A. Hamdani. New York: United Nations University Press, 12–50.

——. 1998. Location and the multinational enterprise: a neglected factor. *Journal of International Business* Studies, 29(1), 45.

——. (ed.). 2000. *Regions, Globalization and the Knowledge-Economy*. New York: Oxford University Press.

——. 2002. *Determinants of Foreign Direct Investment: Globalization Induced Changes and the Role of FDI Policies*. Annual Bank Conference on Development Economics in Europe, Oslo, 2002.

Dunning, J.H. and K.A. Hamdani (eds). 1997. *The New Globalism and Developing Countries*. New York: United Nations University Press.

Dunning, J.H. and F. Zhang. 2008. Foreign direct investment and the locational competitiveness of countries. *Transnational Corporations*, 17(3), 1.

Duran, J.J. and F. Ubeda. 2005. The investment development path of newly developed countries. *International Journal of the Economics of Business*, 12(1), 123.

Easterly, W. 2001. *The Elusive Quest for Growth*. Cambridge, MA: The MIT Press.

Easterly, W. and R. Levine. 2003. Tropics, germs, and crops: how endowments influence economic development. *Journal of Monetary Economics*, 50, 3.

Eberhard, A. 2007. Infrastructure regulation in developing countries: an exploration of hybrid and transition models. *Public-Private Infrastructure Advisory Facility, Working Paper No. 4*. Washington D.C.

Economist, The. 2009. Special report on telecoms in emerging markets. 26 September.

——. 2012. The Rise of State Capitalism. 21 January.

Edquist, C. (ed.). 1997. *Systems of Innovation: Technologies, Institutions and Organizations*. Abingdon, England: Routledge.

Edquist, C. and B. Johnson. 1997. Institutions and organizations in systems of innovation, in *Systems of Innovation: Technologies, Institutions and Organizations*, edited by C. Edquist. Abingdon, England: Routledge, 41–63.

Ernst, D. 2008. Asia's 'upgrading through innovation' strategies and global innovation networks: an extension of Sanjaya Lall's research agenda. *Transnational Corporations*, 17(3), 31.

Esfahani, H.S. and M.T. Ramirez. 2003. Institutions, infrastructure and economic growth. *Journal of Development Economics*, 70, 443.

Estache, A. and M. Fay. 2007. Current debates on infrastructure policy. *World Bank Policy Research Working Paper 4410*. Washington, D.C.: The World Bank.

Estache, A., A. Goicoechea, and M. Manacorda. 2006. Telecommunications performance, reforms and governance. *World Bank Policy Research Working Paper 3822*. Washington, D.C.: The World Bank.

Estavao, M. and J. Levy. 2000. France: selected issues. *International Monetary Fund, Staff Country Report 148*. Washington, D.C.: IMF.

Etounga-Manguelle, D. 2000. Does Africa need a cultural adjustment program? in *Culture Matters: How Values Shape Human Progress*, edited by L.E. Harrison and S.P. Huntington. New York: Basic Books, 65–77.

Evans, P. 1995. *Embedded Autonomy: States and Industrial Transformation*. Princeton: Princeton University Press.

Farrell, G., S. Isaacs, and M. Trucano (eds). 2007. *Survey of ICT and Education in Africa: 53 Country Reports*. Vol 2. Washington, D.C.: infoDev.

Findlay, R. and S. Wellisz (eds). 1993. *The Political Economy of Poverty, Equity, and Growth: Five Small Open Economies*. New York: Oxford University Press.

Fink, C. and C. Kenny. 2003. Whither the digital divide [Online: ITU]. Available at: http://www.itu.int/wsis/docs/background/themes/digital_divide/fink-kenny. pdf [accessed: 7 May 2010].

Finland, Ministry of Education. 2004. *Education and Research 2003–08: Development Plan*. Helsinki: Helsinki University Press.

Finland, Official Statistics of [Online: Statistics Finland]. Available at: http:// www.stat.fi/index_en.html [accessed: 8 May 2010].

Fitzmaurice, G. 1956. The Foundations of the Authority of International Law and the Problem of Enforcement. *The Modern Law Review* 1.

Fong, C.O. 1986. *Technological Leap: Malaysian Industry in Transition*. Singapore: Oxford.

Frankel, J. and D. Romer. 1999. Does trade cause growth? *The Economic Journal*, 114, 379.

Fratianni, M., P. Savona and J. Kirton (eds). 2003. *Sustaining Global Growth and Development*. Aldershot: Ashgate.

Fraunhofer Institute Systems and Innovation Research. 2004. *Benchmarking National and Regional Policies in Support of the Competitiveness of the ICT Sector in the EU*. Karlsruhe, Germany: Fraunhofer Institute Systems and Innovation Research.

Frieden, R. 2005. Lessons from broadband development in Canada, Japan, Korea and the United States. *Telecommunications Policy*, 29, 595.

Friedman, T.L. 2005. *The World is Flat*. New York: Farrar, Straus and Giroux.

——. 2012. Made in the World. New York Times, 29 January http://www.nytimes.com/2012/01/29/opinion/sunday/friedman-made-in-the-world.html?partner=rssnyt&emc=rss.

Fukuyama, F. 2001. Social capital, civil society and development. *Third World Quarterly.* 22(1), 7.

Fuller, L. 1964. *The Morality of Law.* New Haven: Yale University Press.

G-7. 2000. *Impact of the IT Revolution on the Economy and Finance.* Report from G7 Finance Ministers to the Heads of State and Government [Online]. Fukuoka. Available at: http://www.mof.go.jp/english/international_policy/convention/summit/cy2000/if020.htm [accessed: 22 June 2011].

G-8. 2000. *Okinawa Charter on Global Information Society.* Okinawa [Online]. Available at: http://www.mofa.go.jp/policy/economy/summit/2000/pdfs/charter.pdf [accessed: 22 June 2011].

G-20. 2005. *Institution Building in the Financial Sector.* Washington: G-20 Secretariat.

Gan, K.P. 1995. Human capital formation: public policy approach. *The Singapore Economic Review,* 40(2), 159.

Gani, A. and B. Sharma. 2003. The effects of information technology achievement and diffusion on foreign direct investment. *Perspectives on Global Development and Technology,* 2(2), 161.

Gerschenkron, A. 1962. *Economic Backwardness in Historical Perspective.* Cambridge MA: The Belknap Press of Harvard University Press.

Gershenberg, I. 1987. The training and spread of managerial know-how: a comparative analysis of multinational and other firms in Kenya. *World Development,* 15(7), 931.

Ghatak, S. 2003. *Introduction to Development Economics* (4th edition). New York: Routledge.

Ghesquiere, H. 2007. *Singapore's Success: Engineering Economic Growth.* Singapore: Thomson.

Gilardi, F. 2002. Policy credibility and delegation to independent regulatory agencies: a comparative empirical analysis. *Journal of European Public Policy,* 9(6), 873.

——. 2005. The institutional foundations of regulatory capitalism: the diffusion of independent regulatory agencies in western Europe. *Annals AAPSS,* 598, 84.

Gilbert, A.L. 1989. Singapore: a case study in international telecommunications technology transfer. *IEEE Technology and Society Magazine,* 8(4), 25.

Glaeser, E.L., R. La Porta, F. Lopez-de-Silanes, and A. Shleifer. 2004. Do institutions cause growth? *Journal of Economic Growth,* 9, 271.

Glewwe, P. 2002. Schools and skills in developing countries: education policies and socioeconomic outcomes. *Journal of Economic Literature,* 40(2), 46.

Goh, C.B. and S. Gopinathan. 2006. *The Development of Education in Singapore Since 1965.* Asia Education Study Tour for African Policy Makers, Singapore and Vietnam, June 18–30, 2006. Available at: http://intlalliance.org/Singapore.pdf [accessed: 7 May 2010].

Goh, K.S. 1958. Entrepreneurship in a plural economy. *Malayan Economic Review*, 3(1), 1.

——. 1968. Budget day speech, in *Wealth of East Asian Nations* by K.S. Goh. Singapore, Federal Publications, 1995.

——. 1976. A socialist economy that works, in *The Practice of Economic Growth* by K.S. Goh. Singapore: Federal Publications, 1995.

——. 1983. Public administration and economic development in LDCs. *World Economy*, 6(3), 229.

——. 1986. Transformation of Singapore's economy, 1960–1985, in *Wealth of East Asian Nations* by K.S. Goh. Singapore, Federal Publications, 1995, 23–33.

——. 1992. Experience and prospect of Singapore's economic development: strategy formulation and execution, in *Wealth of East Asian Nations* by K.S. Goh. Singapore, Federal Publications, 1995, 34–55.

——. 1995a. *The Practice of Economic Growth*. Singapore: Federal Publications.

——. 1995b. *Wealth of East Asian Nations*. Singapore: Federal Publications.

——. 1996. The technology ladder in development: the Singapore case. *Asian-Pacific Economic Literature*, 10(1), 1.

Goh, K.S. and the Education Study Team. 1979. *Report on the Ministry of Education 1978*. Singapore: Ministry of Education.

Goh, K.S. and L. Low. 1996. Beyond 'miracles' and total factor productivity. *ASEAN Economic Bulletin*, 13(1), 1.

Goldin, C. and L.F. Katz. 2008. *The Race Between Education and Technology*. Cambridge, MA: The Belknap Press of Harvard University.

Gopinathan, S. 1997. Education and development in Singapore, in *Education in Singapore*, edited by J. Tan, S. Gopinathan, and W.K. Ho. Singapore: Prentice Hall, 33–53.

——. 1999. Preparing for the next rung: economic restructuring and educational reform in Singapore. *Journal of Education and Work*, 12(3), 295.

——. 2007. Globalisation, the Singapore developmental state and education policy: a thesis revisited. *Globalisation, Societies and Education*, 5(1), 53.

Gorg, H. and D. Greenaway. 2002. Much ado about nothing? Do domestic firms really benefit from foreign direct investment? *Centre for Economic Policy Research Discussion Paper No. 3485*. London: Centre for Economic Policy Research.

Gough, N. 2005. Introduction. *The Vodafone Policy Paper Series*, 3.

Grace, J., C. Kenney, and C.Z-W. Qiang. 2004. *ICT and Broad-Based Development: A Partial Review of the Evidence*. Washington, D.C.: World Bank.

Grameenphone: Village Phone Program [Online: Grameenphone]. Available at: http://www.grameenphone.com/index.php?id=79 [accessed: 8 May 2010].

Gramlich, E.M. 1994. Infrastructure investment: a review essay. *Journal of Economic Literature*, 32, 1176.

Greenwood, R., C. Oliver, K. Sahlin and R. Suddaby. 2008. *The Sage Handbook of Organizational Institutionalism*. London: Sage Publications.

Groenewegen, J., A. Spithoven and A. van den Berg. 2010. *Institutional Economics*. Palgrave Macmillan: Houndmills.

Grondana, M. 2000. A cultural typology of economic development, in *Culture Matters: How Values Shape Human Progress*, edited by L.E. Harrison and S.P. Huntington. New York: Basic Books, 44–55.

Gual, J. and F. Trillas. 2006. Telecommunications policies: measurements and determinants. *Review of Network Economics*, 5(2), 249.

Guermazi, B. and D. Satola. 2004. Creating the 'right' enabling environment for ICT, in *Telecommunications Trade Liberalization and the WTO, Final Report for the GICT Department*. Washington, D.C.: World Bank, 23–46.

Guislain, P., M.A. Ampah, L. Besançon, C. Niang, and A. Serot. 2005. Connecting sub-Saharan Africa. *World Bank Working Paper No. 51*. Washington, D.C.: The World Bank.

Gutierrez, L.H. 2003. The effect of endogenous regulation on telecommunications expansion and efficiency in Latin America. *Journal of Regulatory Economics*, 23(3), 257.

Haacker, M. and J. Morsink. 2002. You say you want a revolution: information technology and growth. *IMF Working Paper WP/02/70*. Washington, D.C.: International Monetary Fund.

Halimah, A. 2004. Human capital and technology development in Malaysia. *International Education Journal*, 5(2), 239.

Hanna, N. 2003a. *Why ICT Matters for Growth and Poverty Reduction*. Washington D.C.: World Bank. Available at: http://old.developmentgateway.org/node/133831/sdm/blob?pid=4770 [accessed: 5 May 2010].

——. 2003b. Why national strategies are needed for ICT-enabled development. *ISG Staff Working Papers, No. 3*. Washington D.C.: World Bank. Available at: http://wsispapers.choike.org/national_strategies.pdf [accessed: 5 May 2010].

Hargreaves, A. and P. Shaw. 2007. *Knowledge and Skill Development in Developing and Transitional Countries*. Washington D.C.: World Bank. Available at: http://info.worldbank.org/etools/docs/library/235729/Knowledge%20and%20Skills%20Development%20in%20Developing%20and%20Transitional%20Economies.pdf [accessed: 5 May 2010].

Hariss, J., J. Hunter and C.M. Lewis (eds). 1995. *The New Institutional Economic and Third World Development*. New York: Routledge.

Harrison, L.E. and S.P. Huntington (eds). 2000. *Culture Matters: How Values Shape Human Progress*. New York: Basic Books.

Harrison, L.E. 2006. *The Central Liberal Truth*. New York: Oxford University Press.

Hejazi, W. 2010. Dispelling Canadian myths about foreign direct investment. *IRPP Study No. 1*. Montreal: Institute for Research on Public Policy.

Helliwell, J. and R. Putnam. 1995. Economic Growth and Social Capital in Italy. *Eastern Economic Journal*, 21(3), 295.

Helpman, E. (ed.). 1998. *General Purpose Technologies and Economic Growth*. Cambridge, MA: The MIT Press.

Helpman, E. and M. Trajtenberg. 1994. A time to sow and a time to reap: growth based on general purpose technologies. *NBER Working Papers 4854*. New York: National Bureau of Economic Research, Inc.

Henisz, W. and B.A. Zelner. 2001. The institutional environment for telecommunications investment. *Journal of Economics & Management Strategy*, 10(1), 123.

Heston, A., R. Summers and B. Aten. 2011. *Penn World Table Version 7.0*. University of Pennsylvania, Philadelphia: Center for International Comparisons of Production, Income and Prices.

Hilley, J. 2001. *Malaysia: Mahathirism, Hegemony and the New Opposition*. New York: Zed Books.

Hodges, J.T. and G. Dellacha. 2007. Unsolicited infrastructure proposals: how some countries introduce competition and transparency. *Working Paper 1*. Washington, D.C.: Public-Private Infrastructure Advisory Facility.

Hsiao, C. and S. Yan. 2003. Foreign direct investment and economic growth: the importance of institutions and urbanization. *Economic Development and Cultural Change*, 51(4), 883.

Huff, W.G. 1995. The developmental state, government, and Singapore's economic development since 1960. *World Development*, 23(8), 1421.

Hukill, M., and M. Jussawalla. 1989. Telecommunications policies and markets in the ASEAN countries. *Columbia Journal of World Business*, 43.

Hukill, M., R. Ono and C. Vallath (eds). 2000. *Electronic Communication Convergence*. New Delhi: Sage Publications.

Hussein, S.M. 2000. The Malaysian Communications and Multimedia Act 1998 – Its implications on the information technology (IT) industry. *Information & Communications Technology Law*, 9(1), 79.

Hwang, H. and W.W. Powell. 2005. Institutions and entrepreneurship, in *Handbook of Entrepreneurship Research: Disciplinary Perspectives*, edited by S.A. Alvarez, R. Agarwal and O. Sorenson. New York: Springer Science & Business Media, 179–210.

Ignatieff, M. 2005. Introduction: American Exceptionalism and Human Rights in *American Exceptionalism and Human Rights*, by M. Ignatieff. Princeton: Princeton University Press, 1–26.

Infocomm Development Agency [Online: Government of Singapore]. Available at: http://www.ida.gov.sg/ [accessed: 7 May 2010].

Infocomm Development Authority of Singapore. 2000. *Infocomm 21*. Singapore.

——. 2002. *Infocomm 21 Status Update Report*. Singapore.

——. 2003. *Connected Singapore: A New Blueprint for Infocomm Development*. Singapore.

——. 2005a. *iN2015 Master Plan: Innovation, Integration, Internationalisation, Report by the iN2015 Steering Committee*. Singapore.

——. 2005b. *Totally Connected Wired and Wireless: Report by the iN2015 Infocomm Infrastructure, Services and Technology Development Sub-Committee*. Singapore.

Institute of Strategic and International Studies. 2002. *Knowledge-Based Economy Master Plan*. Kuala Lumpur: ISIS.

Institute of Strategic and International Studies and Penang Development Corporation. *Penang Strategic Development Plan 1991–2000*. Kuala Lumpur: ISIS, 1991.

International Bank for Reconstruction and Development (IBRD). 1955. *The Economic Development of Malaya*. Baltimore, MD: The Johns Hopkins Press.

——. 1963. *Report on the Economic Aspects of Malaysia*. A Mission of the IBRD under the Chairmanship of Jacques Rueff. Singapore: Government Printing Office.

International Country Risk Guide. 2009. East Syracuse, NY: Political Risk Services.

International Monetary Fund. *Balance of Payments Manual*. 1993. Washington, D.C.: IMF.

International Telecommunications Union. *ICT Regulation Toolkit* [Online]. Available at: http://www.ictregulationtoolkit.org/en/index.html [accessed: 5 May 2010].

——. *ITU Statistical Database* [Online]. Available at: http://www.itu.int/ITUD/ict/statistics/ict/index.html [accessed: 5 May 2010].

——. 2009. *Measuring the Information Society: The ICT Development Index*. Geneva: ITU.

——. 2010. *Measuring the Information Society: The ICT Development Index 2010*. Geneva: International Telecommunications Union.

——. 2010. *National e-Strategies for Development: Global Status and Perspectives 2010*. Geneva: International Telecommunications Union.

——. 2010. *World Telecommunication/ICT Development Report: Monitoring the WSIS Targets – A Mid-Term Review*. Geneva: International Telecommunications Union.

——. 2011. *Measuring the Information Society: The ICT Development Index 2009*. Geneva: International Telecommunications Union.

——. 2011. *Trends in Telecommunications Reform 2010–11: Enabling Tomorrow's Digital World*. Geneva: International Telecommunications Union.

Ismail, M.N. 1999. Foreign firms and national technological upgrading: the electronics industry in Malaysia, in *Industrial Technology Development in Malaysia: Industry and Firm Studies*, edited by K.S. Jomo, G. Felker, and R. Rasiah. New York: Routledge.

Ismail, M.Y. 1987. *Malaysia's New Economic Policy: Its Impact on Urban, Regional and Sectoral Distribution of Income, Inequality and Poverty 1970–1980*. Ann Arbor, Michigan: UMI Dissertation Information Service [Doctoral Dissertation].

Iyanda, O. and J.A. Bello. 1979. Employment effects of multinational enterprises in Nigeria. *Working Paper No.10*. Geneva: International Labour Organization.

JBIC Institute. 2002. Foreign direct investment and development: where do we stand? *JBICI Research Paper No. 15*. Japan Bank of International Cooperation.

Jalava, J. and M. Pohjola. 2001. Economic growth in the new economy: evidence from advanced economies. *Discussion Paper No. 2001/5*. Helsinki: UNU-WIDER.

Jayakumar, D. 2004. Has Malaysia really eradicated poverty? *Aliran* [Online], 2. Available at: http://www.aliran.com/oldsite/monthly/2004a/2j.html [accessed: 5 May 2010].

Jensen, R. 2007. The digital provide: information (technology), market performance, and welfare in the south Indian fisheries sector. *The Quarterly Journal of Economics*, 122(3), 879.

Johnson, C. 1982. *MITI and the Japanese Miracle: The Growth of Industrial Policy, 1925–1975*. Stanford: Stanford University Press.

———. 1986. The Nonsocialist NICs: East Asia. *International Organization* 40(2), 557.

———. 1989. South Korean democratization: the role of economic development. *The Pacific Review*. 2(1), 1.

———. 1998. Economic crisis in East Asia: the clash of capitalisms. *Cambridge Journal of Economics* 22, 653.

———. 1999. Johnson, C. The developmental state: odyssey of a concept, in *The Developmental State*, edited by M. Woo-Cumings. Ithaca: Cornell University Press, 32–60.

Jomo, K.S. 1986. *A Question of Class: Capital, the State, and Uneven Development in Malaya*. Oxford: Oxford University Press.

Jomo, K.S. and S.K. Ng (eds). 1996. *Malaysia's Economic Development: Policy & Reform*. Petaling Jaya, Malaysia: Pelanduk Publications.

Jomo, K.S. and W.S. Ngan (eds). 2008. *Law, Institutions and Malaysian Economic Development*. Singapore: NUS Press.

Jomo, K.S., G. Felker, and R. Rasiah (eds). 1999. *Industrial Technology Development in Malaysia: Industry and Firm Studies*. New York: Routledge.

Jorgenson, D. 2001. Information technology and the US economy. *The American Economic Review*, 91(1), 1.

Jorgenson, D. and K. Stiroh. 2000. US economic growth at the industry level. *American Economic Review*, 90(2), 161.

Jovanovic, B. and P.L. Rousseau. 2003. General purpose technologies. *NBER Working Paper W11093*. New York: National Bureau of Economic Research.

Jutting, J. 2003. Institutions and development: a critical review. *Working Paper No. 210*. Paris: OECD.

Kaitila, V., H. Koski, J. Routti, P. Tiihonen, and P. Yla-Anttila. (2006) Changes in the economic and institutional regimes, in *Finland as a Knowledge Economy: Elements of Success and Lessons Learned*, edited by C.J. Dahlman, J. Routti, and P. Yla-Anttila. Washington, D.C.: World Bank Institute, 25–38.

Kapstein, E.B. 2002. Virtuous circles? Human capital formation, economic development and the multinational enterprise. *OECD Development Centre Working Paper 191*. Paris: OECD.

Kaufmann, D., A. Kraay, and P. Zoido-Lobaton. 1999. *Governance Matters.* Washington, D.C.: The World Bank Group.

——. 2002. *Governance Matters II: Updated Indicators for 2000/01.* Washington, D.C.: The World Bank Group.

Kaufmann, D., A. Kraay, and M. Mastruzzi. 2005. *Governance Matters IV: New Data, New Challenges.* Washington, D.C.: The World Bank.

——. 2007. *Governance Matters VI: Aggregate and Individual Governance Indicators 1996–2006.* Washington, D.C.: The World Bank.

——. 2009. *Governance Matters VIII: Aggregate and Individual Governance Indicators 1996–2008.* Washington, D.C.: The World Bank.

——. 2010. The worldwide governance indicators: methodology and analytical issues. *Policy Research Working Paper 5430.* Washington, D.C.: The World Bank.

Kenny, C. 2002. The internet and economic growth in least developed countries: a case of managing expectations. *Discussion Paper No. 2002/75.* Helsinki: UNU-WIDER.

Kenny, C. and C.Z.-W. Qiang. 2003. Information and communication technologies and broad-based development, in *ICT and Development*, edited by The World Bank. Washington, D.C.: World Bank, 14–19.

Kiessling, J. 2007. *Institutions and ICT Technology Adoption.* Helsinki: Stockholm University. Available at: http://www.ne.su.se/paper/wp06_07.pdf [accessed: 5 May 2010].

Khalil, M. 2006. Evolution of telecoms in emerging markets. *Telecom Finance 137.* Washington, D.C.: World Bank.

Khalil, M., P. Dongier, and C.Z.-W. Qiang. 2009. Overview, in *Information and Communications for Development: Extending Reach and Increasing Impact*, edited by The World Bank. Washington, D.C.: World Bank, 3–17.

Khan, K. and Koh B.L. 1997. Foreign direct investment, exports and economic growth in the three little dragons: evidence from co-integration and causality tests. *The Singapore Economic Review*, 42(2), 40.

Kharas, H., A. Zeufack and H. Majeed. 2010. *Cities, People & the Economy: A Study on Positioning Penang.* Kuala Lumpur: Khazanah Nasional and the World Bank.

Khoo B.K. 2006. Malaysia: balancing development and power, in *The Political Economy of Southeast Asia: Markets, Power and Contestation* (3rd edition), edited by G. Rodan, K. Hewison and R. Robison. Oxford: Oxford University Press, 170–196.

Khosrowpour, M. (ed.). 1994. *Managing Social and Economic Change with Information Technology.* Hershey, PA: Idea Group Inc.

King, E.M. and L.A. Lillard. 1987. Education policy and schooling attainment in Malaysia and the Philippines. *Economics of Education Review*, 6(2), 167.

Kirton, J., M. Larionova and P. Savona (eds). 2010. *Making Global Economic Governance Effective.* Farnham: Ashgate.

Knowles, S. 2006. Is social capital part of the institutions continuum and is it a deep determinant of development? *Research Paper 2006/25*. Helsinki: UNU-WIDER.

Kodres, L. 2001. The 'new economy' in the United Kingdom. *International Monetary Fund, Staff Country Report 124*. Washington, D.C.: IMF.

Koh, A.I. and K.L. Lim. 2002. Singapore: an infocomm hub, in *Singapore Economy in the 21st Century*, edited by A.I. Koh, K.L. Lim, W.T. Hui, B. Rao, and M.K. Chng. Singapore: McGraw-Hill, 238–257.

Koh, A.I., W.T. Hui, B. Rao and M.K. Chng (eds). 2002. *Singapore Economy in the 21st Century*. Singapore: McGraw-Hill.

Koh. H.H. 1997. Why do nations obey international law? Book Review of *The New Sovereignty: compliance with International Regulatory Agreements* by A. Chayes and A. Handler Chayes, and of *Fairness in International Law and Institutions* by T.M. Franck. *Yale Law Journal* 106, 2599.

———. 1998. The 1998 Frankel Lecture: bringing international law home. *Houston International Law Journal* 35, 623.

Koh, T.H. and P.K. Wong. 2003. Competing at the frontier: the changing role of technology policy in Singapore's economic strategy [Online]. Singapore. Available at: http://papers.ssrn.com/sol3/papers.cfm?abstract_id=626342 [accessed: 5 May 2010].

Kokko, A. 2002. *Globalization and Foreign Direct Investment Incentives*. Annual Bank Conference on Development Economics in Europe, Oslo, 2002.

Koski, H., L. Leijola, C. Palmberg, and P. Yla-Anttila. 2006. Innovation and education strategies and policies in Finland, in *Finland as a Knowledge Economy: Elements of Success and Lessons Learned*, edited by C.J. Dahlman, J. Routti, and P. Yla-Anttila. Washington, D.C.: World Bank Institute, 39–62.

Koski, H., P. Rouvinene, and P. Yla-Anttila. 2001. ICT clusters in Europe: the great central banana and small nordic potato. *Discussion Paper No. 2001/6*. Helsinki: UNU-WIDER.

Koski, H. and P. Yla-Anttila. 2006. Structural changes in the Finnish economy: from agriculture to high-tech, in *Finland as a Knowledge Economy: Elements of Success and Lessons Learned*, edited by C.J. Dahlman, J. Routti, and P. Yla-Anttila. Washington, D.C.: World Bank Institute, 17–24.

Kortum, S. and J. Lerner. 1998. Stronger protection or technological revolution: what is behind the recent surge in patenting? *Carnegie-Rochester Conference Series on Public Policy*, 48(1), 247–304.

Kraemer, K.L. and J. Dedrick. 2001. Information technology and economic development: results and policy implications of cross-country studies, in *Information Technology, Productivity and Economic Growth*, edited by M. Pohjola. Oxford: Oxford University Press, 257–279.

———. 2002. Information technology in southeast Asia: engine of growth or digital divide? in *Information Technology in Asia: New Development Paradigms*, edited by S.Y. Chia and J.J. Lim. Singapore: Institute of Southeast Asian Studies, 22–47.

Krause, L.B., A.T. Koh, and T.Y. Lee. 1987. *The Singapore Economy Reconsidered*. Singapore: Institute of Southeast Asian Studies.

Kremer, M. and A. Holla. 2009. Pricing and access: lessons from randomized evaluations in education and health, in *What Works in Development? Thinking Big and Thinking Small*, edited by J. Cohen and W. Easterly. Washington, D.C.: Brookings Institution Press, 91–129.

Kreps, D.M. and K.F. Wallis. 1997. *Advances in Economics and Econometrics: Theory and Applications, Seventh World Congress*, vol. 2. Cambridge, England: Cambridge University Press.

Krugman, P. 1994. The myth of Asia's miracle. *Foreign Affairs*, 73(6), 62.

Kuemmerle, W. 1999. The drivers of foreign direct investment into research and development: an empirical investigation. *Journal of International Business Studies*, 30(1), 1.

Kuo, C.Y. 1983. Communication policy and national development, in *Singapore Development Policy and Trends*, edited by P. Chen. Singapore: Oxford University Press, 268–281.

Kuruvilla, S., C.L. Erickson, and A. Hwang. 2002. An assessment of the Singapore skills development system: does it constitute a viable model for other developing countries. *World Development*, 30(8),1461.

Kwong, K.S., L.C. Chau, F.T. Lui, and L.D. Qiu. 2001. *Industrial Development in Singapore, Taiwan, and South Korea*. Singapore: World Scientific Publishing.

Lai, Y.W. and S. Narayanan. 1999. Technology utilization level and choice: the electronics and electrical sector in Penang, Malaysia, in *Industrial Technology Development in Malaysia: Industry and Firm Studies*, edited by K.S. Jomo, G. Felker, and R. Rasiah New York: Routledge, 107–124.

Lall, S. 1980. Vertical inter–firm linkages in LDCs: an empirical study. *Oxford Bulletin of Economics and Statistics*, 209.

———. 1994. The East Asian miracle: does the bell toll for industrial strategy, *World Development*, 22(4), 645.

———. 1997. Investment technology and international competitiveness, in *The New Globalism and Developing Countries*, edited by J.H. Dunning and K.A. Hamdani. Tokyo: United Nations University Press, 232–259.

———. 2001. *Competitiveness, Technology and Skills*. Northampton, MA: Edward Elgar.

———. 2002. Linking FDI and technology development for capacity building and strategic competitiveness. *Transnational Corporations*, 11(3), 39.

Lall, S. and R. Narula. 2004. Foreign direct investment and its role in economic development: do we need a new agenda. *The European Journal of Development*, 16(3), 447–464.

Lall, S. and S. Urata (eds). 2003. *Competitiveness, FDI and Technological Activity in East Asia*. Northampton, MA: Edward Elgar.

Landes, D. 2000. Culture makes almost all the difference, in *Culture Matters: How Values Shape Human Progress*, edited by L.E. Harrison and S.P. Huntington. New York: Basic Books, 2–13.

Larionova, M. 2010. The new partnership between multilateral organizations and the G-8, in *Making Global Economic Governance Effective*, edited by J. Kirton, M. Larionova and P. Savona. Farnham: Ashgate.

Lee, C. 2004. Malaysia: telecommunications reform and beyond, in *Telecommunications Reform in the Asia-Pacific Region*, edited by A. Brown, M. Hossain, and D.-T. Nguyen. Cheltenham, UK: Edward Elgar, 119–138.

Lee, E. 2008. *Singapore: The Unexpected Nation*. Singapore: ISEAS Publishing.

Lee, H.H. and Tan H.B. 2006. Technology transfer, FDI and economic growth in the ASEAN region. *Journal of the Asia Pacific Economy Research*, 11(4), 394.

Lee, I.H. and Y. Khatri. 2003. Information technology and productivity growth in Asia. *IMF Working Paper WP/03/15*. Washington, D.C.: International Monetary Fund.

Lee, K.Y. 2000. *From Third World to First*. Singapore: Times Editions.

——. 1950. *The Returned Student*. Talk given to the Malayan Forum at Malaya Hall London, 28 January. Available at: http://stars.nhb.gov.sg/stars/tmp/lky19500128.pdf [accessed: 6 May 2010].

Lee, N.N. 1999. Education in Malaysia: towards vision 2020. *School Effectiveness and School Improvement*, 10(1), 86.

Lee, T.Y. 1997. Infrastructure geared to international economic activity: Singapore, in *Infrastructure Strategies in East Asia: The Untold Story*, edited by A. Mody. Washington D.C.: Economic Development Institute of the World Bank.

Lee, Y., J. Oh and H. Seo. 2002. Digital divide and growth gap: a cumulative relationship. *Discussion Paper No. 88*. Helsinki: UNU-WIDER.

Leijola, L. 2004. The education system in Finland: development and equality. *ETLA Discussion Paper 909*. Helsinki: The Research Institute of the Finnish Economy.

Levy, B. and P.T. Spiller. 1994. The institutional foundations of regulatory commitment: a comparative analysis of telecommunications regulation. *Journal of Law, Economics & Organization*, 10(2), 201.

Lim, C.Y. 1983. Singapore's economic development: retrospect and prospect, in *Singapore Development Policy and Trends*, edited by P.S.J. Chen. Singapore: Oxford University Press, 87–104.

Lim, C.Y. and P.J. Lloyd (eds). 1986. *Singapore: Resources and Growth*. New York: Oxford University Press.

Lim, C.Y. and Associates. 1988. *Policy Options for the Singapore Economy*. Singapore: McGraw-Hill.

Lim, E.-G. 2001. *Determinants of and the Relation Between, Foreign Direct Investment and Growth: A Summary of the Recent Literature*. Washington. D.C.: International Monetary Fund.

Lim, J.J. 2000. *Singapore's ICT Policy for the New Millennium: Implications for SMEs* [Online]. Available at: http://www.jamus.name/research/id1.pdf [accessed: 6 May 2010].

Lim, L. and P.E. Fong. 1982. Vertical linkages and multinational enterprises in developing countries. *World Development*, 10(7), 585.

Lim, L. and R. Findlay. 1993. Singapore, in *The Political Economy of Poverty, Equity, and Growth: Five Small Open Economies*, edited by R. Findlay and S. Wellisz. New York Oxford University Press.

Lin, J.Y. and J.B. Nugent. 1995. Institutions and economic development, in *Handbook of Economic Development, Volume 3A*, edited by J. Behrman and T.N. Srinivasan. Amsterdam: North-Holland, 2301–2370.

Lipsey, R. and C. Bekar. 1995. A structuralist view of technical change and economic growth. *Bell Canada Papers on Economic and Public Policy*, 3.

Lipsey, R., C. Bekar, and K. Carlaw. 1998. The consequences of changes in GPTs, in *General Purpose Technologies and Economic Growth*, edited by E. Helpman. Cambridge, MA: The MIT Press, 193–218.

——. 2005. *Economic Transformations: General Purpose Technologies and Long-term Economic Growth*. Oxford: Oxford University Press.

Liu, X. and C. Wang. 2003. Does foreign direct investment facilitate technological progress? Evidence for Chinese industries. *Research Policy*, 32, 945.

Loewendahl, H. 2001. A framework for FDI promotion. *Transnational Corporations*, 10(1), 1.

Loh, C.M., P.H. Ang, and M. Hukill. 2000. Convergence development in Singapore's digital environment, in *Electronic Communication Convergence*, edited by M. Hukill, R. Ono, and C. Vallath. New Delhi: Sage Publications.

Loh, F.K.W. and B.T. Khoo. 2002. *Democracy in Malaysia: Discourses and Practices*. Richmond, Surrey, England: Curzon.

Loh, F.K.W. 2009. *Old vs. New Politics in Malaysia: State and Society in Transition*. Petaling Jaya: Strategic Information and Research Development Centre and Penang.

Loh, K.W. 2006. Balancing the pursuit of academic excellence and the massificiation of tertiary education. *Aliran Monthly*, 25(10). http://aliran.com/archives/monthly/2005b/10h.html Accessed October 16, 2012.

Lopez, L. 2009. Malaysia's cash cow posting lower profits. *The Straits Times* (Singapore), 26 June, A15.

Love, J.H. 2003. Technology sourcing versus technology exploitation: an analysis of US foreign direct investment flows. *Applied Economics*, 35, 1667.

Low, L., M.H. Toh, and T.K. Soon. 1991. *Economics of Education and Manpower Development: Issues and Policies in Singapore*. Singapore: McGraw Hill.

——. 2006. *The Political Economy of a City-State*. Singapore: Marchall Cavendish.

Low, S.L. 2001. McKinsey's MSC study was leaked, says MDC chief. *CNET* [Online], 28 March. Available at: http://www.zdnetasia.com/news/hardware/0,39042972,10035838, 00.htm [accessed: 6 May 2010].

Luke, A., P. Freebody, S. Lau, and S. Gopinathan. 2005. Towards research-based innovation and reform: Singapore schooling in transition. *Asia Pacific Journal of Education*, 25(1), 5.

Mahathir, M. 1991. *Vision 2020*. Kuala Lumpur: Institute of International and Strategic Studies.

——. 1998. *Multimedia Super Corridor*. Subang Jaya, Malaysia: Pelanduk Publications.

Maiorano, G. and J. Stern. 2007. Institutions and infrastructure investment in low and middle-income countries: the case of mobile communications. *City University London, Department of Economics, Discussion Paper 07/06*. London: City University London, Department of Economics.

Malaya, Federation of. 1961. *Second Five-Year Plan 1961–1965*. Kuala Lumpur: Government Press.

——. 1963. *Interim Review of Development in Malaya under the Second Five-Year Plan*. Kuala Lumpur: Government Press.

Malaya, Office of the Member for Economic Affairs. 1953. *Progress Report on the Development Plan of the Federation of Malaya 1950–1952*. Kuala Lumpur: The Treasury, Government Press.

Malaysia External Trade Development Corporation. *Malaysia's Trade Performance 2008* [Online]. Available at: http://www.matrade.gov.my/cms/content.jsp?id=com.tms.cms.article.Article_hide_TradePerformance2008 [accessed: 8 May 2010].

Malaysia, Government of. 1965. *First Malaysia Plan 1966–1970*. Kuala Lumpur: Government Press.

——. 1969. *Mid-Term Review of the First Malaysia Plan 1966–1970*. Kuala Lumpur: Government Press.

——. 1971. *Second Malaysia Plan 1971-1975*. Kuala Lumpur: Government Press.

——. 1973. *Mid-Term Review of the Second Malaysia Plan 1971–1975*. Kuala Lumpur: Government Press.

——. 1976. *Third Malaysia Plan 1976–1980*. Kuala Lumpur: Government Press.

——. 1979. *Mid-Term Review of the Third Malaysia Plan 1976–1980*. Kuala Lumpur: Government Press.

——. 1981. *Fourth Malaysia Plan 1981–1985*. Kuala Lumpur: Government Press.

——. 1986a. *Fifth Malaysia Plan 1986–1990*. Kuala Lumpur: Government Press.

——. 1986b. *Industrial Master Plan 1986–1995*. Kuala Lumpur: Ministry of International Trade and Industry, Government Press.

——. 1991. *Sixth Malaysia Plan 1991–1995*. Kuala Lumpur: Government Press.

——. 1994a. *National Telecommunications Policy*. Kuala Lumpur: Ministry of Energy, Telecommunications & Posts, Government Press.

——. 1994b. *Review of the Industrial Master Plan 1986–1995*. Kuala Lumpur: Ministry of International Trade and Industry, Government Press.

——. 1996. *Seventh Malaysia Plan 1996–2000*. Kuala Lumpur: Government Press.

——. 1998a. *Communications and Multimedia Act 1998*. Laws of Malaysia Act 588. Kuala Lumpur: Percetakan Nasional Malaysia Berhad.

——. 1998b. *Malaysian Communications and Multimedia Commission Act 1998*. Laws of Malaysia Act 589. Kuala Lumpur: Percetakan Nasional Malaysia Berhad.

——. 2001. *Eighth Malaysia Plan 2001–2005*. Kuala Lumpur: Government Press.

——. 2006. *Ninth Malaysia Plan 2006–2010*. Kuala Lumpur: Government Press.

——. 2010. Tenth Malaysia Plan 2011–2015. Kuala Lumpur: Government Press.

Malaysian Communications and Multimedia Commission. 2002. *Framework for Industry Development 2002–2006*. Kuala Lumpur.

Mansell, R. 2001. Digital opportunities and the missing link for developing countries. *Oxford Review of Economic Policy*, 17(2), 282.

Mantzavinos, C., D.C. North, and S. Shariq. 2003. *Learning, Institutions and Economic Performance*. Bonn: Max Planck Institute for Research on Collective Goods.

Markusen, J.R. and A.J. Venables. 1999. Foreign direct investment as a catalyst for industrial development. *European Economic Review*, 43, 335.

Mascarell. C. 2007. The Macedonia community development project: empowerment through targeting and institution building. *SP Discussion Paper No. 0710*. Washington, D.C.: The World Bank.

Maskus, K.E. 1990. Normative concerns in the international protection of intellectual property rights. *World Economy*, 13(3), 387.

Mathews, R.C.O., C.H. Feinstein and J.C. Odling-Smee. 1982. *British Economic Growth: 1856–1873*. Stanford, CA: Stanford University Press.

Mazelan, N.A., M. Harneive, and A.C. Valida. 1999. *Multimedia Super Corridor: A Journey to Excellence in Institutions of Higher Learning*. London: ASEAN Academic Press.

Menard, C. and M.M. Shirley (eds). 2005. *Handbook of new Institutional Economics*. Dordrecht: Springer.

Mesher, G. 1999. *Malaysia's Multimedia Super Corridor (MSC)*. Sacramento, CA: Asian Technology Information Program.

Meyer, J.W. and B. Rowan. 1983. The structure of educational organizations, in *Organizational Environments: Ritual and Rationality*, edited by J.W. Meyer and W.R. Scott. London: Sage Publications, 71–97.

Milhaupt, C.J. and K. Pistor. 2008. *Law & Capitalism*. Chicago: The University of Chicago Press.

Ming, Y.U. and R. Ghulam. 2007. Knowledge gap and earnings differential in the knowledge-based economy. *Applied Economics Letters*, 14, 219.

Mirza, H. 1986. *Multinationals and the Growth of the Singapore Economy*. London: Croom Helm.

Mitchell, M. and B. Gillis. *Making Sense of the Relationship between Information Communication Technologies and Economic Development* [Online]. Center to Bridge the Digital Divide, Washington State University. Available at: http://dgss.wsu.edu/di/docs/MakingSenseoftheRelationshipbetweenICTandEconomicDevelopment.pdf [accessed: 7 May 2010].

Mody, A. (ed.). 1997. *Infrastructure Strategies in East Asia: The Untold Story*. Washington D.C.: Economic Development Institute of the World Bank.

Mohnen, P. 2001. International R&D spillovers and economic growth, in *Information Technology, Productivity and Economic Growth*, edited by M. Pohjola. Oxford: Oxford University Press, 50–71.

Montaner, C.A. 2000. Culture and the behavior of elites in Latin America, in *Culture Matters: How Values Shape Human Progress*, edited by L.E. Harrison and S.P. Huntington. New York: Basic Books, 56–64.

Morales-Gomez, D. and M. Melesse. 1998. Utilising information and communication technologies for development: the social dimensions. *Information Technology for Development*, 8(1), 3.

Moran, T.H., E.M. Graham, and M. Blomstrom (eds). 2005. *Does Foreign direct Investment Promote Development?* Washington, D.C.: Institute for International Economics and Center for Global Development.

Mortimore, M. and S. Vergara. 2004. Targeting winners: can foreign direct investment help developing countries industrialise? *The European Journal of Development Research*, 16(3), 335.

Motiwalla, J., M. Yap, and L.H. Ngoh. 1995. Building the national Information infrastructure: some key issues. *Singapore Management Review*, 17(1), 1.

Multimedia Super Corridor Malaysia [Online]. National ICT Initiative. Available at:http://www.mscmalaysia.my/topic/12073050330739 [accessed: 6 May 2010].

Myint, H. 1971. *Economic Theory and the Underdeveloped Countries*. New York: Oxford University Press.

——. 1973. *The Economics of the Developing Countries*. London: Hutchinson & Co.

Mytelka, L.K. and L.A. Barclay. 2004. Using foreign investment strategically for innovation. *The European Journal of Development Research*, 16(3), 531.

Nair, M. and M. Kuppusamy. 2004. Trends of convergence and divergence in the information economy: lessons for developing countries. *Electronic Journal on Information Systems in Developing Countries*, 18(2), 1.

Najib, M.T.A.R. 2009. *Keynote Address*. Invest Malaysia Conference, Kuala Lumpur, 30 June. Available at: http://www.pmo.gov.my/?menu=speech&page=1676&news_id=146& speech_cat=2 [accessed: 6 May 2010].

Narula, R. 1996. *Multinational Investment and Economic Structure: Globalisation and Competitiveness*. London: Routledge.

Narula, R. and J.H. Dunning. 1998. Globalisation and new realities for multinational enterprises: developing host country interaction. *MERIT Research Memorandum, 2/98-015*. The Netherlands: MERIT.

Nathan, Robert T. and Associates Inc. 1970. *Penang Master Plan*.

National Computer Board [Online]. Government of Mauritius. Available at: http://www.gov.mu/portal/site/ncbnew/menuitem.e6c78af276b0a4c9fff04a10a0208a0c/ [accessed: 6 May 2010].

National Electronics and Computer Technology Center. Government of Thailand. Available at:http://www.nectec.or.th/intro/e_background.php [accessed: 7 May 2010].

Nonnemberg, M. B. and M. J. Cardoso de Mendonca. 2002. *The Determinants of Foreign Direct Investment in Developing Countries* [Online]. Rio de Janeiro: IPEA. Available at: http://www.anpec.org.br/encontro2004/artigos/A04A061.pdf [accessed: 6 May 2010].

Noorbakhsh, F., A. Paloni, and A. Youssef. 2001. Human capital and FDI inflows to developing countries: new empirical evidence. *World Development*, 29(9), 1593.

North, D. 1990. *Institutions, Institutional Change, and Economic Performance*. New York: Cambridge University Press.

——. 1994. Economic performance through time: the limits to knowledge. *American Economic Review*, 84(3), 359.

——. 1995. The new institutional economics and third world development, in *The New Institutional Economics and Third World Development*, edited by J. Hariss, J. Hunter and C.M. Lewis. New York: Routledge, 17–26.

——. 2005. *Understanding the Process of Economic Change*. Princeton, NJ: Princeton University Press.

Nunnenkamp, P. 2001. Foreign direct investment in developing countries: what policymakers should (not) do and what economists (don't) know. *Kiel Discussion Paper No. 380*. Kiel: Kiel Institute for World Economics.

——. 2002. Determinants of FDI in developing countries: has globalization changed the rules of the game? *Kiel Working Paper 1122*. Kiel: Kiel Institute for World Economics.

——. 2004. To what extent can foreign direct investment help achieve international development goals? *The World Economy*, 27(5), 657.

Nunnenkamp, P. and J. Spatz. 2003a. Foreign direct investment and economic growth in developing countries: how relevant are host-country and industry characteristics? *Kiel Working Paper 1176*. Kiel: Kiel Institute for World Economics.

——. 2003b. Intellectual property rights and foreign direct investment: the role of industry and host country characteristics. *Kiel Working Paper 1167*. Kiel: Kiel Institute for World Economics.

OECD PISA Survey [Online: Ministry of Education and Culture, Finland]. Available at: http://www.minedu.fi/OPM/Koulutus/artikkelit/pisa-tutkimus/index.html?lang=en [accessed: 8 May 2010].

Oliner, S. and D. Sichel. 2000. The resurgence of growth in the late 1990s: is information technology the story? *The Journal of Economic Perspectives*, 14(4), 3.

Oliva, M.-A. and L.A. Rivera-Batiz. 2002. Political institutions, capital flows, and developing country growth: an empirical investigation. *Review of Development Economics*, 6(2), 248.

Olken, B.A. 2009. Comment on L. Pritchett, The policy irrelevance of the economics of education: is 'normative as positive' just useless, or worse? in *What Works in Development? Thinking Big and Thinking Small*, edited by J. Cohen and W. Easterly. Washington, D.C.: Brookings Institution Press, 165–169.

Ooi Kee Beng and Goh Ban Lee (eds). 2010 *Pilot Studies for a New Penang* (Singapore: ISEAS Publishing)

Organisation for Economic Co-operation and Development. 1996. *Detailed Benchmark Definitions of Foreign Direct Investment*. Paris: OECD.

——. 2000. *Knowledge-Based Industries in Asia*. Paris: OECD.

——. 2001. *Understanding the Digital Divide*. Paris: OECD.

——. 2002. *Towards a Knowledge Based Economy: Recent Trends and Policy Directions for the OECD*. Paris: OECD.

——. 2003. *Seizing the Benefits of ICT in a Digital Economy*. Paris: OECD.

——. 2004a. *Access Pricing in Telecommunications*. Paris: OECD.

——. 2004b. *The Economic Impact of ICT*. Paris: OECD.

——. 2004c. *Information Technology Outlook 2004*. Paris: OECD.

——. 2004d. *Innovation in the Knowledge Economy: Implications for Education and Learning*. Paris: OECD.

——. 2005. *Innovation Policy and Performance: A Cross-Country Comparison*. Paris: OECD.

——. *OECD Glossary of Statistical Terms* [Online: Organisation for Economic Co-operation and Development]. Available at: http://stats.oecd.org/glossary/index.htm [accessed: 6 May 2010].

Oshikoya, T.W. and N. Hussain. 1999. Information technology and the challenge of economic development in Africa. *Economic Research Papers No. 36*. Tunis-Belvedère, Tunisia: African Development Bank.

Ostrom, E. 1986. An agenda for the study of institutions. *Public Choice*, 48, 3.

——. 2005. *Understanding Institutional Diversity*. Princeton: Princeton University Press.

Pack, H. and K. Saggi. 1997. Inflows of foreign technology and indigenous technological development. *Review of Development Economics*, 1(1), 81.

Painter, M. and S.-F. Wong. 2006. Varieties of the regulatory state? Government-business relations and telecommunications reforms in Malaysia and Thailand. *Policy and Society*, 24(3), 27.

——. 2007. The telecommunications regulatory regimes in Hong Kong and Singapore: when direct state intervention meets indirect policy instruments. *The Pacific Review*, 20(2), 173.

Pande, R. and C. Udry. 2006. *Institutions and Development: A View From Below*. New Haven, Connecticut: Yale University. Available at: http://www.econ.yale.edu/~rp269/ website/papers/institutions_revisionjan.pdf [accessed: 6 May 2010].

Pang, E.F. 1982. *Education, Manpower and Development in Singapore*. Singapore: Singapore University Press.

Peebles, G. and P. Wilson. 2002. *Economic Development in Singapore: Past and Present*. Northampton, MA: Edward Elgar.

Penang, State Government. 2001. *The Second Penang Strategic Development Plan 2001–2010*. Penang.

People's Action Party. 1959. *The Tasks Ahead: P.A.P.'s Five-Year Acton Plan 1959–1964*. Singapore: People's Action Party.

———. 2006. *Staying Together Moving Ahead: PAP Manifesto 2006*. Singapore: People's Action Party.

Perkins, D. 1994. There Are At Least Three Models of East Asian Development, *World Development*, 22(4), 655.

Pilat, D. 2004. Introduction and summary, in *The Economic Impact of ICT*, edited by OECD. Paris: OECD, 7–18.

Pilat, D. and A. Devlin. 2004. The diffusion of ICT in OECD economies, in *The Economic Impact of ICT,* edited by OECD. Paris: OECD, 19–36.

Pilat, D. and A. Wolfl. 2004. ICT production and ICT use: what role in aggregate productivity growth? in *The Economic Impact of ICT*, edited by OECD. Paris: OECD, 85–104.

Pohjola, M. (ed.). 2001. *Information Technology, Productivity and Economic Growth*. Oxford: Oxford University Press.

———. 2002a. The new economy: facts, impacts and policies. *Information Economics and Policy*, 14, 133.

———. 2002b. The new economy in growth and development. *Oxford Review of Economic Policy*, 18(3), 380.

Portelli, B. and R. Naurla. 2004. Foreign direct investment through acquisitions and implications for technological upgrading: case evidence from Tanzania. *MERIT Research Information Series 2004-008*. Maastricht: MERIT. Available at: http://www.merit.unimaas.nl/publications/rmpdf/2004/rm2004-008.pdf [accessed: 6 May 2010].

Porter, M. 1990. *The Competitive Advantage of Nations*. New York: The Free Press.

———. 2000. Attitudes, values, beliefs, and the microeconomics of prosperity, in *Culture Matters: How Values Shape Human Progress*, edited by L.E. Harrison and S.P. Huntington. New York: Basic Books, 14–28.

Posner, R.A. 1998. Creating a legal framework for economic development. *The World Bank Research Observer*, 13(1), 1.

Pournarakis, M. and M.C. Varsakelis. 2004. Institutions, internationalisation and FDI: the case of economies in transition. *Transnational Corporations*, 13(2), 77.

Powell, W.W. and J.A. Colyvas. 2008. Microfoundations of institutional theory, in *The Sage Handbook of Organizational Institutionalism*, edited by R. Greenwood, C. Oliver, K. Sahlin and R. Suddaby. London: Sage Publications.

Prado, M. and M. Trebilcock. 2009. Path dependence, development, and the dynamics of institutional reform. *University of Toronto Law Journal*, 59(3), 341.

Pritchett, L. 2009. The policy irrelevance of the economics of education: is 'normative as positive' just useless, or worse? in *What Works in Development? Thinking Big and Thinking Small*, edited by J. Cohen and W. Easterly. Washington, D.C.: Brookings Institution Press, 130–164.

Przeworski, A. 2003. *The last Instance: Are Institutions the Primary Cause of Economic Development?* [Online]. Meeting on Institutions, Behavior, and Outcomes, CEBRAP, Sao Paulo, 12–14 March. Available at: http://www.nyu.edu/fas/institute/dri/ DRIWP/DRIWP11.pdf [accessed: 6 May 6 2010].

Putnam, R.D., R. Leonardi and R. Nanetti. 1993. *Making Democracy Work: Civic Traditions in Modern Italy*. Princeton: Princeton University Press.

Putnam, R.D. 2000. *Bowling Alone: The Collapse and Revival of American Community*. New York: Simon & Schuster Paperbacks.

Qiang, C.Z.-W. and A. Pitt. 2004. Contribution of information and communication technologies to growth. *The World Bank Working Paper No. 24*. Washington D.C.: The World Bank.

Qiang, C.Z.-W. and C.M. Rossotto with K. Kimura. 2009. Economic impacts of broadband, in *Information and Communications for Development: Extending Reach and Increasing Impact*, edited by The World Bank. Washington, D.C.: World Bank, 35–50.

Quah, D. 2001. The weightless economy in economic development, in *Information Technology, Productivity and Economic Growth*, edited by M. Pohjola. Oxford: Oxford University Press, 72–96.

Quibria, M.G., S.N. Ahmed, T. Tsang, and M.-L.Reyes-Macasaquit. 2003. Digital divide: determinants and policies with special reference to Asia. *Journal of Asian Economics*, 13, 811.

Rahim, S.A. and A.J. Pennings. 1987. *Computerization and Development in Southeast Asia*. Singapore: Asian Mass Communication Research and Information Centre.

Rajaratnam, S. 1964. PAP's first ten years, in *S. Rajaratnam: The Prophetic and the Political*, edited by H.C. Chan and O. ul Haq. Singapore: Graham Brash, 1987, 26–64.

——. 1987. An epistle to the Synod of the Socialist Orthodox Church, in *S. Rajaratnam: The Prophetic and the Political*, edited by H.C. Chan and O. ul Haq. Singapore: Graham Brash, 1987, 76–91.

Ramasamy, B., A. Chakrabarty, and M. Cheah. 2004. Malaysia's leap into the future: an evaluation of the Multimedia Super Corridor. *Technovation*, 24, 871.

Rasiah, R. 1995. *Foreign Capital and Industrialization in Malaysia*. London: Macmillan.

——. 1996. Lessons from Penang's industrialization, in *Malaysia's Economic Development: Policy & Reform*, edited by K.S. Jomo and S.K. Ng. Petaling Jaya, Malaysia: Pelanduk Publications, 189–210.

——. 2002a. Manufactured exports, employment, skills and wages in Malaysia. *International Labour Organization Employment Paper No. 35*. Geneva: International Labour Organization.

———. 2002b. Systemic coordination and the development of human capital: knowledge flows in Malaysia's TNC-driven electronics clusters. *Transnational Corporations*, 11(3), 89.

———. 2003a. Foreign ownership, technology and electronics exports from Malaysia and Thailand. *Journal of Asian Economics*, 14, 785.

———. 2003b. Industrial technology transition in Malaysia, in *Competitiveness, FDI and Technological Activity in East Asia*, edited by S. Lall and S. Urata. Northampton, MA: Edward Elgar, 305–333.

———. 2004. *Foreign Firms, Technological Capabilities and Economic Performance: Evidence from Africa, Asia and Latin America*. Cheltenham, UK: Edward Elgar.

Rasiah, R. and G. Rasagam. 2004. Economic performance, local sourcing and technological intensities in Malaysia, in *Foreign Firms, Technological Capabilities and Economic Performance: Evidence from Africa, Asia and Latin America*, edited by R. Rasiah. Cheltenham, UK: Edward Elgar, 115–141.

Rasiah, R. and J. Schmidt (eds). 2010. *The New Political Economy of Southeast Asia* Cheltenham UK: Edward Elgar.

Rebelo, S. 2001. The role of knowledge and capital in economic growth, in *Information Technology, Productivity and Economic Growth*, edited by M. Pohjola. Oxford: Oxford University Press.

Rhee, Y.W. and T. Belot. 1990. Export catalysts in low-income countries: a review of eleven success stories. *World Bank Discussion Paper 72*. Washington D.C.: World Bank.

Riaz, A. 1997. Telecommunications in economic growth of Malaysia. *Journal of Contemporary Asia*, 27(4), 489.

Ritchie, B.K. 2002. Foreign direct investment and intellectual capital formation in southeast Asia. *OECD Development Centre, Working Paper 194*. Paris: OECD.

Rochon, L. 2011. Architect creates a play of solid and wood. *The Globe and Mail*, A16, (9 April), Toronto.

Rockoff, H. 1990. The Wizard of Oz as a monetary allegory. *Journal of Political Economy*, 98(4), 739.

Rodan, G. (ed.). 2001. *Singapore*. Aldershot: Ashgate.

———. 2006. Singapore: Globalisation, the State, and Politics in *The Political Economy of Southeast Asia: Markets, Power and Contestation* (3rd edition), edited by G. Rodan, K. Hewison and R. Robison. Oxford: Oxford University Press, 137–169.

Rodan, G., K. Hewison and R. Robison. 2006. Theorising Markets in South-East Asia: Power and Contestation in *The Political Economy of Southeast Asia: Markets, Power and Contestation* (3rd edition), edited by G. Rodan, K. Hewison and R. Robison. Oxford: Oxford University Press, 1–38.

Rodriguez-Clare, A. 1996. Multinationals, linkages and development. *American Economic Review*, 86, 852.

Rodrik, D. 1999. *Institutions for High Quality Growth: What They Are and How to Acquire Them*. Cambridge, MA: Harvard University. Available at: http://ksghome.harvard.edu /~drodrik/institutions.PDF [accessed: 6 May 2010].

——. (ed.). 2003. *In Search of Prosperity*. Princeton, NJ: Princeton University Press.

——. 2004a. *Getting Institutions Right*. Cambridge, MA: Harvard University. Available at: http://ksghome.harvard.edu/~drodrik/ifo-institutions%20 article%20_April%202004_.pdf [accessed: 6 May 2010].

——. 2004b. *Growth Strategies*. Cambridge, MA: Harvard University.

——. 2004c. *Rethinking Growth Policies in the Developing World*. Cambridge, MA: Harvard University.

——. 2007. *One Economics, Many Recipes*. Princeton, NJ: Princeton University Press.

——. 2009. The new development economics: we shall experiment, but how shall we learn? in *What Works in Development? Thinking Big and Thinking Small*, edited by J. Cohen and W. Easterly. Washington, D.C.: Brookings Institution Press, 24–47.

——. 2011. *The Globalization Paradox*. New York: W.W. Norton & Co.

Rodrik, D., A. Subramanian, and T. Francesco. 2004. Institutions rule: the primacy of institutions over geography and integration in economic development. *Journal of Economic Growth*, 9, 131–65.

Rolfe, R.J., D.A. Ricks, M.M. Pointer, and M. McCarthy. 1993. Determinants of FDI incentive preferences of MNEs. *Journal of International Business Studies*, 24(2), 35.

Roller, L.-H. and L. Waverman. 2001. Telecommunications infrastructure and economic development: a simultaneous approach. *The American Economic Review*, 91(4), 909.

Romer, P.M. 1990. Endogenous technological change. *The Journal of Political Economy Part 2*, 98(5), S71.

——. 1994. The origins of endogenous growth. *Journal of Economic Perspectives*, 81, 3.

Rostow, W.W. 1960. *The Stages of Economic Growth: A Non-Communist Manifesto*. London: Cambridge University Press.

Ruggie, J.G. 1998. What makes the World Hang Together?: Neo-untilitarianism and the Social Constructivist Challenge. *International Organization* 52, 855.

——. 2005. American exceptionalism, exemptionalism, and global governance, in *American Exceptionalism and Human Rights*, edited by M. Ignatieff. Princeton: Princeton University Press, 304–338.

Ryan, N.J. 1963. *The Making of Modern Malaya*. London: Oxford University Press.

Sachs, J.D. 2001. Tropical underdevelopment. *Working Paper 8119*. New York: National Bureau of Economic Research.

———. 2003. Institutions don't rule: direct effects of geography on per capita income. *National Bureau of Economic Research Working Paper No. 9490*. Cambridge, MA: NBER.

———. 2005. *The End of Poverty*. New York: Penguin Books.

Salazar, L.C. 2007. *Getting a Dial Tone: Telecommunications Liberalization in Malaysia and the Philippines*. Singapore: Institute for Southeast Asian Studies.

Sarji, A.H. 1993. *Malaysia's Vision 2020: Understanding the Concept, Implications and Challenges*. Petaling Jaya, Malaysia: Pelanduk Publications.

Schein, E.H. 1996. *Strategic Pragmatism: The Culture of Singapore's Economic Development Board*. Cambridge, MA: The MIT Press.

Schreyer, P. 2000. The contribution of information and communication technology to output growth: a study of the G7 countries. *STI Working Paper 2*. Paris: OECD.

Schumpeter, J.A. 2008. *Capitalism, Socialism and Democracy*. New York: First Harper Perennial Modern Thought.

Scott-Kennell, J. and P. Enderwick. 2005. FDI and inter-firm linkages: exploring the black box of the investment development path. *Transnational Corporations*, 14(1), 105.

Seah, C.M. and L. Seah. 1983. Education reform and national integration, in *Singapore Development Policy and Trends*, edited by P.S.J. Chen. Singapore: Oxford University Press, 240–267.

Sen, A. 1999. *Development as Freedom*. New York: Anchor Books.

———. 2006. *Identity and Violence*. London: Allen Lane/Penguin.

Sharpe, L. and S. Gopinathan. 2002. After effectiveness: new directions in the Singapore school system? *Journal of Education Policy*, 17(2), 151.

Sheriff, M.K. 1993. Vision 2020's linkages with the sixth Malaysia Plan and the second outline perspective plan, in *Malaysia's Vision 2020: Understanding the Concept, Implications and Challenges*, edited by A.H. Sarji. Petaling Jaya, Malaysia: Pelanduk Publications, 67–87.

Shin, J.S. 2005. The role of the state in the increasingly globalized economy: implications for Singapore. *The Singapore Economic Review*, 50(1), 103.

Shionoya, Y. and M. Perlman (eds). 1994. *Innovation in Technology, Industries, and Institutions*. Ann Arbor: The University of Michigan Press.

Shirley, M.M. 2005. Institutions and development, in *Handbook of New Institutional Economics*, edited by C. Menard and M.M. Shirley. Dordrecht: Springer, 611–638.

Singapore, Budget 2012. [Online] Available at: http://app.singaporebudget.gov.sg/budget_2012/default.aspx

Singapore, Economic Development Board. *EDB Singapore* [Online]. Available at: http://www.edb.gov.sg/edb/sg/en_uk/index/about_edb/vision__mission__.html [accessed: 8 May 2010].

Singapore, Government of. 1991. *Singapore: The Next Lap*. Singapore.

Singapore, Ministry of Communications and Infrastructure. 1987. *Singapore: Into the Nineties*. Singapore.

Singapore, Ministry of Education. 2000. The Singapore education system. *Journal of Southeast Asian Education*, 1(1), 185.

———. 2009. *2009 Education Statistics Digest*. Singapore.

Singapore, Ministry of Finance. 1961. *State of Singapore Development Plan 1961–1964*. Singapore.

Singapore, Ministry of Trade and Industry. 2002. Singapore's changing growth engines since 1965: an economic history of nimble adaptability. *Economic Survey of Singapore (Second Quarter)*. Singapore.

Singh, C. 1975. Regional economic cooperation in northern Malaysian development: its rationale and the role of Penang, in *Malaysian Economic Development and Policies*, edited by S. Chee and S.M. Khoo. Kuala Lumpur: Malaysian Economic Association, 269–278.

Slaughter, M. J. 2002. Skill upgrading in developing countries: has inward foreign direct investment played a role? *OECD Development Centre, Working Paper 192*. Paris: OECD.

Smith, A. 2008. *An Inquiry into the Nature and Causes of the Wealth of Nations*. New York: Oxford University Press.

Solow, R. 1987. We'd better watch out. *New York Times Book Review*, 12 July, New York.

Soon, T.K. 1988. *Singapore's New Education System: Education Reform for National Development*. Singapore: Institute of Southeast Asian Studies.

Soon, T.K. and C.S. Tan. 1993. *Singapore: Public Policy and Economic Development*. Washington, D.C.: World Bank.

Spanning the Digital Divide [Online: Bridges.org]. Available at: http://www.bridges.org/files/active/1/spanning_the_digital_divide.pdf [accessed: 5 May 2010].

Spinanger, D. 1986. *Industrialization Policies and Regional Economic Development in Malaysia*. Singapore: Oxford University Press.

Stephens, G. 2010. Information and communication: G8 institutionalization and compliance in the DOT Force, in *Making Global Economic Governance Effective*, edited by J. Kirton, M. Larionova and P. Savona. Farnham: Ashgate, 201–216.

Stern, J. 2007. *Evaluating Regulatory Decisions and Sector Outcomes in Infrastructure Industries: Results from Africa and Other Developing Countries*. Washington D.C.: PPIAF/World Bank.

Stiglitz, J.E. 1994. Endogenous growth and cycles, in *Innovation in Technology, Industries, and Institutions*, edited by Y. Shionoya. and M. Perlman. Ann Arbor: The University of Michigan Press.

———. 2003. Globalization, technology and Asian development. *Asian Development Review*, 20(2), 1.

Straub, S. 2008. Infrastructure and growth in developing countries. *Policy Research Working Paper 4460*. Washington, D.C.: The World Bank.

Tan, F.B. 1994. Beyond industry policy to information society: a framework for government involvement in IT policy, in *Managing Social and Economic*

Change with Information Technology, edited by M. Khosrowpour. Hershey, PA: Idea Group Publishing, 290–295.

Tan H.H. 1999. *Official Efforts to Attract FDI: Case of Singapore's EDB*. 1999 EWC/KDI Conference on Industrial Globalization in the 21st Century: Impact And Consequences For East Asia And Korea, 2–3 August. Available at: www.fas.nus.edu.sg/ecs/pub /wp/previous/AHTAN2.pdf [accessed: 7 May 2010].

Tan, J., S. Gopinathan and W.K. Ho (eds). 1997. *Education in Singapore*. Singapore: Prentice Hall.

Tan, K.Y. 1987. Economic change and the formulation of economic policy, in *Singapore: Into the Nineties*, edited by Ministry of Communications and Infrastructure of Singapore. Singapore, 1–24.

Tavares, A.T. and S. Young. 2005. FDI and multinationals: pattern, impacts and policies. *International Journal of the Economics of Business*, 12(1), 3.

te Velde, D.W. 2001. *Policies Towards Foreign Direct Investment in Developing Countries: Emerging Best Practices and Outstanding Issues*. London: Overseas Development Institute.

——. 2002. Government policies for inward foreign direct investment in developing countries: implications for human capital formation and income inequality. *OECD Development Centre, Working Paper 193*. Paris: OECD.

TEKES Annual Report 2007 [Online: Tekes: The Finnish Funding Agency for Technology and Innovation]. Available at: http://www.tekes.fi [accessed: 8 May 2010].

Telecommunication Services [Online: World Trade Organization]. Available at: http://www.wto.org/english/tratop_e/serv_e/telecom_e/telecom_e.htm [accessed: 8 May 2010].

Temple, J. 2002. The assessment: the new economy. *Oxford Review of Economic Policy*, 18(3), 241.

Thangavelu, S.M. and G. Rajaguru. 2004. Is there an export or import-led productivity growth in rapidly developing Asian countries? A multivariate VAR analysis. *Applied Economics*, 36, 1083.

Thatcher, M. 2002a. Delegation to independent regulatory agencies: pressures, function and contextual mediation. *West European Politics*, 25(1), 125.

——. 2002b. Regulation after delegation: independent regulatory agencies in Europe. *Journal of European Public Policy*, 9(6), 954.

Thio Li-ann and Kevin Y.L. Tan (eds). 2009. *Evolution of a Revolution: Forty Years of the Singapore Constitution*. Abingdon: Routledge-Cavendish.

Todaro, M.P. and S.C. Smith (eds). 2009. *Economic Development* (10th edition). Boston: Pearson Addison Wesley.

Toh, M. H. and L. Low. 1990. Towards greater competition in Singapore's telecommunications. *Telecommunications Policy*, 14(8), 303.

Total Factor Productivity [Online: About.com]. Available at: http://economics.about.com/od/economicsglossary/g/tfp.htm [accessed: 8 May 2010].

Trebilcock, M.J. and R. Howse. 2005. *The Regulation of International Trade* (3rd edition). New York: Routledge.

Trebilcock, M.J. and M. Prado. 2011. *What Makes Poor Countries Poor? Institutional Determinants of Development*. Cheltenham, UK: Edward Elgar.

Treasury Department, Ministry of Finance. 2009. *Economic Report 1994/1995– 2008–2009*. Kuala Lumpur: Government of Malaysia.

Turnbull, C.M. 1989. *A History of Malaysia, Singapore and Brunei*. Sydney: Allen and Unwin.

United Nations Conference on Trade and Development. 1996. *World Investment Report 1996: Investment, Trade and International Policy Arrangements*. New York: UNCTAD.

——. 1998. *World Investment Report: Trends and Determinants*. New York: UNCTAD.

——. 1999. *World Investment Report: Foreign Direct Investment and the Challenge of Development*. New York: UNCTAD.

——. 2001. *World Investment Report: Promoting Linkages*. New York: UNCTAD.

——. 2003. *World Investment Report 2003: FDI Policies for Development*. New York: UNCTAD.

——. 2004. *The Impact of FDI on Development: Globalization of R & D by Transnational Corporations and Implications for Developing Countries*. New York: UNCTAD.

——. 2005. *The Digital Divide: ICT Development Indices 2004*. New York: UNCTAD.

——. 2008a. *Information Economy Report 2008*. New York: UNCTAD.

——. 2008b. *World Investment Report 2008: Transnational Corporations and the Infrastructure Challenge*. New York: UNCTAD.

——. 2009. *Information Economy Report 2009*. New York: UNCTAD.

United Nations Development Programme. 2005. *Malaysia: Achieving the Millennium Development Goals*. Kuala Lumpur: United Nations Development Program.

United Nations Commissioner for Technical Assistance. 1963. *Proposed Industrialization Programme for Singapore. Department of Economic and Social Affairs, Report 63-42027*. New York: United Nations.

United Nations Economic and Social Council. 2005. *Third Annual Report of the Information and Communications Technologies Task Force*. New York: UN.

United Nations Educational, Scientific and Cultural Organization, Institute for Statistics and Organisation for Economic Co-operation and Development. 2005. *Education Trends in Perspective: Analysis of the World Education Indicators*. Paris: UNESCO.

University of Toronto G8 Working Group. 2002. *Issue Objectives for the 2002 G8 Kananaskis Summit – Digital Opportunities Task Force (DOT Force)*. Toronto.

Ure, J. (ed.). 1995. *Telecommunications in Asia: Policy, Planning and Development*. Hong Kong: Hong Kong University Press.

——. 2008. *Telecommunications Development in Asia*. Hong Kong: Hong Kong University Press.

van Ark, B., R. Inklaar, and R.H. McGuckin. 2003a. ICT and productivity in Europe and the United States: where do the differences come from? *Economics Program Working Paper Series, EW#03-05*. New York: The Conference Board.

van Ark, B., J. Melka, N. Mulder, M. Timmer, and G. Ypma. 2003b. ICT investments and growth accounts for the European Union 1980–2000. *Research Memorandum GD-56*. Groningen, The Netherlands: Groningen Growth and Development Centre.

van Elkan, R. 1995. Singapore's development strategy, in *Singapore: A Case Study in Rapid Development*, edited by K. Bercussan. Washington, D.C.: IMF, 11–19.

Vernon, R. 1996. International investment and international trade in the product cycle. *Quarterly Journal of Economics*, 80, 190.

VTT Annual Report 2007 [Online: VTT Technical Research Centre of Finland]. Available at: http://www.vtt.fi [accessed: 8 May 2010].

Wade, R. 1992. East Asia's Economic Success: Conflicting Perspectives, Partial Insights, Shaky Evidence. *World Politics* 44 (January), 270.

———. 2002. Bridging the digital divide: new route to development or new form of dependency? *Global Governance* 8, 443.

———. 2004. *Governing the Market: Economic Theory and the Role of Government in East Asian Industrialization* (2nd paperback edition), Princeton: Princeton University Press.

Wallsten, S. 2002. Does sequencing matter?: Regulation and privatization in telecommunications reform. *Policy Research Working Paper 2817*. Washington, D.C.: World Bank.

Wang, E.H-H. 1999. ICT and economic development in Taiwan: analysis of the evidence. *Telecommunication Policy*, 23, 235.

Warda, J. 2005. *Incentives of ICT Adoption: Canada and Major Competitors*. Ottawa: Information Technology Association of Canada.

Waverman, L., M. Meschi, and M. Fuss. 2005. The impact of telecoms on economic growth in developing countries. *The Vodafone Policy Paper Series* 3.

Wee, V. 2001. *Imperatives for the K-Economy: Challenges Ahead*. InfoSoc Malaysia Conference, Penang, Malaysia, 14–16 June. Available at: http://www. digitalibrary.my/dmdocuments/malaysiakini/668_Imperatives%20for%20 the%20K%20Economy_%20challenges%20ahead.pdf [accessed: 7 May 2010].

———. 2001. *K-Economy: Basis for Malaysia's Economic Transformation*. National Conference on the National Vision Policy, the Eighth Malaysia Plan, and Privitization, Petalong Jaya, Malaysia, 27–28 August.

———. 2003. *Vision 2020 and enhancing competitiveness. Prime Leadership and Management Course (JUSA) Series 28 No. 2/2003. Kuala Lumpur: INTAN*.

Wellenius, B. 2006. Extending communication and information services: principles and practical solutions, in *Information and Communications for Development: Global Trends and Policies,* edited by The World Bank. Washington, D.C.: World Bank, 41–55.

Wendt, A. 1992. Anarchy is what states make of it: the social construction of power politics. *International Organizations*, 46(2), 391.

——. 1994. Collective identity formation and the international state. *American Political Science Review*, 88, 385.

——. 1999. *Social Theory of International Politics*. Cambridge, UK: Cambridge University Press.

Wheelwright, E.L. 1965. *Industrialization in Malaysia*. Melbourne: Melbourne University Press.

Williamson, O. 1998. The institutions of governance. *The American Economic Review*, 88, 75.

——. 2000. The new institutional economics: taking stock, looking ahead. *Journal of Economic Literature*, 38, 595.

Winsemius, A. 1984. *The Dynamics of a Developing Nation: Singapore*. Text of a speech delivered at General Electric Personnel Council Meeting, Singapore, 19 June.

Wint, A.C. and D.A. Williams. 2005. Attracting FDI to developing countries: a changing role for government? *The International Journal for Public Sector Management*, 15(5), 361.

Wong, J. 2011. *Betting on Biotech: Innovation and the Limits of Asia's Developmental State*. Ithaca: Cornell University Press.

Wong, P.-K. 2001. The contribution of information technology to the rapid economic growth of Singapore, in *Information Technology, Productivity and Economic Growth*, edited by M. Pohjola. Oxford: Oxford University Press, 221–241.

——. 2002. ICT production and diffusion in Asia: digital dividends or digital divide? *Oxford Review of Economic Policy*, 14(3), 167.

——. 2003. From using to creating technology: the evolution of Singapore's national innovation system and the changing role of public policy, in *Competitiveness, FDI and Technological Activity in East Asia*, edited by S. Lall and S. Urata. Northampton, MA: Edward Elgar, 191–238.

——. 2004. The information society and the developmental state: the Singaporean model. *Entrepreneurship Centre Working Papers*. Singapore: National University of Singapore.

Wong, P.-K., Ho Y.P., and A. Singh. 2005. Singapore as an innovative city in east Asia: an explorative study of the perspectives of innovative industries. *Policy Research Working Paper 3568*. Washington, D.C.: World Bank.

Woo-Cumings, M. (ed.). 1999. *The Developmental State*. Ithaca: Cornell University Press.

World Bank. 2002. *Constructing Knowledge Societies: New Challenges for Tertiary Education*. Washington, D.C.: World Bank.

——. 2003. *Lifelong Learning in the Global Knowledge Economy: Challenges for Developing Countries*. Washington, D.C.: World Bank.

——. 2004. *Morocco: Developing Competition in Telecommunications*. Washington, D.C.: World Bank, GICT Policy Division.

——. 2005a. *Expanding Opportunities and Expanding Competencies for Young People: A New Agenda for Secondary Education*. Washington, D.C.: World Bank.

——. 2005b. *Financing Information and Communication Infrastructure Needs in the Developing World: Public and Private Roles*. Washington, D.C.: World Bank.

——. 2005c. *The Digital Divide: ICT Development Indices 2004*. Washington, D.C.: World Bank.

——. 2006. *Information and Communications for Development: Global Trends and Policies*. Washington, D.C.: World Bank.

——. 2009. *Information and Communications for Development: Extending Reach and Increasing* Impact. Washington, D.C.: World Bank.

World Bank Data Services. *India: Data* [Online]. Available at: http://data.worldbank.org/country/india [accessed: 8 May 2010].

World Economic Forum. *Global Information Technology* [Online]. Available at: http://www.weforum.org/en/initiatives/gcp/Global%20Information%20Technology%20Report/index.htm [accessed: 7 May 2010].

——. 2002. *The Global Competitiveness Report 2001–2002*. New York: Oxford University Press.

——. 2008. *The Global Competitiveness Report 2008–2009*. Geneva: World Economic Forum.

——. 2009. *Global Information Technology Report 2008–2009*. Geneva: World Economic Forum.

——. 2010. *The Global Information Technology Report 2009–2010*. Geneva: World Economic Forum.

——. 2010a. *The Global Competitiveness Report 2010–2011*. Geneva: World Economic Forum.

——. 2010b. *Global Information Technology Report 2010–2011*. Geneva: World Economic Forum.

——. 2011a. *The Global Competitiveness Report 2010–2011*. Geneva: World Economic Forum.

——. 2011b. *The Global Information Technology Report 2010-2011*. Geneva: World Economic Forum.

World Summit on the Information Society. 2003. *Geneva Plan of Action*. Geneva.

——. 2005. *Tunis Agenda for the Information Society*. Tunis.

World Urbanization Prospects: The 2007 Revision Population Database [Online: United Nations Department of Statistics]. Available at: http://esa.un.org/unup/ [accessed: 8 May 2010].

Wu, R. and G. Leung. 2008. *Hong Kong and Singapore: Two Models of Telecommunications Regulation?* Hong Kong: University of Hong Kong. Available at: www.imaginar.org/its2008/36.pdf [accessed: 7 May 2010].

Yap, S., R. Lim and L. Weng Kam. 2009. *Men in White: The Untold Story of Singapore's Ruling Political Party*. Singapore: Singapore Press Holdings.

Yip, S.K., S.P. Eng, and Y.C. Yap. 1997. 25 years of education reform, in *Education in Singapore*, edited by J. Tan, S. Gopinathan and W.K. Ho. Singapore: Prentice Hall, 3–32.

Young, A. 1994. Lessons from the east Asian NICs: a contrarian view. *European Economic Review*, 38, 964.

——. 1995. The tyranny of numbers: confronting the statistical realities of the east Asian growth experience. *Quarterly Journal of Economics*, 110(3), 641.

Yusuf, S. and K. Nabeshima. 2009a. *Tiger Economies Under Threat: A Comparative Analysis of Malaysia's Industrial Prospects and Policy Options*. Washington: World Bank.

——. 2009b. Can Malaysia escape the middle income trap? A strategy for Penang. *World Bank Policy Research Working Paper 4971*. Washington: World Bank.

Zhang, Z. (ed.). 2011. *Dynamics of the Singapore Success Story: Insights by Ngaim Tong Dow*. Singapore: Cengage Learning.

Index

Global Finance Series

Full series list